RANALD MacDONALD
1824-1894

Ranald MacDonald

From an old daguerreotype taken about 1853,
in the possession of Mr. A. T. MacDonald, of Great Falls, Montana.

Ranald MacDonald.

The Narrative of his early life on the Columbia under the Hudson's Bay Company's regime; of his experiences in the Pacific Whale Fishery; and of his great Adventure to Japan; with a sketch of his later life on the Western Frontier

1824-1894

※

Edited and annotated from the original manuscripts by

William S. Lewis and Naojiro Murakami

※

Oregon Historical Society Press

Produced by the Oregon Historical Society Press.

The paper used in this publication meets the minimum requirements of the American National Standard for Information Sciences—Permanence of Paper for Printed Library Materials, ANSI 739.48-1984.

Library of Congress Cataloging in Publication Data

MacDonald, Ranald, 1824 – 1894.
    Ranald MacDonald: the narrative of his early life on the Columbia under the Hudson's Bay Company's regime, of his experiences in the Pacific whale fishery, and of his great adventure to Japan: with a sketch of his later life on the Western Frontier, 1824 – 1894 / edited and annotated from the original manuscript by William S. Lewis and Naojiro Murakami; foreword by Donald Sterling; afterword by Jean Murray Cole.
        p.   cm.—(North Pacific studies series; 16)
    Reprint, with new foreword and afterword. Originally published for the Eastern Washington State Historical Society by the Inland-American Printing Co., 1923.
    Includes bibliographical references (p.   ).
    ISBN 0-87595-229-1
    1. MacDonald, Ranald, 1824 – 1894. 2. Pioneers—Columbia River Valley—Biography. 3. Frontier and pioneer life—Columbia River Valley. 4. Columbia River Valley—History. 5. Hudson's Bay Company. 6. Japan—Description and travel—1801 – 1900. 7. Americans Japan History—19th century. I. Lewis, William S. (William Stanley), 1876 – 1941. II. Murakami, Naojiro, 1868 – 1966. III. Title. IV. Series: North Pacific studies series; no. 16.
    F853.M13   1990
    979.7'02'092—dc20
    [B]   90-7219
                                                                              CIP

Printed in the United States of America.

Support for the production of this volume was provided primarily by the Friends of MacDonald through funds generously donated by Epson Portland Inc.

ラナルド・マクドナルドの生涯

The characters shown here are the Japanese version of this book's title, and they are read top to bottom, right to left. They also appear on the last page of this edition and debossed on the back cover, both the traditional locations of Japanese book title pages and front covers, respectively.

TO THE PIONEER

The history of mankind is little less than a narrative of designs which have failed and hopes that have been disappointed——*Johnson*

Better to be a crystal, though shattered, than lie as a tile unbroken on the housetop——*Old Chinese Classic*

CONTENTS

MAPS AND PLANS

Map showing Ranald MacDonald's route on leaving ship and landing in the island of Yankeshiri. Compiled from Mr. MacDonald's original sketch, imposed on a map of Yezo of 1854. *Facing 152*

Map of the west coast of Yezo (now called Hokkaido) showing route by which Ranald MacDonald reached Matsmai (now Fukuyama). From Commodore Perry's map of 1855, compiled from that of van Seibold.   *186*

Plan of the place and court of examination at Nagasaki. Drawn from an original sketch by Ranald MacDonald.   *215*

ILLUSTRATIONS

Portrait of Ranald MacDonald from an old daguerreotype taken about 1853. Original in possession of Mr. A.T. MacDonald of Great Falls, Montana.   *Frontispiece*

Portrait of Archibald MacDonald, our author's father, from an old daguerreotype taken about 1851.   *Facing 26*

Log cabin in which Ranald MacDonald died on August 5, 1894. From a photograph by Mr. J.A. Meyers.   *Facing 68*

Grave of Ranald MacDonald, near Toroda, Washington. From a photograph by Mr. J.A. Meyers.   *Facing 68*

Portrait of Ranald MacDonald, from a photograph taken July 5, 1891, in the possession of Mrs. Jennie Lynch, Toroda, Washington.   *Facing 71*

Chinook Indian grave in canoe. From a drawing by H.J. Warre.   *Facing 76*

King Com-Comly's grave. From a drawing in Wilkes' Narrative. IV, 221.   *Facing 76*

Chinook (or Flathead) Indian woman, with child undergoing the process of head flattening. From Catlin's North American Indians, II, 125.   *Facing 82*

FOREWORD

IMAGINE a young man hunched restlessly over a bank clerk's ledger in St. Thomas, Ontario, Canada, in the early 1840s. He had been born in 1824 at Fort George at the mouth of the Columbia River and had spent his boyhood in frontier posts in northwestern North America. His Scottish father was an official of the powerful fur-trading Hudson's Bay Company. His mother was a Chinook Indian princess, a daughter of Chief Comcomly, who welcomed Lewis and Clark and the Astor party to the mouth of the Columbia River.

The young man was educated at academies to which the company's chief officers sent their children, but the collar and coat of a banker fit him awkwardly. He smarted from the social rejection he attributed to the Indian side of his ancestry. Besides, he said, he felt "uncontrollably in my blood, the wild strain of wandering freedom."

From his boyhood on the Pacific coast he had learned something about the Japanese, the people of the forbidden land on the far side of the ocean. He may even have seen a racial connection between them and his own North American Indian ancestors. Out of his unhappiness and his hunger for adventure he contrived a daring mission: to solve the mystery of Japan.

That young man was Ranald MacDonald, and the heart of this book is his account of the supreme experience of his life.

After some preliminary wanderings, he reached the waters of his desire on an American whaling vessel in June 1848, when for two centuries Japan had been a closed kingdom. To preserve their regime and to protect the harmony of the nation, its Tokugawa rulers had expelled foreign missionaries and traders and shut off the islands from almost all outside intercourse. Foreigners who landed risked imprisonment and even death, as did Japanese who went abroad and attempted to return.

Into this seemingly dangerous place MacDonald ventured— alone, at the age of 24, with no knowledge of the Japanese language. He had arranged to have himself put adrift from the whaler in a small boat and was washed ashore on Rishiri Island off the northwestern tip of Yezo, the major northern island now called Hokkaido.

The natural charm that acquaintances acknowledged even at the end of MacDonald's life must have helped him. Japanese officials soon took him prisoner. They sent him by ship the entire length of the Japanese chain to Nagasaki, the southern port where a Dutch trading post provided Japan's one window to the outside world. But although he was kept in close captivity for nearly the entire ten months of his stay in Japan, he declared later that he had "never ceased to feel most kindly and ever grateful to my fellow men of Japan for their really generous treatment of me."

MacDonald recorded observations on the Japanese language, customs, and government. In turn, fourteen Japanese who served as interpreters at the Dutch trading post visited him frequently in the room where he was confined, to take lessons from him in English. On these contacts MacDonald based his claim to having been the first teacher of English to the Japanese. A few years later, in 1854, several of those men served as interpreters when Commodore Matthew C. Perry arrived in Japan to force its leaders to sign the treaty that opened its ports and ended its long self-imposed isolation.

MacDonald's captivity lasted until April 1849, when the United States Navy sent its warship *Preble* into Nagasaki harbor to demand the release of fifteen deserters from an American whaler whom the Japanese had been holding there also. Two of those sailors had died, under conditions of imprisonment that by the survivors' accounts were much harsher than those Mac-

Donald described. The Japanese turned over the other thirteen and MacDonald along with them.

MacDonald continued a wandering life, much of it in the frontier mining camps of British Columbia. In the end he lived in dignified poverty on a farm in eastern Washington, near the site of the Hudson's Bay post at Fort Colvile where his father had once been in command. Some forty years after his supreme adventure he wrote prophetically of the Japanese: "To what their march in the progress of nationhood will ultimately attain no man can tell. In this they may yet lead the world; their autonomy being of the strongest among men; and now, the most active in national progress." When he died in 1894 his last word was the Japanese farewell, "*Sayonara.*"

Interest in MacDonald's story, once near forgotten, has been revived in recent years. In 1951 a substantial stone was set over his grave in an Indian cemetery near Toroda, Washington, close to the British Columbia border. The Rishiri Rotary Club unveiled a monument in 1987 at MacDonald's landing place on Notsuka Cape. It marks, one of its proposers said, "the first spontaneous cultural exchange between Japan and North America." In Oregon a monument at MacDonald's birthplace in Astoria tells his story in English and Japanese. The Clatsop County Historical Society erected it in 1988, and in the same year formed a committee, the Friends of MacDonald, to collect and disseminate information about him and other pioneers in the developing relationship between the United States and Japan.

In 1923, nearly three decades after MacDonald's death, the Eastern Washington Historical Society brought out this account of his adventures that he had struggled unsuccessfully to publish in his lifetime. That edition has long been out of print, and this re-publication by the Oregon Historical Society ensures that MacDonald's story will survive, as it deserves to do.

Donald J. Sterling, Jr. *Portland, Oregon*

EDITORS' PREFACE

THE Japan Story of Adventure of Ranald MacDonald is printed as it appears in the duplicate manuscripts of Ranald MacDonald in the possession of the Eastern Washington State Historical Society at Spokane, Washington, and the Provincial Library at Victoria, B. C.

The author, but twenty-four years old at the time of his Japan adventure (1848-1849), spent his entire life on the frontiers of civilization, and it was not until forty years later (about 1888) that he undertook to prepare from his notes for publication his own story of his youthful adventure in Japan.

As shown by the bibliography attached, Ranald MacDonald's experiences in Japan excited some interest in the press of the time, and have been alluded to by many present-day writers on Japan. Had the story been published immediately after his return from Japan or even after the opening of Japan for foreign commerce by Commodore Perry's treaty in 1854,[1] the book would doubtless have met with great success and conferred deserved fame on its author. But in later years the public was deluged with volumes on the islands, and Ranald MacDonald was able neither to secure a publisher nor to finance the publication of the book at his own expense.

While on a visit to his father's home at St. Andrews,

---

[1] The treaty was signed at Kanagawa, Japan, March 31, 1854.

Quebec, in 1853, Ranald MacDonald left his original manuscript notes and papers with an old family friend, Malcolm McLeod, a barrister of Ottawa, Canada, and then proceeded to the Northwest Coast, where he engaged in various remote mining and ranching ventures for many years, and entirely lost touch with his family and friends at St. Andrews, Quebec; many of whom believed he was dead. Nearly a quarter of a century elapsed before he renewed correspondence with his friend. [2]

In 1857 Mr. McLeod edited Ranald MacDonald's notes, and to some extent rewrote and prepared the manuscript for publication—to just what extent the present editors are unable to say. [3] In March of that year the story was submitted to Messrs. Dix, Edwards & Company of Boston for publication. In a letter to Ranald MacDonald of date of November 8, 1890, Malcolm McLeod says: "The book is yours in utmost sense." Little of Ranald MacDonald's original manuscript has been preserved, but having acquired some familiarity with Ranald MacDonald's personality and read many of his letters, including the Ranald Mac-Donald-Malcolm McLeod correspondence in the Provincial Library at Victoria, B. C., the present editors concur in Mr. McLeod's statement, though evidences of Mr. McLeod's composition are apparent.

---

[2] "It is over a quarter of a century since I wrote you from Victoria, British Columbia." Letter from Ranald MacDonald at Old Fort Colvile, Marcus, P. O., to Malcolm McLeod, undated (1888), in the Provincial Library, Victoria, B. C.

[3] "Mr. MacDonald was my guest about three years ago. I have adhered most strictly to his text. Mr. MacDonald was perfectly competent to write his own story, having received a good education, but his nature, bold but modest, would not allow him. In aught that seems to contradict this in the course of the narrative, blame me." Letter from Malcolm McLeod to Messrs Dix Edwards & Co., March 18, 1857, in the Provincial Library, Victoria, B. C.

The first draft of the story was completed in 1857 [4]
and another in 1887. A third draft was prepared in
1891, revised and corrected by Ranald MacDonald. A
prospectus was issued for the publication of this draft
by Messrs. W. Foster Brown & Co. of Montreal in 1891
under the title *A Canadian in Japan*, and a number of
subscriptions therefor were secured by the author [5] and
by Mr. McLeod.

The present revised draft was finished in 1893.
Three copies of this manuscript were prepared by Mr.
McLeod. One was sent to a friend, the Rev. H. M.
Fletcher, Crasmere, County Westmoreland, England,
in expectation that he might interest some English publisher; the second was retained by Mr. McLeod himself;
while the third was forwarded to Ranald MacDonald,
then living at Old Fort Colvile, Washington. The
manuscript was now submitted in turn to various Canadian and American publishers [6] without success. In a
series of letters from Ranald MacDonald to his friend,
Malcolm McLeod (1890-1893) in the Provincial Library at Victoria, B. C., we have a rather pathetic account of Ranald MacDonald's desperate efforts to raise
the amount of money required to secure publication of
his book.

In the fall of 1893 Mrs. L. C. P. Haskins, a local
writer of some ability and then editor of a newspaper

---

[4] "Twenty-four years ago I wrote the manuscript ready for publication." Malcolm McLeod, *Pacific Railway, Canada*, Ottawa, February 4,
1875. The reader will note a discrepancy in Malcolm McLeod's dates.

[5] "I can dispose of 150 here and in Spokann." Letter Ranald Mac-
Donald to Malcolm McLeod, Sept. 5, 1893, in the Provincial Library, Victoria, B. C. In another letter dated Dec. 26, 1891, our author mentions
having secured 87 subscriptions.

[6] The manuscript was submitted, among others, to Appleton, the
Harpers and the Putnams, New York, and to McClurg & Co., Chicago
all of whom spoke highly of the work, but did not think it would take
with the general reader.

near his home, published the first chapters of it in the
Kettle Falls (Wash.) *Pioneer*,[7] in an effort to arouse
interest in the manuscript. In a letter[8] in February,
1894, our author hopefully mentions Mrs. Haskins' intention to interest Mr. Penrose (President of Whitman
College) in the proposed publication. Up to the time
of his death, in the summer of 1894, Ranald MacDonald was still endeavoring to publish his book.

Some years after Ranald's death, his copy of the
manuscript came into the possession of the Eastern
Washington State Historical Society at Spokane,
Washington, through Mr. A. D. Burnett, a newspaper
man, to whom it had been entrusted by Ranald Mac-
Donald some months before his death, with a view of
his assisting in its publication. A chapter of the narrative was published in the Spokane (Wash.) *Spokes-
man-Review* by Mr. Burnett.

Later, on the death of Malcolm McLeod, his duplicate copy of the manuscript, with some notes and correspondence from Ranald MacDonald, was acquired
from the estate of Malcolm McLeod by the Provincial
Library at Victoria, B. C. During all these years most
writers on the evolution of modern Japan were in ignorance as to Ranald MacDonald's survival and the details of his life.

In 1905 Mrs. Eva Emery Dye, who had exchanged
some letters[9] with Ranald MacDonald in 1892 at the

---

7 The publication commenced with the issue of Nov. 16, 1893—see
bibliography.

8 Letter to Malcolm McLeod Feb. 13, 1894, in the Provincial Library,
Victoria, B. C.

9 Our author apparently never had the pleasure of meeting Mrs. Dye
in person. In a series of letters exchanged with her (principally in the
months of July, August, September and October, 1892), he informed her
that his book was completed and that he was then endeavoring to find
a publisher. Part of the correspondence with Mrs. Dye is in the Provincial Library at Victoria, B. C.; the remainder is in the Oregon Historical
Society's collections at Portland, Oregon.

time she was gathering materials for the writing of her *McLoughlin and Old Oregon*, had access to the duplicate manuscript in the Provincial Library at Victoria, B. C., and copied it; later publishing a considerable portion of it verbatim in a book entitled *MacDonald of Oregon* without mention of Ranald MacDonald's actual authorship of the material so published.

Thus Ranald MacDonald wrote, and up to the time of his death was endeavoring to publish his own narrative of his Japan adventure. The editors have thought his story of sufficient literary merit and historic value to warrant its publication as his own story, just as written. The style, perhaps a little florid for some cold readers of today, was addressed to the readers of the past century. By copious footnotes an attempt has been made to verify statements in the manuscript and to add to its historical interest and value. Such errors and seeming inaccuracies as have occurred through the lapse of forty years between the occurrence of the events and the final compilation of the story by Ranald MacDonald have been indicated in footnotes in preference to any alteration of the text of the narrative. Some contemporary records, confirming MacDonald's story, are included in an appendix. The editors have also added a bibliography and a brief biographical sketch of some portions of Ranald MacDonald's life not touched on in his story; the latter confessedly could have been better done a quarter of a century ago than now when the only sources of information are a few public records and the failing recollection of his few surviving contemporaries and associates.

Historically, the story is of interest because of the insight it gives into the restless spirit of inquiry, stirring among educated classes of Japan at the time, and to the current of thought then developing, a demand for the radical governmental changes which took place a few years later.[10]

The admiration, respect and affection which Ranald MacDonald felt for his pupils, his deep insight into the Japanese character, his remarkable appreciation of the Japanese national aspirations and his early forecast of the development of Japan into a nation of the first rank cannot fail to impress the American and British readers and will, we hope, tend to a better mutual understanding and to stronger ties of friendship between Japan and the great English-speaking nations of the world.

The editors acknowledge their indebtedness to and desire to thank many historical societies, libraries and individuals[11] for their unfailing courtesy, cheerful cooperation and assistance in the search for data relating to Ranald MacDonald's life and the events narrated by him.

William S. Lewis
N. Murakami[12]

[10] This fact, the self reformation of Japan from interior causes, was predicted by early writers,—V. M. Golowin, *Memoirs of a captivity in Japan, 1811-1813* (English Ed. London, 1824) iii, 34-35; and has been strongly insisted on by Dr. Wm. Elliot Griffis in *The Mikado's Empire* (New York 1876), chapter xxvii; see also note on Nakahama Manjiro and Yoshida Torajiro, note 138, pages 128, 129 hereof.

[11] The editors acknowledge their special indebtedness to Wm. Elliott Griffis, D. D. L. H. D. of New York, Mr. Steward Culver of the Brooklyn Institute Museum, Brooklyn, New York, his Honor, F. W. Howay, F. R. S. C. of New Westminster, B. C., and Mr. Jacob A. Meyers of Meyers Falls, Washington, for information furnished and for pertinent suggestions made by them. Mr. Frederick Perry Noble, Ph. D., of Spokane, Washington, has assisted by a critical reading of the manuscript and footnotes prior to publication.

[12] Naojiro Murakami is at present head of the School of Music at the Imperial University, Tokyo, Japan. He was formerly at the head of the Department of Foreign Languages at the Imperial University, and sometime Commissioner of Historical Compilation for Japan, and known among historical students in the United States for occasional papers and encyclopedia articles in English on matters of Japanese and Pacific Coast history. Any merit in this work may be attributed to him and the errors and mistakes to his associate editor, William S. Lewis.

BIOGRAPHICAL ACCOUNTS OF RANALD MACDONALD

OUR author, Ranald MacDonald, was a simple, great and many-sided character. As noted in the preface, most of his active life was spent in world wanderings or in the transient mining communities of the Northwest frontier, and it is extremely difficult, at this late day, to give an adequate or satisfactory account of the various incidents of his life to supplement that which he has told to us in his *Japan Story of Adventure*.

His mother, Princess Sunday, died a few months after Ranald's birth—the date being given as "the salmon running time" (which is usually in the months of May and June), 1824. The infant, Ranald, was then taken by his mother's sister, Car-cum-cum, and the two resided in an Indian lodge at Fort George under care of Archibald McDonald, who, a year later, proceeded to Fort Garry (now Winnipeg, in the Province of Manitoba), where he married his second wife, Jane Klyne, on the first day of September, 1825—the Rev. Mr. Cochran officiating—and returned with his bride to the Columbia River district.

When about two years old, young Ranald was taken to the family home at Kamloops (now in British Columbia), where he spent part of the years 1826-1830, though he appears to have passed much time up to the tenth year among his Chinook relatives. Writing in 1891, our author says that he had a clear remembrance of the "Princess," and recalled that an old Chinook

woman used to call him "Qua-ame, Qua-ame," meaning my grand child; he said that his last recollection of
the old King was when he was taken in Com-Comly's
arms when on the way to Fort Langley.[13]

BOYHOOD.

His step-mother, Jane Klyne McDonald, was a most
admirable character and seems to have truly loved and
cared for her little, half-breed stepson as well as, if not
better than, her own children. Here at Kamloops the
little boy met and remembered the kindly Frank Ermatinger. Writing of him in later years, Ranald Mac
Donald says: "He would sometimes give me a cake—
then a great rarity, for our allowance of flour was two
sacks brought from London[14] by way of Cape Horn,
then transported to the interior—tea and sugar in like
limited proportions. I must not forget, to us children,
that great luxury—a few cakes of gingerbread—how
Mr. Frank Ermatinger[15] would say: 'I won't tell.' My
foster mother would miss them and I was sure to be
blamed."

[13] Letter Ranald MacDonald to Malcolm McLeod, dated June 4, 1891,
in the Provincial Library, Victoria, B. C.

[14] The first shipments from the pioneer grist mill at Fort Colvile were
some bags of barley and corn meal, from the 1827 crop, taken down to
Fort Okanogan by John Work in May, 1828. Part of this cargo, with
three pigs, was assigned to New Caledonia, where doubtless a portion of
it reached our author's family. Wheat flour was probably not supplied
to the New Caledonia posts until a year or two later.

[15] Francis (Frank) Ermatinger, whose name appears as Nos. 123, 95
and 84, respectively, on the List of Employees for the years 1821, 1822
and 1823, remained in the employment of the company between 30 and
40 years; a great part of the time on the Pacific side of the mountains;
he spent much time in the vicinity of Fort Colvile, old Spokane House
and the Flathead country, in what is now the State of Montana. He retired about 1850. He married Catherine, a daughter of Wm. Sinclair,
and a niece of Mrs. Dr. John McLoughlin. He died in 1857 and his
remains rest in the old churchyard at St. Thomas, Ontario, beside those
of his brother. See note 121, page 115, 116.

The family was stationed at Fort Langley, on the Northwest Coast, in 1828-1833, with frequent visits to Forts Colvile and Vancouver, the centers of the Columbia River fur trade. Journeys along the Columbia River to Fort Vancouver were usually by bateaux, but the return into the interior was usually in part by horseback; Ranald MacDonald describing it as "my brother (Angus) in one basket and me in another."

At Fort Langley the education of Ranald and his younger brothers was begun under the personal supervision of his father, a reputed graduate of the University of Edinburgh, Scotland.

In the winter of 1833-1834 Ranald for a short time attended the school of Mr. Ball,[16] an American gentleman who taught at Fort Vancouver. This was the first school in the Pacific Northwest. Describing it, Ranald MacDonald has said:

"I attended the school to learn my A. B. C. and English. The big boys had a medal put over their necks, if caught speaking French or Chinook, and when school was out had to remain and learn a task. I made no progress."

In 1834 Ranald was sent overland to Fort Garry to attend the Red River Missionary School, supported by

---

[16] John Ball was a Yankee schoolmaster who reached Fort Vancouver in Nathan J. Wyeth's employ in the fall of 1832. On Nov. 17, 1832, he opened school at the fort for two dozen half-breed Indian children of the Hudson's Bay Company's employees. These children ranged in age from six to sixteen years and talked the Cree, Nez Perce, Chinook, Klickitat and other Indian languages. Mr. Ball said: "I found them both docile and attentive, and they made good progress." Dr. McLoughlin, whose son was one of the pupils, was a frequent visitor to the school. Mr. Ball was succeeded as a teacher at Vancouver by Solomon H. Smith in March, 1833. He was the first American to teach school and the first American to raise wheat in what is known as "Old Oregon"; see Ball's *Journal*, Oregon Historical Society's *Quarterly*, vi, 82, 100, 219; H. H. Bancroft's *History of Oregon*, i, 75; Chapman's *Story of Oregon*, 53, 74, note; Holman's *Dr. John McLoughlin*, 257-8.

the Hudson's Bay Company and then the most westernly educational institution in Canada. He went with the fall brigade from Fort Colvile in 1834 under charge of Mr. Finlayson. Recalling the trip, Ranald MacDonald has said that the trip was made in the late fall or early winter when the snow was deep in the mountains about Athabasca Pass and that he suffered greatly from the cold. After crossing the mountains he rode part of the way in one of the panniers on a pony.

At the Red River school Ranald was shortly followed by his younger brothers, and many children of the Columbian clerks, chief traders and factors. During Archibald McDonald's furlough in Europe, 1834-1835, the family stayed with the Rev. Mr. Cochran at Red River. Among the students then there, Ranald MacDonald recalled Miss Catherine Sinclair—later the wife of Frank Ermatinger. We know of no better source of information concerning this period of Ranald MacDonald's life than to quote from contemporary letters written by his father, Archibald McDonald, chief trader at Fort Colvile, on the Columbia River, to his friend, Edward Ermatinger, an old associate in the Hudson's Bay Company's service, then retired and engaged in banking at St. Thomas, Ontario.

Extracts concerning Ranald MacDonald from letters of Archibald McDonald to Edward Ermatinger, from the originals in the Provincial Library at Victoria, B. C.

Letter of Archibald McDonald written at Fort Colvile, April 1, 1836:

"Taking us altogether, we are men of very extraordinary ideas—a set of selfish drones, incapable of entertaining liberal or correct notions of hu-

Archibald McDonald
Chief trader and chief factor of the Hudson's Bay Company

From an old daguerreotype, taken about 1850, copied
from the original in possession of the late Benjamin MacDonald by Mr. T. C. Elliot,
of Walla Walla, Wash.

man life.—Our great password is a *handsome provision for our children*, but behold the end of this mighty provision, which we are amassing like exiled slaves; the off-spring is let loose upon the wide, wild world while young, without guide or protection (but always brimful of his own importance) to spend money and contract habits at his own free will and pleasure. The melancholy examples resulting from this blind practice are, I am sorry to say, but too common—much better to dream of less, to set ourselves down with them in time, and to endeavour to bring them up in habits of industry, economy and morality, than expire at all this visionary greatness for them. All the wealth of Rupert's land will not make a *half-breed* either a good parson, a shining lawyer or an able physician, if left to his own discretion while young.

"With this impression, I am myself for being off with them as soon as possible. Three of them are at present at the Red River Academy. Ranald, or if you will have it *Toole*, was removed there from Pritchard's[17] last summer and now costs me £30 a year. As I hinted to you before, I am very anxious to send him down before us; by 1838, I think he ought to be qualified enough to begin the world for himself. Will you then do me a favor to take him in hand? Without flattery I feel confident he cannot be under a better guardian. You

[17] Richard Mortimer Pritchard's school, a sort of grade or primary school for preparation for the Rev. David Thomas Jones' High School. Letters from our author to Malcolm McLeod dated October 24, 1893, in the Provincial Library at Victoria, B. C. Pritchard was related to the John Pritchard mentioned in Prof. E. H. Oliver's *The Canadian Northwest* (Ottawa, 1914), i, 55.

know their facility with the pen, and indeed their aptness altogether while young. He will not at the time I am speaking of be a learned lad, but with the help he can pick up with you will have knowledge enough to develop what may be in him as a man. Bear in mind he is of a particular race, and who knows but a kinsman of King Concomly is ordained to make a great figure in the new world; as yet he bears an excellent character. Unless he takes it after his father and Prince Cass-acas (I do not mention the princess) he won't have an itching for *Law*. Be good enough next spring to write me your sentiments about him and suggest the best way of getting him on in summer '38 from the Sault St. Marie by way of the Lakes."

Letter dated Fort Colvile, January 25, 1837:

"I am glad you notice the allusion I made about my young Chinook, as in my last I have expressed myself. Still more serious as regards him, indeed my mind is made up to send him down in '38, if your letter of '37 will not absolutely prevent me. I heard very favorable accounts of him this fall from Mr. Jones, [18] and who knows but he may turn out a rare exception to the case. I tell him to keep him at a Jointer plane and Beauvit's Sledge hammer when the younger boys are at play, and he will in reality be trained to the one or the other should we unfortunately discover a leaning to unsettled habits. Two of our other boys are with Mr. Jones

---

[18] The Rev. David T. Jones. He came to Red River in 1823 as successor to the Rev. Mr. West and founded St. Pauls (the middle) and St. Johns (the upper) churches. He returned to England in 1838. See note 119 on Red River Missionary School, herein page 114.

also; a young one is there with the Klynes, another and the young lady with ourselves."

Fort Colvile, February 2, 1838:

"I am exceedingly obliged to you for the readiness with which you come into my views respecting my own boy. If Frank goes down he is to take him, but if not I will for a year or two yet have him at Mr. Jones', which must finish all the education I intend for him. Were I certain of the time I can get down myself, I could with more ease say how I would like to have him begin the world. In short, my aim is to try how useful he can make himself to me in the first place, and in the next to acquire those habits of industry and good conduct that might at a future day be useful to himself. Upon the strength of your suggestion I have made up my mind to send my other two boys at R. R. down to Toronto as soon as possible."

Fort Colvile, February 1, 1839:

"Should Frank be going down this summer, he will be taking Ranald along with him and indeed should he not it is still my intention that the youngster should accompany some one to the Sault. I will enclose him a letter for you, suggesting what we will endeavour to make of him. He has a high character for application and good behaviour from Mr. Macallum.[19]

[19] The Rev. John Macallum, M. A. Sometime councilor and coroner of Assiniboia. He succeeded the Rev. Mr. Jones in charge of the Red River Boarding School in 1837. See minutes of Council, Prof. E. H. Oliver, op. cit. i, 88, 769. The Red River Academy, later St. John's College, Winnipeg, founded by the Rev. John West, rose to importance under him. He died in 1849.

Continued March 20th in the same letter:

"This I hope will be handed you by my son, together with another letter entirely about himself, and I trust in God the poor fellow may be a credit to us both. I have written to Mr. Christie[20] and to Mr. Nourse[21] about him, also to Mr. Keith.[22] Should it so happen that he goes by way of Lachine, I hope there will be no difficulty about a passage for him as far as the Sault. Mr. Christie is directed not to send him to Norway House if it is possible to meet the canoes at 'Bas de la Riviere,' direct from Red River."

Letter carried by Ranald MacDonald.

"Fort Colvile, March 10, 1839.
"Edward Ermatinger Esqr.
"Dear Sir:

"This will be handed you by my son, Ranald, of whom I have already made mention. Having seen nothing of him myself for the last four years, I am much at a loss how to speak of him to you now. All say he is a promising, good-natured lad. Before he went to Red River in '34, I had him myself pretty well advanced in arithmetic, so that one would suppose he is now something of a scholar; yet, I am aware, boys of his age leaving school not infrequently are very deficient, and that a little practical learning about that time brushes them up amazingly. I will just quote you a sentence about him from the Rev. Mr. Cochran's letter to me last

20 Alexander Christie, Chief Factor at Red River Settlement (Fort Garry) for some years.

21 William Nourse, Chief Trader.

22 James or George Keith, both Chief Factors.

fall: 'I preached at the upper church last Sunday, and saw the boys; they were all well then. Angus (the little white-headed boy you saw crawling about at Okanogan House) still takes the lead;but Ranald has certain indescribable qualities which lead me to imagine that he will make the man that is best adapted for the world.' So far good; still I cannot divest myself of *certain indescribable fears,* which you can conceive as well as I can; but in your hands, without flattery, I feel the grounds for those fears are considerably removed.

"I should like to give him a trial in the way of business, and with this view have him bound to yourself, sir, as an apprentice. By the spring of '40 you will be able to judge of his conduct and capacity, when I shall trouble you for a full expose of all you think about him. My reply to that letter you will have in the fall of '41, which will either confirm all our plans of making a gentleman *tout de bon* of him or have him enter on a new apprenticeship at any trade he may select for himself. In either case I will with great pleasure attend to all the little demands you may make on his account, and by the first opportunity direct how the remittance is to be made.

"You know the Rock on which split all the hopes and fortunes of almost all the youth of the Indian Country. Ranald, I hope, will have none of those fatal notions. His success in the world must solely depend on his good conduct and exertions. He has a few letters his father and mother lately addressed him, with the very best advice we could give, situated as we are; which you will have the goodness to see that, the better to impress their import upon his mind, he will frequently peruse.

"Above all, let him be a constant attendant at church. Had I known the name of your Episcopalian preacher, I would certainly have taken the liberty to address him a few lines about the moral duties of my son, which I dare say the reverend gentleman would not take amiss. We had him vaccinated some years ago, but, as the inflammation was scarcely perceptible, there would be no harm in giving it him again. I am, my dear sir, very truly yours,

"Arch'd McDonald."

Regarding the trip to St. Thomas, our author himself has written:

"I left Red River School in 1839 in a canoe brigade of four bark canoes in charge of Roderick McLeod. We crossed Lake Winnepeg, then to Rainy Lake, Lake of the Woods, to Fort William on Lake Superior, across Lake Superior to Sault St. Marys, where the canoe left me in charge of Mr. Norse, to whom I delivered letter of introduction. He then turned me over to the agent of the American Fur Company at Fort Bradly, on the opposite side of the river. Here I saw the first steamboat (the Governor Marcy), the first negro and the first American soldier. The agent secured me a passage on the Governor Marcy to Mackena, armed with letters to the agent there. From there I got on board a large steamer for Detroit. When it was known that I was born at Astoria I was much made of, particularly by a dignified gentleman, a Mr. Ralph Gurney of Washington, D. C., who gave me his card. On arrival at Detroit I was taken care of by a Mr. Abbott, the agent of the American Fur Company. After enjoying his hospitality I was transferred to charge of Captain Ebberts of the little Canadian steamer (the Brothers). We crossed over to Windsor, Canada, from there to Chatam, and from there by stage to London, where I saw the first British soldiers. From there I proceeded to St. Thomas."[23]

We continue to quote from the letters of our author's father, Mr. McDonald, a chief trader of the Hudson's Bay Company, written to his friend, Edward Ermatinger of St. Thomas, Ontario.

From letter written at Fort Colvile, April 2, 1840:

"Without your express desire to that effect, I have sent you Ranald, and am satisfied you will do towards him all that one friend can consistently expect from another. After you have an opportunity of seeing the best of his own inclinations, you will have the goodness to suggest to me what we can best do with him—but you have my ideas on this head already, and I beg you to act up to them according to circumstances—without my saying it you can imagine the source of anxiety he is to me. I do not like this country for them, yet how many of them have done well out of it. With him it rests to develop the character of the *Westsidian*, and God send it may be a creditable one."

Fort Colvile, March 5, 1841:

"About my son I am truly at a loss what to say,

---

[23] Letter of our author to his friend, Malcolm McLeod, Oct. 24, 1893, in the Provincial Library, Victoria, B. C.

and as it is probable your brother will be going down to see you, I shall refrain from saying anything till I see him. I fear much the stupid fellow takes no right view of his situation, he is now approaching the age of manhood, and he must be given to understand that I cannot afford to make a gentleman of him, nay, to put him even in the way of gaining a decent livelihood for himself, without the proper exertion on his own part. What in the universe could have put the army in the head of the baby—does he forsooth think I am going to buy a commission for him? Please have the goodness to tell him I am exceedingly displeased at his notions and that the sooner he drops them the better, otherwise, though it galls me to say it, he must speedily shift for himself. My wife, too, is much concerned to hear of the little satisfaction he is likely to afford us."

Continued April 21:

"From all you write about my son I am placed in a very awkward situation; so much so, that, with the view of relieving my anxiety at once about him, I have resolved on trying the Indian country again, and to this end have written Governor Simpson[24] and Mr. Finlayson[25] to R. R. [Red Riv-

---

24 (Sir) George Simpson, an exceedingly able man, whose activity and intelligence soon elevated to a high position in the Hudson's Bay Company's affairs. Shortly after the coalition he was made Governor in Chief of all the Hudson's Bay Company's territories in America—a position of great power, which he maintained for forty continuous years. He made three trips across the mountains, received knighthood and died at Lachine, Canada, in 1861. His name is preserved in Fort Simpson and Port Simpson. He was the author of *Narrative of a Journey Around the World During the Years 1841 and 1842*, London, Henry Colburn, 1847, 2 vols.

25 Duncan Finlayson, see note 105, page 107.

er]. My letter to Ranald himself is enclosed to the latter, who will add a postscript to it, according to the answer his excellency may give. April, '42, is the ordinary time he could embark at Lachine, but I have suggested that probably they could employ him at some one of the near forts for some months prior to that date by way of initiation, and thus avoid further incumbrance to you and Mrs. E., to whom I am much indebted for her kindness. Herewith I enclose you a bill on the company for £35 Sterling., and any further claim you may have, let me know it and I shall attend to it cheerfully. Should the plan of mine with respect to Ranald be acceded to, you know how to assist in the execution of it. My paper is done, but all I could say to you, not one-half.

P. S.—Whether Ranald leaves you immediately in receipt of this, or hang about you till spring, have the goodness to drive out of his head his new notions of greatness. Even for the few months he was with you I can see he very much improved in his hand-of-writing and business appearance altogether. In case my application now may not be conceded to, to the full extent of my wishes, I shall after the Governor is [?] renew the charge and write you out by our fall express, which generally reaches Lachine end of March or beginning of April; so that I hope you will have an eye upon the youngster until we can fairly dispose of him in a *conne* [*il*] *faut* manner."

Fort Colvile, March 30, 1842:

"In reference to my son. Seemingly it would be a waste of time to say much. I believe I told you last year of the application I was making on his

behalf to return to the hopeful Indian Country,
and of course would have seen Finlayson's note
from R. R. to my letter to the chap himself. The
Governor himself has since informed me that, to
meet my views he had forwarded my son's name
to Fenchurch Street[26] before he left Red River,
and thought it possible notice of his appointment
would reach St. Thomas early in the spring. He
may or may not make good use of this opening
made for him. One advantage he will have by receiving the appointment through their Honors is
that of being placed on the footing of *apprentice
clerk,* instead of apprentice, as is the case with all
those received into the service from the country.
Unwilling to lose this chance and to make assurance doubly sure, I by the Cape Horn vessel in-
closed Mr. Secretary Smith my own application
direct to the board, for him to present in the event
of his finding the Governor's recommendation
overlooked or mislaid. And this is all I can do for
the future benefit of the gentleman. You will,
however, my dear sir, as I have no doubt either the
one or the other application will be attended to,
have the goodness to continue your kind offices to
him, and keep him about you till you hear from
London comformably to my wish to that effect addressed to Mr. Smith and look to me for a discharge of the bill of expense."

Continued in same letter:

"For God's sake don't lose sight of my son,
until he is fairly embarked in that concern which I
believe is the most suitable for every mother's son
of them, bad as it has proved to many."

---

[26] London—the head office of the Hudson's Bay Company.

Colvile, March 5, 1843:

"From Master Ranald himself I also heard by a few lines dated in March from London. As matters have now turned out, I am not at all sorry that the young buck is made to look more to himself, but I fear from what you say of his thoughtless and indolent disposition that Mr. John Clair's store has too many tempting cordials in it to be a fit nursery for the young gents of the far west. Never mind, my friend, we have done our duty and things must now be allowed to take their course. If he can only keep out of egregious acts of impropriety till we can once more have him back in the Indian country, I shall consider it a great point gained that the experiment with him was made and tested so early in life. Here, for all I shall ever do for him again, he may just crawl through life as the Black Bear does—lick his paws. We are all most unfortunate parents."

Fort Colvile, March 22, 1844:

"The case of unfortunate Ranald gave me great pain. As it is clear, however, that the bent of his inclinations was anything but what we could wish, perhaps the step he has taken is the very best that could have happened. As for the service, in the case of these chaps, I never look upon it but as a mere apology to keep them out of harm's way, and that in all probability is as effectively done on the wide ocean as in the most obscure corner of the Indian Country, and all I hope is that he may stick to the ship "Tuskeny."[27] His miserable scrawl

[27] There were, at this time, several vessels named "Tuscany." The brig of that name, on which our author first reached London, was, ac-

does not enable us to say when he sailed, but that is immaterial; it is enough that we know he was yet in existence, contrary to other rumors that reached the country from Canada. Both Sir George and Mr. Smith wrote me about him, the latter a few days before his death."

MANHOOD.

OF the high-minded, visionary, quixotic youth who single-handed invaded the forbidden realms of the Hermit Kingdom we get our first glimpse at St. Thomas. Sitting perched on his bank-stool, the wanderlust—inherited equally from his Scotch Highland father and Indian mother—took possession of him.

More than fifty years later, Ranald MacDonald related to a friend, Mrs. Eleanor Haskins Holly of Kettle Falls, Wash., how he happened to decide on the attempt to get to Japan. It apparently came about through an unhappy, youthful love affair; when he found that the strain of Indian blood in his veins was considered a barrier to his marrying the young girl who had won his heart. He did not mention her name, but it was some one with whom he was associated in Eastern Canada.

He described some of the parties he used to attend at St. Thomas and elsewhere; the dinner; then the din-

---

cording to Lloyd's Register, of 236 tons, built at Portland, Me., 1832, and owned by C. Prince, New York, G. Dean, Master. It cleared from Hull for New York in the summer of 1841, and entered New York from Marseilles on Dec. 4, 1841, and appears frequently on the New York Custom House records in succeeding years. A contemporary ship of the same name, 288 tons, was bought from Philadelphia in 1842 by John Budd of Sag Harbor, and under Capt. Godbey sailed that year on a whaling voyage to Crozette Island, returning Feb. 26, 1845; it was withdrawn from the fishery in 1855. Starbuck's *History of the American Whale Fishery*, 396, 522-3. Capt. F. W. Beechey (R. N.) [*Narrative of a Voyage to the Pacific*, London, 1834, ii, 321], mentions an English whale ship of somewhat similar name—"The Tuscan."

ing-room (paneled with dark wood and lighted by can-
dles and a flaming fireplace) being cleared, and the
young people—"some of the finest in the land"—to use
his expression, bowing and courtesying, gliding across
the polished floor to the music of the viols.

It was one of those pretty, dainty maids met in these
surroundings whom he loved and wished to marry, and
it was then that he learned for the first time[28] that Jane
Klyne MacDonald was not his own mother, as he had
always supposed, and that some social prejudice existed towards him on account of his Indian blood. In
childhood his father had affectionately called him his
"little Chinook," Mr. Edward Ermatinger and Peter
Warren Dease occasionally addressed him as Com-
comly,[29] and the Indians had respectfully dubbed him
"little chief," but it appears that he took these terms
with childish egotism as his due; or, if he gave them
any consideration, supposed they were given him on account of his father's position. It evidently came to him
as a shock to learn of his Indian birth. He stated that
it was then he decided to go to Japan, of which he had
heard and read, and from which he was convinced that
the North American Indians originally came—"The
land of his ancestors," he termed it. He decided to run
away and get to Japan, if possible, and made his plans
accordingly. He had an idea, he said, that the Japanese were similar to the Indians and probably ignorant,
so that an educated man might make himself something

---

[28] Elsewhere our author has stated that he first learned the story of
his birth and that Jane Klyne was not his mother from Celeste—daughter
of Co-boy or Cobaway, the Clatsop Chief who married Solomon H.
Smith of Clatsop Plains, an early pioneer of Oregon. Smith, as has
been mentioned, page 25, succeeded Mr. Ball as teacher in the first
school established on the Northwest Coast in 1833.

[29] Letter Ranald MacDonald to Malcolm McLeod June 4, 1891, in the
Provincial Library, Victoria, B. C.

of a personage among them; and, though he did not say so, it is evident that he determined, if possible, to achieve some prominence among them.

SAILOR.

Little is known of his experiences after leaving Mr. Edward Ermatinger's home at St. Thomas, Ontario, in 1841 or of his trip down the Mississippi. He walked to the Great Lakes and then proceeded to St. Paul, where he engaged as a deck hand on one of the Mississippi River boats. At New Orleans he shipped for New York City. In later years he described the garb which he wore when he went on the docks at New York City to obtain a berth on some sailing vessel in his first step towards Japan. He thought that he would be more apt to obtain a position as a sailor if he were rudely dressed; so, he said, he wore a buckskin shirt trimmed with fringe, heavy wool trousers tucked into his fur-trimmed leggings and a fur cap, with a tail at the back of it, on his head. He must have looked more like a hunter than a sailor, but he was a strong, broad-shouldered, well-grown fellow and had no difficulty in getting a berth. This ship was evidently the "Tuskeny," and the first voyage was to London, from which port, in March of 1842, he wrote to his father for the first time since his disappearance.

Archibald McDonald and Duncan Finlayson made a trip to New York in 1844 with the object of locating the young man and bringing him back home and having him assert some claim of Indian title in the "old Oregon" country as lineal descendent to King Com-Comly.[30] At the time of the settlement of the Hudson's Bay

---

[30] Letter Ranald MacDonald to Malcolm McLeod May 25, 1889, in the Provincial Library, Victoria, B. C.

Company's claims against the United States, under the Treaty of 1846, the idea of presenting a claim on the part of Ranald MacDonald, as heir and successor of old Chief Com-Com-ly as a Canadian subject was further considered by family friends of our author, but his whereabouts were then unknown. Writing facetiously on the subject in later years, Ranald MacDonald said: "I consider myself the only living descendant of the once powerful King Kumkumly. The lands they have taken away, a heritage that should be mine. Being no lawyer, I could not define their limits and perhaps no one else can. I hear they are going to deprive me of my now empty title (for I had never assumed it). As King Kum Kumly's only surviving representative you will excuse me if I dutifully and loyally enter my protest (for all the good it may do) in this usurping of rights and prerogatives of another. Don't laugh; I mean what I say. Although I may not have enough to jingle on a tombstone, yet such is the case nevertheless."

At the time of the proposed restoration of Queen Liliuokalani to the throne of Hawaii in 1892, the matter was the subject of a characteristic editorial by the late Harvey W. Scott in the Portland *Oregonian*.[31]

Ranald MacDonald was at Yerba Buena (now San Francisco) late in 1842 where, in later years, he mentioned having seen, but not made himself known to Mr. Rae[32] of the Hudson's Bay Company.

It was of this or a later voyage that he related to an intimate acquaintance another story of his sailing experiences which he requested him never to tell while

---

[31] Portland (Ore.) *Oregonian*, November 29, 1893; also Harvey W. Scott, *History of Oregon*, ii., 140-141.

[32] W. Glen Rae, Chief Trader at Yorba Buena in 1842; he had previously been a clerk in the employ of the Hudson's Bay Company at the Sandwich Islands.

he was living; but, now that he has gone, there can be no harm in doing so.

He said that he had sailed from Calcutta on a boat which took on a cargo for Liverpool, England; this consisted of various things, among them several kegs of specie. After making several foreign ports *en route,* they turned and sailed eastward and at last sighted the coast of Southern California, where after the specie had been taken on shore by direction of the officers, the vessel was scuttled and sunk. A number of the crew had been paid off and left at foreign ports and only those absolutely necessary to handle the ship had been retained. The crew which remained, of whom there were only a few, were taken on shore and given some money and told to make their way up into California and on peril of their lives never to disclose what they knew. This also may sound like a rather incredible tale, but his friend certainly believed it, as, after telling it, Mr. MacDonald appeared rather disturbed that he had done so, and again cautioned his friend against repeating it, as, he said, as long as he was living it might cause some trouble he feared, even at that late day.

Another voyage, he said, was on board a ship that proved to be a *slaver,* and Ranald MacDonald stated that, after taking on cargo, they proceeded to the west coast of Africa and took on board a lot of negro slaves —men and women. On their return voyage they were chased by a British man-of-war, and, when it was seen that they would be overhauled, the brutal captain ordered the negroes (who were all kept confined below decks) brought up and made them walk the plank overboard; so when the man-of-war later came up to them, to use MacDonald's graphic expression—"Our decks were clean as a hound's tooth." Ranald Mac-

Donald expressed his horror of the captain's act and his own powerlessness to interfere with the execution of these ruthless orders.

It is hard for us at this late period to believe that such things could be done, but we must remember that this was early in the last century, when such things were possible, if not common, and when many men, then considered Christians and good citizens, regarded negro slaves as little better than cattle. Mr. MacDonald's friends were convinced that he was absolutely truthful in telling of it.

But little is known of Ranald MacDonald's wanderings prior to his re-shipping on board the Plymouth at Sahaina in the Sandwich Islands, in the fall of 1847, for his Japan adventure. From contemporary accounts it is apparent that he had, at that time, made at least two Cape Horn voyages, and had originally shipped on board the "Plymouth" when she sailed from the United States on December 6, 1845.

In a contemporary letter to his father, Ranald MacDonald says: "I again shipped for *another Cape Horn voyage* with the intention of being discharged at some of the islands or on the Spanish main. These intentions I have altered, and, as Captain Edwards was going to China and from there to the Japan sea, I thought it a good opportunity to crown my intentions; that, if I went with him, I should be discharged before he left the sea. He tried to persuade me to give up the adventure, *but I am going.*"[33]

A shipmate (E. P. E.) in a contemporary account describes Ranald MacDonald as "a man of about five feet, seven inches; thick set; straight hair and dark com-

[33] *The Seaman's Friend,* Honolulu, S. I. See appendix herein, page 273.

plexion. . . . He was a good sailor, well educated, a
firm mind, well calculated for the expedition upon
which he embarked. His intentions were to stay at this
island (Yezo) and learn some of the Japanese language, and from there go down to Yeddo, the principal
city of Nipon, and, if the English or Americans ever
open trade with the Japanese, he would find employment as an interpreter. *He had other intentions which
I never mention only in a secret manner.*"[34]

MINER AND MAN.

After leaving Nagasaki, the "Preble" touched at
Shanghai and he reached Macao, China, on board the
"Preble" in June, 1849. Little is known of Ranald
MacDonald's subsequent wanderings in China, India,
Australia and elsewhere in the Orient. At this or a subsequent time he visited Calcutta, Madras, Bombay and
Java ports and, according to an annotation in his Japan
notes, arrived at Singapore Aug. 19, 1849, and sailed
again Aug. 22, 1849. Presumably, he sailed on the
"Sea Witch" of London for Madras, and was wrecked
off the coast of India near Madras. He took part in
the Australian gold-rush and mined for a time at Ballarat, near Melbourne, Australia, where he described
the formation as resembling chalk—specimens of which
he brought back with him to Canada, and demonstrated
and explained to the family and friends how they
washed the gold from this chalk formation by crush-
ing it.

A contemporary has related an incident that occurred
at Ballarat when there was some trouble among the

---

[34] *The Seaman's Friend,* Honolulu, S. I.   See appendix herein, page
272.

miners over the working of the claims. While Ranald
MacDonald was naturally of a very mild and non-com-
bative disposition, in the course of the difficulty and
the melee which occurred thereover, Ranald was attacked by a man who was a total stranger to him, and in
defending himself Ranald, to use the phrase, "knocked
this man out," then went on about his business and gave
the matter no further thought. That evening he heard
a rap on his cabin door and upon opening it he found
some men who stated that they had been appointed a
committee to interview him, and they then handed him
a belt, and on Ranald MacDonald inquiring what they
meant, they informed him that he was now entitled to
the belt as champion of Australia, having "knocked
out" the previous champion. The narrator stated that
Ranald MacDonald informed the committee that he was
not particularly interested in that branch of athletics,
and declined the belt, shaking hands with the committee and thanking them for the honor proffered him.

Returning from Australia, he evidently sailed around
the Cape of Good Hope, as he later remarked on having
visited Rome, Paris and London on his way home to
North America in 1853. At this time, on his way to
British Columbia, Ranald MacDonald visited the family home at St. Andrews—his father had died a short
time before. After a brief visit he set out for British
Columbia, where he joined his half-brother, Allen Mac-
Donald.

The two brothers had a ranch on Bonaparte River,
and conducted a supply-house and ran pack-trains to
the gold mines on the Upper Fraser River in the Cariboo district.

In the year 1861 Ranald MacDonald associated with
Mr. John G. Barnston, a barrister attorney of Lower

Canada, and some capitalists of San Francisco conceived the idea of finding a shorter way to the gold
mines on the upper Fraser River, and searched for a
route from Fort Alexandria to a bay or inlet around
Bentinck Arm, where boats from Victoria, Puget Sound
and the Columbia could go up the Coast and land
freight and passengers. Ranald MacDonald was successful in his explorations, and finally secured a permit from the Provincial Government to establish a toll-
trail there.[35] Ranald MacDonald's report to Governor
Douglas of these explorations is among the archives of
the Provincial Library at Victoria, B. C.

In the course of this enterprise Ranald MacDonald
explored a good part of the country west of the Fraser
River, especially that called the West Road River to
Chiskas' House and on to the Coast, and from Ques-
nelle to Chesecut Lake, British Columbia.[36] The trail
was built and a small quantity of freight was packed
in over it, but it was never a commercial success, and
the promoters failed to secure a line of steamer connection. The original grant was small, simply for a pack-
trail. Soon after their enterprise was started other
parties, perhaps more influential, persuaded the government into building a wagon road; this wagon road when
built took all the business.

In 1859-1861 Ranald and his brother, Allen, in addition to their supply-store at Douglas, on Harrison Lake,

---

[35] The printed prospectus of the enterprise is in the Provincial Li-
brary, Victoria, B. C., entitled "Prospectus of the Bentinck Arm and
Fraser River Road Company, Limited. The company is organized under
the Joint Stock Company's Limited Liability Act, 1860. Victoria, V. I.
Printed at the British Colonist Office, 1862." This route is described in
Macfie's Vancouver Island and British Columbia, London, Loughman,
Green & Roberts, 1865.

[36] Letter Ranald MacDonald to Malcolm McLeod, May 24, 1889, in
the Provincial Library, Victoria, B. C.

secured a government license and ran a ferry across the Fraser River at Lillolet, B. C., charging one dollar a head toll. Ranald MacDonald now became interested in mining and was one of the pioneers in the Bonaparte and Horsefly districts, 1862-1863. He had great faith in the Horsefly Country, but the mines there never proved of any great value. In 1862 his brother, Allen, sold out and returned to Montreal, Canada, but Ranald continued prospecting and developing his mining claims in northern British Columbia for some ten years more, spending his summers in the mountains and his winters on the ranch at Bonaparte.

Ranald MacDonald's father had been a close personal friend and associate of Governor Sir James Douglas of Vancouver Island, and the Governor's wife was a distant relative of Ranald's foster mother, Jane Klyne MacDonald. During his stay in British Columbia Ranald, as well as his brothers, Allen and Benjamin, was an occasional guest at the residence of the Governor in Victoria. While at St. Andrews, Quebec, in 1853, Ranald MacDonald was initiated into the Masonic order at the St. Andrews' lodge, No. 516, A. F. A. M., and became a Master Mason.

While in the Cariboo Country, the character of Ranald MacDonald as a dominant, red-blooded man, brooking no interference by bullies or "bad men," is exemplified by a story told by Mr. J. M. Lynch—long familiar with the Rock Creek and Camp McKinley mining country in British Columbia. During the gold-rush of the early '60s a "tough bunch" came up to the Cariboo Country from San Francisco and tried to carry the camp by force and terrorizing the more peaceful and law-abiding element. Ranald MacDonald, being of the old school, resented their conduct and on various occasions personally encountered and defeated several of them in the rough and tumble fights of that day. One bully—a prize-fighter named McCune, whom he encountered—defeated him in a fist-fight. Ranald MacDonald took his defeat in good grace, but remarked to McCune that, as he had met McCune and had been defeated at his game, McCune should accept a return match at his (MacDonald's) game. McCune, who was plucky, impulsively consented. Ranald·chose single-stick, and at once proceeded to make two large, stout clubs for the contest, in which McCune received a terrible beating.

As the result of this contest, Mr. MacDonald acquired a nick-name which followed him during his residence in the Cariboo District. After the contest McCune, in pique, remarked that he wouldn't have cared a damn if he had been defeated by a white man, but that he hated like hell to be beat by a "siwash." This title, used by the miners as a good-natured expression of their respect and approval, stuck to MacDonald and he was thereafter known in the section as "Siwash" Mac-Donald, to distinguish him from his brothers and other MacDonalds in the camp. Between such manly resistance by the individual miners and the strict enforcement of the law, the Cariboo became a peaceful mining camp, without resort to the "vigilante committees" of the early mining camps of California, Idaho and Montana.

GENTLE MAN.

There was another side of Ranald MacDonald's character; that of a courtly, old-school gentleman, with all the grace, courtesy and gayety of a Frenchman, which is best presented by the accounts of his niece and two cultured and accomplished ladies who met him in his later years.

Mrs. Hannan, a niece at whose home Ranald Mac-Donald spent much time in the early '80s, emphasizes his quiet, gentle, good-natured disposition and courtly manner and his insistence that his young nieces, then growing to womanhood on a remote frontier ranch, should learn and observe all the rules of etiquette for ladies of his day; painstakingly teaching them the old-fashioned minuets and polkas, how to mount to their side saddles from his palm, how to meet and address social equals, and explaining the family "coat of arms" which his father brought from Glencoe, Scotland.

Elizabeth B. Custer, widow of the gallant General Custer, who visited our author's home in the summer of 1890, says: [37]

"The Hudson's Bay Company's fort (Fort Colvile) is another square surrounded by the low log-huts, but individualized by the block-house that still stands as firm as if it were a stone-tower. It has a four-sided roof, and below are three portholes for muskets and one, larger still, under these for a gun.

When we drew up in front of the larger house of the group, an old man came out, bowing and smiling, while half-breed children, chickens and dogs scattered on either side. The men said: "Here comes old Ranald MacDonald himself," but I had not heard his history and consequently could not account for his courteous manner and marked individuality. No one could have invited us to descend from our anything but dignified

[37] Harper's *Weekly*, July 18, 1891.

perch on the high seats with more grace than did this coarsely dressed antiquarian. We felt that if our descent was in keeping with the suave reception and the bared head, we ought properly to be picking our way, in brocaded gown and ruffed stomacher, down the old-time steps that were unrolled from the chariots of the time of the Louises.

We were all presented, and this descendant of Scotch kings led the way about, showing us the huge logs held together with wooden pins, the great rafters with the mark of the ax on them still, and then a broken half of a little cannon covered with verdigris and rust. "This, ladies, was the great gun which defended his majesty King George's subjects from the enemy, and this the ladle in which the bullets were melted for the huge two-inch bore." As he stood laughing to scorn the little three-foot cannon, I discovered that his merry eyes missed no fun. "Now, ladies, can I escort you to our famous bastion?" And we followed him to the block-house that had a liberal sprinkling of bullet holes. "We had once a high stockade," he said, "with a gallery inside, about which the sentinel walked, and down there we made a charge for water. Think of it, ladies, a fort and no well! But then," he added, "when the great gate was closed and the enemy were about, and it was necessary to start a man for the river, why he ran under cover of our guns from the block-houses; for there were two of them."

"Getting water under these circumstances must have enrolled a good many of you under the army of the great unwashed," said we.

His eyes twinkled, and he replied: "Fortunately, we were not always under siege, and daily the Indian servants went and came from the river for all of us."

At last I was so overcome by this prince of paupers[38] that I fell behind to question one of the men of our party, for I could not make the high-flown language, of which I can give but a faint idea, fit the man. Then I was told that his father was a man of great distinction —Archibald McDonald, chief factor in the Hudson's Bay Company. He was forty-two years in the service, coming first as the secretary of the Earl of Selkirk, returning to Scotland, and after two years coming again with Sir George Simpson. The chief factor had married a squaw, as was the custom of the country, and Ranald was one of the several sons born to his father. He had all his early life been associated with English and Scotch, which accounted for the grandiose style of the old-school gentleman and the evidences of vivacity and foreign polish were traceable to the French Canadians who were in the employ of the company in its prosperous day.

As I was receiving this hurried history, the old courtier, sans several articles of toilet that civilization might require, came back as hurriedly as his many years would permit. Uncovering his gray head he said, so that I could hear: "I must make my compliments if it is really she," and such obeisance and lordly bending of his ancient back made me aware that he had not heard who I was at our introduction, and had come back to pay reverence to my husband's name. I can

---

[38] In the Sept. 3rd, 1891, issue of the Kettle Falls (Wash.) *Pioneer*, our author called attention to some slight errors and mistakes in Mrs. Custer's published interview with him. In this, she spoke of him as "The prince of paupers" and described his garb in rather disparaging terms. The article was seen by Mr. MacDonald, and it aroused his indignation. In recounting the matter afterward to friends, he said in his stately old-fashioned way: "I will allow, I was rather carelessly garbed, and had moccasins on my feet; but in a chest on the other side of that very room I had clothes in which I could have appeared before the crowned heads of Europe."

scarcely think of anything more incongruous than this aristocratic old man, with his high-flown expression, of which we knew nothing except in the literature of the style of Sir Charles Grandison, and the tumbled down, dilapidated, untidy old buildings around him. And yet the two clothes he wore and the straggling, gray hair and beard looked to me far more interesting than the dressed-up and commonplace looking man who occupied a panel of the family album, and represented Ranald when he was in the outside world. Then another incongruity was the slip he sometimes made into everyday talk and the introduction, in the very midst of his most lofty flights of rhetoric, of slang phrases, which seemed all the more absurd, associated as they were with the stately language of by-gone days.

"Now," said he, "that you have seen our monster guns"—and he rolled the little cannon with his foot—"and have viewed our lofty palisades"—there was still some of the log-stockade standing—"and have gazed upon the formidable bastions"—and here he waved his hand toward the block-house—"can I persuade you to go into my home?"

We found a large living-room with poor and very shaky furniture, a long alcove on one side, half covered with a calico curtain, where, as it was twice as long as an ordinary bed, I concluded the whole family slept. Three of the presidents were on the walls, and there were a few books. Two cumbrous wooden chairs, held together with wooden pegs; one with arms and a slatted back, dated back to the chapters of Hudson's Bay people. The adobe fireplace had an oval back, and it was so narrow there could be no way of burning logs except to stand them on end. Our host drew our attention to a trap-door, into the cellar, and his eyes danced with

the memories, he recalled as he spoke of the good old
Jamaica rum that was once there in abundance.   There
were guns and deer-horns on ths walls, and in this large,
low, cheerful room I could picture the convivial party
about the open fireplace brewing warm drinks and
pressing the guests to "take a drop more."   One of the
old Hudson's Bay men has since told me that they always expected the company they entertained to end the
evening under the table.[39]

A bright-eyed, half-breed woman was presented to
us as Mrs. MacDonald (wife of Duncan MacDonald—
a cousin of Ranald's); and of some dark-skinned children I asked about, the old man waved his hand over
them and said: "They are all MacDonald"; and no
chief of the clan could have referred to his aristocratic
progeny in a more stately manner.   Then I told him
that I had come out to this country representing an in-

---

[39] Our author's cousin, Angus MacDonald, Chief Trader in charge of
Fort Colvile in 1853 at the time of the arrival of the first territorial governor, Isaac I. Stevens, says: "I had full instructions as to the hospitality
and the discretion of it entirely trusted to myself.   The Governor had
ample credentials from the east crossing the Rocky Mountains by the
Hell Gate defile.   McLellan met him here with an escorting party from
Puget Sound.   I had fifty imperial gallons of extra rations to entertain
the gentlemen. ' McLellan drank but little; the Governor was rather fond
of it and laid back about ten on the first night to sleep the darkness out.
His last words were, 'Mac, this is powerful wine.'   All hands had been
steeped during the day and found the grass and their blankets the best
way they could.   As all the party had disappeared McLellan began to
sip the juice of the vine more freely and we sat on the old sofa together
as closely as space allowed.   Having to undergo the hospitalities of the
day to all hands, I felt my grog inviting me to go to my blankets, but I
was well trained to that splendid brandy and in the prime of life, too, and
hard to make me give in at it.   Suddenly the General put his arm around
my neck and whispered in my ear, 'Mac, my proud father, too, was at
Culloden,' and he quietly slipped down off the sofa to the floor.   I soon
made the sofa an easy place for him and he and the Governor snored
the night till daylight.   This spree has been spoken of, God knows where
not; McLellan spoke of it in the Crimean, when sent as one of the Commissioners to observe the military arrays and genius of the France-Brit-
ish and Russion armies."   *A Few Items of the West, Washington Historical Quarterly*, viii, 196-197.

terrogation-point, and would he tell me something of his life?"

"Gladly, madam, gladly," said he. "In my mind there was only one man born on the third day of February, 1824, and that man was Horace Greeley, but nevertheless I first saw the light on that same February 3, at Astoria, the great trading post in Oregon, and was brought here at the age of 2 years. I flatter myself that I was the instigator of Commodore Perry's expedition to Japan."

I confess myself astonished at this, as it was hard for me to connect that distant world with this peaceful, old man, that seemed never to have left the green basin shut in by the mountains, about us. I found, however, that he had been a wanderer all his early days, and he said in the most pathetic tones:

"I have been all over the world—India, Japan, China, Australia, everywhere—but no matter how far I roamed, my mind always reverted to this little amphitheater. . . . Then he added, with his hands waving about him: It is my home." . . .

He went on to say that he was off on a whaler, and his spirit of adventure made him beg the captain to fit him out with a sail-boat and a few supplies and leave him as near the coast of Japan as possible. For this privilege he paid $2,000—his share in the whaling profits. He told us that the people there gave him to understand that they admired his courage, and paid tribute to it by heaping him with favors.

"I had thirty or forty attendants," said he, "one to arrange my bath, another to light my pipe, another for my wardrobe, another to be my majordomo and take me about, another to fetch coal for my fire. It was all luxury and magnificence, and I tell you, madam, my lord lay back and enjoyed it all." . . . He was so dramatic, that I watched his movements with fascinated eyes. For instance, as he described how the natives brought a warm bath for his feet, he bent to imitate their humble movements, and then thew himself back in the most *dolce far niente* attitude, and expressed by gesture that he could be a high muck-a-muck if he had the opportunity. . . . . He was imprisoned there for eleven months. . . . . The expedition of Commodore Glynn resulted in his release. His depositions are now on file in Washington.

As the quaint old man went on talking about the days when the Hudson's Bay Company was in its most flourishing condition, the whole place became transformed to me. I saw the bustle of traffic, the industry of the little community, the military discipline and precision with which everything was conducted; for, though the governor of the company was not an officer, he was an autocrat, such as can scarcely be conceived in those independent days. The nearest court of justice was 600 miles away. There were forty servants of the company, including all kinds of clerks, artisans, interpreters, and then a swarm of Indian domestics. It was a great distributing fort for the smaller agencies of the company. There were two mills, and the storehouses were bristling with furs, skins and merchandise to be given in exchange. Two brigades came in twice a year, consisting of about fifty men, bringing in eight or nine boats, the supplies of the company, and returned with furs to Vancouver, on the Pacific coast, where they were shipped to England. Whenever these brigades journeyed, gathering up furs from the different stations, the few travelers who were daring enough to go about in those days attached themselves to the column and received protection.

The trails of the Pend d'Oreilles, Kootenais, the Flatheads, the Coeur d'Alenes, Cayuses, indeed all the coast and mountain Indians, centered in this valley, and here they came with pack-horses almost hidden under the loads of beaver, otter, mink, marten, lynx, bear, wolverine and buffalo hides, humps and tongues and the first salmon of the season, that, Mr. McDonald added, "was the royal fish, and his majesty, the governor, got it." We asked if there were caribou, and he said yes, but only two elks had been seen in that part of the country in nearly thirty years. There was no money, but beaver was the standard of value. For instance, twenty beavers would be proffered for a horse, or "I'll give a beaver for that skin"—meaning that the offer was from 5 to 6 bits, equivalent to $1 in the east. "Ah, madam," he said, "those were halcyon days—no taxes, no money, no sheriff, no judge, no jury." . . . .

The Earl of Selkirk, on his return to Scotland to get recruits, tried to induce Scotch women to come out, but the only ones who were willing, Mr. MacDonald said, were induced to do so by the promise of all the tea they wanted. "For a while," he said, "they came in hordes." He explained that it was Labrador or Muskage tea, and grew about thirty inches up from the ground, having leaves an eighth of an inch in width, the outside hard, the inside yellow and downy. The missionaries offered $5 a pound for the flowers for medicinal purposes. He said "the aroma was delicious, and the Scotch would like it." It would have been an article of commerce, but the East India Company had a monopoly of that trade at that time.

It is impossible to describe the merriment in the narrator's eyes and his most expressive gestures as he dwelt on the Scotch women who refused to come to the wilderness with their husbands, till the tea was offered as an allurement. It suddenly came over me how some people I knew in the east would enjoy this witty, dramatic and versatile man, and how I should like to take the droll old fellow and set him in the midst of people who get so tired of each other and long for novelty. So I suddenly said:

"Oh, Mr. MacDonald, how I should like to take you home with me!"

In return I received such an impressive bow, and his hand went instinctively over his heart as he said:

"Oh, madam, take possession of me. I am yours."

I glanced at the squaw, wondering if any of the savage instincts remained in her and how she would look upon this rather open trespassing upon her preserves; but she smiled upon me, and I hastened to lead my new-found friend back to his narrative. I found afterward that she was Mrs. MacDonald, but the wife of the older man's cousin, so the tomahawks ceased to float in the air before my imaginative eyes.

Mr. MacDonald's education was a very serious question for his father, but he was determined, as the old man told me, that it should be "A No. 1. So my brother and I were sent a thousand miles or more to Winnipeg on snow-shoes. I know something of Romanism, but those Episcopalians at that church school knocked the spots out of the Catholics with their doctrines. We used to have pemican for our luncheon, and it was something of which a little goes a long ways. Buffalo meat is dried and pounded, mixed with fat boiled, berries, sugar, raisins (if you had 'em), and then sewed up in a sack of buffalo hide; and if you are very hungry

you eat it raw; if you are delicate, why, put in a frying
pan and cook it in slices." Then he asked me if I would
like to hear of his first naval engagement. By this time
I found that it made little difference what he said, his
manner of telling what he had to say was something
that I was not likely to encounter every day.

He left home with a brigade of the company to go to
Vancouver to meet his father, who had traveled with
Sir George Simpson 3,000 miles in a canoe, through the
various rivers and lakes between Hudson's Bay and the
mouth of the Fraser River, on the shores of the Pacific
Ocean. At Vancouver, while waiting, he met his maternal grandfather, old King Com-Comly, a blind Indian, who was very faithful to the whites. When the
annual ships that came from England reached them,
they took passage for Fort Astoria. Arriving, they
found two or three other vessels of the Hudson's Bay
Company, all carrying guns, and they signaled to prepare to engage in a fight; for a short time before a vessel was wrecked and the captain came on shore among
the Indians to get dry and find assistance, leaving his
crew with orders not to follow him. A cowardly Indian
shot him, and then all the village ran to the ship and
plundered it. They filled their huts with bales of blankets, cases of guns, hogsheads of tobacco and every
kind of merchandise. Governor Connolly, the father
of Lady Douglas, was in command of the brigade, and
at a signal from the ships all opened fire on the village.
The Indians fled back into the forest, and the crews
and Hudson's Bay Company's employes landed in
small boats, under fire of the guns, and set a torch to
the cabins and tents. They were stored with sturgeons'
heads and the tails and with oil, and there soon was little left of the village. "While the guns were firing, I

was eager to have a hand," he said, "and so ran out from where I had been hiding and jumped on one of the guns, but what was my mortification, even at 6 years of age, to be slapped by the captain and ordered off to the steward, and this was the ignominous end of my first engagement at sea."

When we came to say a reluctant goodby to this man, whose life had been crowded so full of adventure, he said so simply, but with admiring tones in his voice: "I wish, madam, you would speak of one man who loved this life and his duties here so well he did not want to return to England, even when offered knighthood for having attained by his exertions the furtherest point north then known, and he was Peter Warren Dease."

As soon as we had driven far enough away, we all fell to talking at once of his quaintness, his animation, his Scotch and French manner. The railroad official told us that the old man had said that he might perhaps come and see me, if he could be slipped on as baggage in the freight car, and was told by him that he would do better than that, he would ship him as an original package. The old Sir Ranald, however, was driven out of our minds soon by the grandeur of Kettle Falls, on which we looked from the banks of the Columbia, 200 feet above.

Eleanor Haskins Holly has furnished the following reminiscences of our author:—

I met Ranald MacDonald many times, but my first meeting with him is very vivid in my memory. It was on New Year's day, 1893. I was living at the new town of Kettle Falls (Wash.) which had been started shortly before on the Columbia River, just below the falls of that name in the Columbia. On the flat above the upper fall were the old block-house and log-buildings built for a trading post of the Hudson's Bay Company in 1826 and occupied 1835-1844 by Archibald McDonald, Esq., the father of Ranald, and later by Angus MacDonald, Ranald's cousin, the last Hudson's Bay Trader or Factor in this region.

My maid, a German girl who spoke but little English, came to call me, saying: "There is a 'gross Mann' wants to see you." And when I entered the room, as the imposing personage arose from his chair, I saw that her description was not amiss, for he was a 'gross' man. The height of his figure did not impress you at first glance, on account of comparison with the breadth of his shoulders and general proportions, but as he seemed to tower up beside his companion, who was quite an average-sized man, I realized how imposing a figure he really was. He wore a light-blue, army overcoat, made with capes and brass buttons, such as, I believe, was used during the Civil War, and where he could have obtained it at that late day I cannot imagine; but it certainly added to his size and dignity.

He carried a wide-brimmed hat of black felt, with which he made a sweeping bow—then crossing the room he clasped my hand and lifted it to his lips with a courtly obeisance. We women of this period not being accustomed to such ceremonious greetings, I saw that I was fortunate enough to have encountered an interesting character, although I did not then know who he was.

His companion was a man who was then living on the Colville Indian reservation, and had married a half-blood Indian girl who had been educated at Walla Walla, He himself was a man of education, closely related (a cousin I believe) to one of the members of President Cleveland's cabinet. He had, years before in the east, when a mere boy, been involved in an escapade which had had national notoriety, and had come to the west, and through some whirl of fortune's wheel had landed up here on the Columbia River and there stayed. He[40] was almost as interesting a character in himself as was Mr. MacDonald.

My husband had been interested in starting the Town of Kettle Falls, and Mr. Ranald MacDonald and his companion had with old-fashioned courtesy decided to call upon me and extend their New Year's greeting. Also, I found later, Mr. MacDonald, having learned that my mother, Mrs. L. C. P. Haskins, was a writer, wished to enlist her aid in the publication of the book which he had written of his experiences in Japan before Commodore Perry opened its doors to the western world.

At that time Mr. MacDonald was about 69 years of age, but from his erect bearing and strong vigorous appearance you would not have thought him more than 60. His hair, worn rather long, was gray, thick and *curling;* he wore a full beard cut rather short, but not close, which was quite gray and also very curly. His features were rather rough-hewn, but the high cheekbones and rather large and *flat* nose (with peculiarly wide nostrils) were the only features which would appear to show his Indian ancestry. His complexion, while dark, was not more so than that of many men who have spent much of the time in the open. His rather small and deep-set eyes were *gray,* and peculiar in that the gray iris was encircled at the outer edge by a distinct line of hazel-brown.

---

[40] This gentleman was at one time U. S. Customs Collector.

I have seen eyes with that peculiar combination of colors a few times since, but it appealed to me then as being very odd, and I used to think of it as showing the two races to which he belonged, which in him met and harmonized, but did not blend. His face, while not handsome, had a look of power which interested.

I saw him many times afterward as he used to come to see my mother, Mrs. Haskins, concerning his book of his experiences in Japan, which he was very anxious to have published, and she endeavored to assist him in interesting some one to do so, printing the first chapters in the Kettle Fall's newspaper and copying out several long extracts from it for him and sending them off to parties who might bring it out; but she was not successful in having it done.

I had many long and interesting talks with him of the early times there on the Columbia and his own early days. I remember his describing to me, one time, the festivities which would ensue when the boats of the "voyageurs" came back up the Columbia with supplies. The "bateaux" landed at the rapids about six miles below the Kettle Falls of the Columbia at what is now known as Rickey Rapids, from whence the supplies were carried by cart and pack to the trading post, Fort Colvile, just above the falls.

The canoes and bateaux went down the river to Fort Vancouver and Fort George at the mouth of the Columbia in the spring and returned in the fall. Every white man and Indian in the employ of the Company, with their wives and children, were given their yearly ration at the time of their return, Mr. MacDonald said, and they were all there to receive it. In reply to my question as to what the rations consisted of, he enumerated, among other things, salt, molasses, tea, beans, cloth, I recall; so much, he said, was allotted to each man, woman and child in any way connected with the Hudson's Bay Company. The trappers and hunters, even those who were located at far-distant points for the trapping and to gather up the furs of the Indians at those places, would all be there at those times.

He described the scene of festivity the night of the arrival of the boats; the long table which was spread o accommodate all those in any position of authority— his father at the head and the others seated according to the importance of their positions—the Indians at the foot; some of the squaws and children at the very lowest end of the table; and others at another table in the same room. There, amid jollity and a buzz of conversation, his father would read aloud items of interest from the letters received from the outside world or orders and instructions from the Company.

One can fancy the scene: the great fire of flaming pitch logs glowing in the huge fireplace and throwing its red light over the low ceiled room, lighting up the curiously diversified company.

His reminiscences had a great fascination for me, and I would always encourage him to talk, which was perhaps why he told me so much of his past.

He also told me many curious anecdotes of the past up there on the Columbia River. Among one which I remember was that of the burning of the last "witch" among the Indians on the Columbia River at that point below the falls. My husband had a tract of land a mile in length along the river (where the town of Kettle Falls now is) and we were building a house at the southern end not far above where the Colville River flows into the Columbia, where the high bank curved back, making a point from where there is a beautiful view far down the river.   In speaking of that point one day Mr. Mac Donald said, "there is a curse on it."   In surprise I asked why?   He replied that years before an Indian woman had been burned there as a witch. It seemed she was an Okanogan and had in some way caused a great deal of trouble (there was always much friction between the Okanogan and the Colville Indians, he told me) and at last she was burned as a witch. That point was selected because it could be seen far down and across the river.   Dying, she cursed the ground, and he said that the Indians had a superstitious feeling in regard to it even then.

One day shortly before I came away from there—it was in the summer just before Mr. MacDonald went up the Kettle River on the Reservation to make the visit from which he never returned—he came down to see my mother about something concerning his book, and, as he was a little lame and walked with difficulty, I had my horse brought out to take him back home.   The Colville Indian Reservation across the Columbia from the town of Kettle Falls was about to be opened and land allotted to all who had Indian blood entitling them to it.   As we drove along the river bank, I looked across the river to the Indian Reservation where there were some beautiful tracts of farm land, and said to him: "Why do you not take a farm over there, Mr. MacDonald?"   The old man drew himself up indignantly— "Why should I take a farm over there?   I am not an Indian.   I have no wish for any land there—let them have their farms."

It was curious how, with the pride which he in one way held in his Indian descent, he at the same time repudiated being classed in any way with them.   When I heard that he was dead and had been buried up there on the Colville Reservation, I was sorry to know it, as I felt sure he would have wished some other spot for his final resting place.

At one time I said to him: "Mr. MacDonald why did you never marry?"

"Well," he replied with a little, whimsical smile which used to light up his face at times—"I suppose it was because the women I would have married would not marry me, and the women who would have married me, I would not marry." The reply exemplified the old man's pride very well.

He told me many details of his stay in Japan, most of which, I think, are embodied in his book. He used to carry in walking, when he came down to our house, a handsome, ivory-headed cane which, he told me, was given to him by the son of one of his Japanese pupils; but I can not remember if it was sent to him at the same time the carved box which was sent to Montreal for him was received or at some other time. He valued it very highly and generally carried it when he went to make a ceremonious call. His manner always had a rather stately, old-time courtesy which was pleasing; and his language was well chosen and more than inclined to grandiloquence."

During his twenty odd years' residence in the Cariboo mining country Ranald MacDonald was at all the various mining camps of that region and engaged in many different businesses and employments, and experienced many vicissitudes of fortune. He is reported to have made $60,000.00 at one time in the Cariboo gold mines, but lost it all through ill luck and the dishonesty of some of his associates.

At one time he kept the Hotel at Hat Creek for George Dunn; at another time he was connected with the Bonaparte House, owned by Semlin and Parke; at another time he was in the employ of the stage line operated by Steve Tingley and Bernard; and in 1875 he worked for a time on the books in his cousin's trading post at Kamloops, B. C.   Changes in fortune apparently had little effect on his character, and he was ever ready to assist, serve, or entertain his contemporaries; whether this consisted of gallant attentions to an occasional lady visiting those crude settlements; or in joining his comrades in their amusements in the saloons and gambling houses which then furnished their sole means of recreation in western mining towns; or in performing his full share of the arduous duties on trail and in camp.   In the latter 70's he visited the Peace River country for a time.

He is remembered in British Columbia as a jolly, likeable character, the friend of everyone and, notwithstanding his occasional grand manner and high-flown speech, he has been characterized by a few surviving contemporaries (all now over four score years) as a "good sport," the *ne plus ultra* of frontier commendation.

In 1877 he spent some time at the ranch of a second-cousin, Mrs. Christina MacDonald McKenzie, at Shuswaps Prairie on Thompson's River, B. C.   Having disposed of his mining and other interests our author returned to Washington Territory about 1882 and later moved to old Hudson's Bay Company Fort Colvile where his second-cousin, Donald MacDonald resided. In September 1885 he settled on a preemption claim of 153 acres adjoining the old fort, and embracing a part of the old fort grounds.   Here he remained, living in a rough board shack and engaged in farming, prospecting and similar pursuits.   He secured a United States patent to the land Oct. 13, 1891 and sold six acres of his land to the Spokane Falls and Northern Railway Company for railway right of way. His homestead shack which burned down that spring was never rebuilt by him. Later he erected a log house on the Colville Indian reservation opposite the "big Island."

He never married, and spent much of his time with Donald MacDonald and his family at the old abandoned Hudson's Bay Company trading post, where he was interviewed by Mrs. Custer, and made occasional visits to his cousins after they removed to Montana. He was delightful and interesting company, full of strange tales of adventure in many lands, in the telling of which he drew from both fact and fancy. He enjoyed the discussion of current topics and pioneer history and was an occasional contributor to the Kettle Falls Pioneer. He refuted from personal knowledge of pioneer events the Whitman saved Oregon legend. [41]

He never desired to hoard or keep money, and the earnings and profits of his mining and business ventures in earlier years had been freely spent or loaned to improvident acquaintances. In his later years he spent much time planning to run a drift on Boundry Creek at the mouth of Norwegian Creek to catch the lost run of gold on the celebrated "Norwegian" placer ground.

These later years were passed in comparatively straitened circumstances and his principal ambition and desire at this time was to see the story of his Japan adventure in print before he died. A number of his letters in the Provincial Library at Victoria, B. C., recite a pathetic attempt to raise money for this purpose by borrowing from friends and mortgaging of his homestead.

[41] Letter Ranald MacDonald to Malcolm McLeod, Feb. 25, 1891, Provincial Library, Victoria, B. C.

Prior to his death he felt the infirmities of old age, suffering from "pains in the joints" and partial deafness, both probably attributable to the exposure and hardships of his pioneer life.   He died near Toroda post office, on Kettle River, in Ferry County, State of Washington, about seventy-five miles northwest of Marcus or old Fort Colvile, on the 5th day of August, 1894, while on a visit to the home of his niece, Mrs. Nelson, now Mrs. Jennie Lynch, a daughter of his younger half brother, Benjamin MacDonald.   His remains are buried in a neglected Indian grave yard near Toroda, Washington; a spot unmarked by any monument and known and remembered by only a few near relatives and friends.

His last words as he sank to eternal sleep in the arms of his niece were: "Sionara, my dear, sionara".[42]

Ranald MacDonald was certainly a unique character, not only interesting in himself, but as a bond between those early days and our own time, with the added interest we have in his early efforts in gaining access to the then inaccessible country of Japan and attempting to teach them something of the civilization and Christianity of the Occident.

As to the motives impelling him to his great Japan adventure we have the following in the introduction to his autograph manuscript notes:—"My principal motive in this way, it must be confessed the mere gratification of a love of adventure—the world within a mysterious veil which then hung, as it still hangs over Japan, unaccountably attracted my roving mind and at any risk I determined to solve it."[43]

---

[42] Sayonara, Japanese for "farewell." This meaning of the term was not known to Mrs. Lynch until informed by the editors of its meaning.

[43] *Original Manuscript* of Ranald MacDonald, in the Provincial Library, Victoria, B. C.

Cabin (in center) in which Ranald MacDonald died on August 5,
1894

From a photograph by J. A. Meyers.

Grave of Ranald MacDonald (indicated by small cross at left of
enclosure) near Torodo P. O., Washington

From photograph by J. A. Meyers.

Offspring from a union of the best blood of the old and new world, Ranald MacDonald was of the stuff that heroes are made of. Why the promise and early achievements of his youth did not reach a greater fruition in his mature years his editors are unable to say.

His father's letters disclose that Ranald MacDonald early displayed some unusual traits of character, distinguishing him somewhat from his half-brothers and the other boys at the Red River Missionary School. He was not only a promising, good natured lad, with a high chaɪacter for application and good behaviour, concerning whom his instructors gave very favorable accounts; but he possessed "certain indescribable qualities" indicating that he would make "the kind of man best adapted for the world". Archibald McDonald ventures this prediction concerning his offspring: "Who knows but a kinsman of King Concomly is ordained to make a great figure in the new world."

In the carrying out of his bold design to enter the forbidden realm of Japan, our author displayed unusual enterprise, intelligence, courage, and steadfastness of purpose; a combination of qualities which, applied in the same measure to the ordinary pursuits of life, would have achieved more than average success for him in later years.

Incidents at random in his life, occasional remarks to intimate acquaintances, a few paragraphs in his letters, and the pages of his narrative, here published, suggest that the bold and rugged exterior of Ranald MacDonald covered an unusually proud and sensitive spirit which was deeply wounded by occasional affronts to which he was subjected on account of his Indian blood from crude and self-satisfied people encountered in the business and social life of his time;

causing him, as he himself has expressed it, "to withdraw from highly honorable enterprise".

His Scotch and Indian pride keenly resented, and his sensitive nature shunned the slight and implied inferiority of his Indian blood, and the man whose youthful exploit placed among the great adventurous spirits of his age was doubtless moved by the affronts of a few thoughtless and bigoted contemporaries to shun the centers of the business and social life of his compeers, and spend his remaining days in the more liberal atmosphere of the northwestern mining camps. In his *Narrative* [page eighty-four] he mentions this unreasonable hatred of race, acknowledges his Indian blood, and declares his quick resentment to any insult on that score.

Whatever the cause, our author passed the remainder of his life in retirement from society, in the peace and contentment of simple ambition and accomplishment, among the crude and unpolished, but manly characters of the northwest frontier.

His life was gentle, and the elements
So mix'd in him, that nature might stand up
And say to all the world, 'This was a man!'
—*Shakespeare.*

Ranald MacDonald
From a photograph taken July 5, 1891, in possession of his
niece, Mrs. Jennie Lynch, Toroda, Washington.

Japan
Story of Adventure

of

Ranald MacDonald
FIRST TEACHER OF ENGLISH IN JAPAN
A. D. 1848-1849

———

"The Gates, of Brass, Were Opened!"

By
RANALD MacDONALD
Original Manuscript

PREFACE

This story, is now given, at the solicitation of many —most of them strangers to me—to meet what would seem to be a want in solution of the problem—mysterious, and certainly exceptional in many regards—of Japanese national development.

It was, and is, essentially internal; due to their own inherent sense of fitness in national life, a fact which the writer, in his accidental position of first teacher of English to them, had the singular opportunity of learning. The statement may have been advanced by others, but the writer is not aware of the fact, and he feels it but right, and in justice to his old friends across the way, that they should have his testimony of that fact.

Ranald MacDonald.

Old Fort Colvile, [44] Columbia River,
State of Washington, U. S. A.
September, 1893.

---

[44] The spelling of the name, conferred in honor of Andrew Colvile, has in later years been changed to Colville; the editors have adhered to the original spelling.

CHAPTER I: INTRODUCTORY

First Connection of Whites and Natives—Columbia-
King Com-Comly-Royal Marriage—Hudson's Bay
Company and Northwest Company—Pioneer Ex-
ploration—David Thompson.

Now verging on the alloted three score and ten of
human life, but still alive to the events of the hour, it
has struck me that it might be of some passing interest
to the now fast increasing crowd of travel by this new
western way to the "East", to hear my humble story of
pioneer development of it.   I have often, in years long
gone bye, when a wanderer in older countries, been
advised to publish it; but circumstances—chiefly nar-
rowed means; and with no ambitions in that way; and
moreover, the loss of most of my notes—prevented me.
Happily, nature has endowed me with a good memory;
and in my oldening, I find no loss of it—at least not yet
perceptibly; but, on the contrary, by some inexplicable
natural process, those earlier incidents and scenes of
my life come up, to my mind's eye, with all the glow
and vividness of recurring morn, as if sunlit for ever
on my page of time.
   What I have to say in this way is, essentially, merely
personal narrative, but, incidentlly, it may—so many
have urged me on—be of more than mere personal interest.   As to that I make no pretension.   Like others,
in common with my race, I have ever done what I considered was my duty, when thereunto called in public
or private behest.   Native, and denizen almost through-

out life, of the great Columbia Valley of the Pacific
Slope of America, I claim to be, in the broadest sense,
a true American.

True it was the British flag covered my cradle [45] but
that makes no difference. The Oregon Treaty of 1845
made me a citizen of the United States of America. But
further: on this point I may state, that on my mother's
side, I am by direct legal succession, of the blood of the
sole King (known to history as such) of the Columbia,
and of the Pacific Slope in those latitudes, viz: King
Com-Comly [46] of Washington Irving's *Astoria*, the

[45] Astoria, mouth of the Columbia River. The Fort—within which I
was born on February 3, 1824—had, in 1818, under the treaty between
Britain and the United States, of that date, been formally "restored" to
the latter—Commander Biddle of the U. S. Sloop of war, "Ontario,"
formally hoisting the flag of the United States on the occasion. How,
exactly, it was changed, and so remained changed for many years, is
more than I can explain. The Northwest Fur Company (Canadian)
bought out Astor in 1813, and in 1821 the Hudson's Bay Company
bought out (by coalition and absorption) the latter. That is the only
explanation I ever heard of the matter.—[Original.]

[46] The meaning of this Chinook name is unknown; it is of the type
of birds' names, common among the Chinook Indians and, according to
Dr. Franz Boas of Columbia University, cannot be analyzed. Elliott
Coues' statement, [*New Light on the Early History of the Greater
Northwest*, ii, 750] "that the name has something to do with salmon, for
a map before me letters 'Con-con-ully or White Salmon on a certain
creek,' " shows the danger of mere surmises. Con-con-ully, an Okanogan Indian word now applied to the Conconully lake, creek and town in
Okanogan County, State of Washington, is not of Chinook origin and
has no relation whatever to the Chinook name, Com-com-le. This Chinook name has been variously spelled by early explorers and fur traders as: Com-comly, Ross Cox, *Adventures on the Columbia River*, i, 67;
Washington Irving, *Astoria*, chap. vii; Elliott Coues, *op. cit.*, pp. 850, 750,
Com-com-le, Gabriel Franchere, *Narrative of a Voyage to the Northwest
Coast of America*, 100; Te-cum-le, Pierre Jean de Smet, *Life, Letters and
Travels*, ii, 442; Comcomli, Dr. John Scouler, *Journal, Oregon His-
torical Quarterly*, vi, 165. Come-Comly, Alexander Ross, *Adventures of
First Settlers on the Oregon or Columbia River*, 68. Com-com-moly,
Lewis and Clarke Journals, 716. Com-com-mo-ley, Reuben Gold
Thwaites, *Original Journals of the Lewis and Clark Expedition*, iii, 238,
294. Com-comly and Kum-Kumly in our *author's correspondence*. Kom-
komle, in J. B. Tyrell, *David Thompson's Narrative of his Explorations
in Western America*, 505, and Com-comly, Maduse or Thunder, David
Douglas, *Journals Kept During His Travels in North America*, 61, 147.

truly royal host of the Astor expedition there in 1811-
1813 and of all other whites since, in his realm.   His
palace was on the north side of the Columbia where the

Madsu, Dr. Scouler, *op. cit.*   See also Peter Corney, *Voyages in the
Northern Pacific,* 27-68.

Whatever his correct name, all visitors at the mouth of the Columbia
make mention of the old Chief.   On Nov. 20, 1805, Lewis and Clarke met
the Chief with his sub-chief, Chil-lai-la-wil and gave them both medals
in commemoration of the occasion, also presenting Com-com-mo-ly, as
they called him, with a flag.   Thwaites, *op. cit.,* iii, 238.

David Thompson described him in 1811 as "a strong, well-made man,
his hair short, of dark brown, and naked except a short kilt around his
waist to the middle of the thigh"; Washington Irving as "a shrewd old
savage with one eye"; Corney, as "a short elderly man . . . . . the
richest and most powerful chief on the River," *op. cit,* 65; Dr. Scouler,
in 1824, describes him as then being sixty years of age. *Op. cit,* vi, 167.
Many interesting stories are told of the old chief.   On one occasion he
saved the lives of Messrs. McDougal and Stewart from drowning, entertained them in his lodge,   and was in many ways of service to the
Astorians, who were at first suspicious of him, but later acknowledging
him a staunch supporter of the Americans, and even offering to fight
the British in their behalf.   Mr. Edward Ermatinger mentions his "marching into Vancouver with all his naked aids and followers, rigged out in a
British general's   uniform"—minus   the pantaloons. *Washington Historical Quarterly,* v, 205.   At a dinner given in his honor on board the
"Pedlar," March 5, 1814, he appears to have donned the trousers and
to have been still more elaborately dressed. Coues, *op. cit.,* 850.   He
was the principal chief of the confederacy of all the tribes of the lower
Columbia (except the Clatsops) who spoke the Chinook language, between the Cascade Mountains and Cape Disappointment.   He had a
wife, according to Indian custom, from nearly every tribe in the confederacy, and some from the neighboring tribes.   With these wives he
possessed a considerable family and many slaves. See Corney, *op. cit.,*
65.   Mr. Henry [Coues, *op. cit.,* p. 750]mentions him as seated in his
canoe alongside of his favorite woman, Le Blanche.

Chief Com-comly was treated as an equal and often sat at the table
with Dr. McLoughlin and (Sir) James Douglas. He was in high feather.
His principal palace, or royal lodge, was at Scarborough head, where the
new fort, Columbia, has now been erected.   The bald place high up on
the slope that catches the attention of all passers was the eerie from
which he spied out the approach of the Hudson's Bay Company's ships
which came every spring.   Com-com-ly was made chief bar and river
pilot for the company (the first on the Columbia, James Scarborough
being the second) and wore the uniform of their service.   When a ship
came in sight, he had 20 of his slaves launch the royal canoe and take
him out to meet the vessel.   His canoe and all its crew would be taken
aboard, and Com-com-ly would guide the craft up to headquarters at
Vancouver.—Portland (Ore.) *Oregonian,* Dec. 17, 1899, p. 28.

He had several sons. Ross, [*op. cit.,* 83], mentions two; the eldest was
Che-nam-us, a child by Com-comly's Multnomah wife. A younger brother, the favorite son and intended heir of the old chief, was named Sha-la-

great river, at its discharge, is about six miles wide. His
relations with the whites had ever been most amicable.

---

pau. He learned to talk, read and write English fluently and was much
beloved by the tribe. Among the men at the fort these two sons were
known as the "Prince of Wales" and the "Duke," respectively. Irving,
[*op. cit.*, lvi] gives the name of another son as "Gassacop"; Corney,
[*op. cit.* 65] gives the name of another as "Selechel." See also Coues,
op. cit., 890, 901, 906. Sha-la-pau and a younger brother died of sick-
ness April, 1824; and Dr. Scouler states that another brother promptly
assassinated the medicine chief under whose care they died. *Op. cit.*,
vi, 166, 277. A brother of Com-comly, named Tha-a-muxi, or Bear, was
also a chief and resided in the vicinity. David Douglas, *op. cit.*, 147.

Chief Com-comly had several daughters; the eldest, "the Princess,"
the daughter of Com-Comly's Scappoose wife, married the Astor partner, Duncan McDougal; the second married our author's father; a third
married Calpso, a chief of the Chinook village near Cape Disappointment. The Rev. Samuel Parker in his *Journal of an Exploring Tour*,
245, describes the latter as a "woman of more than common talents and
respectability and relates that she slew two female slaves to attend her deceased daughter to the world of the spirits. He had still another daughter named Car-cum-cum. E-lo-wah-ka was a daughter of Com-comly by
a Willapa woman; she married into the tribe and died in 1861 at Ilwaco,
a thriving village named for her. The "Princess Margaret," Kah-at-lau,
Com-comly's daughter by his Chehalis wife, married Louis Rondeau, a
Hudson's Bay Company's trapper in 1825. Another daughter of the old
Chief married a Scotchman named McKay, also a Hudson's Bay Company's employee.

After his oldest daughter's marriage to Mr. McDougal, the Chief appears to have fully appreciated his position as father-in-law to the mana-
ger of the establishment. Father de Smet, writing in later years says:
"When he used to come to Vancouver in the days of his glory, 300
slaves would precede him and he used to carpet the ground that he had
to travel from the main entrance of the fort to the Governor's door, several hundred feet, with beaver and other skins." de Smet, *op. cit.*, ii,
442-443. His opposition to the surrender of Astoria to the British has
been noted. Com-Comly's tribe and immediate family fell easy victims
to the measles, smallpox and other diseases of civilization brought to
the Columbia River by the whites. Dr. Scouler [*Op. cit.*, vi, 276] mentions that Com-comly lost eight members of his family in the two years
preceding September, 1825. The family burial place was near Point
Ellis, and the Chief's two sons, previously mentioned, were buried in
canoes with fowling pieces by their side, with loaded pistols in each
hand, and surrounded by all their possessions. The old Chief regularly
visited their graves to see that their property and the remains of his
relatives were undisturbed.

Chief Com-comly died suddenly in 1830 of virulent intermittent
fever, an epidemic that carried off about a thousand of his people at
the same time, and his remains were buried with great ceremony as be-
fitting his rank in life, in a canoe near Fort George, according to Chinook
custom. Later, for greater security, his body was taken out of the canoe

Chinook Indian Grave in Canoe
From a drawing by H. J. Warre.

King Com Comly's grave
From drawings in Wilkes' *Narrative*, iv, 321.

A leading officer of the name of MacDougall [47] (Duncan) on the Astor staff had, before the sale and transfer of the establishment to the North-west Company in

_____

by relatives and placed in a long box in a lonely part of the woods. The precaution to preserve his remains from molestation was, however, idle. James Dunn, who was either present or had first-hand knowledge, states in his *History of the Oregon Territory* (London, 1844), 132: "His head is now in the possession of some eminent physician in Edinburgh and, strange to say, although he had been buried about five years, his skin was quite dry and not decayed. It required a very sharp knife to penetrate the skin and his hair was still on his head." His grave was located by Commodore Wilkes in 1841 and a picture of it is preserved in *The Narrative of United States Exploring Expedition*, iv, 321, where mention is made of the skull having been carried to Glasgow by a Hudson's Bay Company's agent. Father de Smet, who visited his grave with Mr. Birnie on Aug. 1, 1844, seems to have been among the last to do honor to the famous Com-Comly.

Indian graves were frequently desecrated then and ever since. J. K. Townsend, in 1836, mentions his own acts of carrying off the mummy of an Indian woman and the taking of four skulls from another Chinook Indian cemetery in the vicinity of Fort George and near Fort William, Weyeth's transient settlement on Wapato Island. John K. Townsend, *Narrative of a Journey Across the Rocky Mountains* (Phila., 1839), 236-238; 255-256.

Chief Com-comly has several living descendants residing along the Columbia River, some of whom have grown wealthy from the development of the salmon fishing industry. Portland (Ore.) *Oregonian*, Dec. 17, 1899, 28. Until the summer of 1888 a street in Astoria bore the old chief's name, it was then changed to First street.

[47] Duncan McDougal was a clerk of the Northwest Company when he joined the Astor enterprise in 1810. Franchere, *op. cit.*, p. 20; Irving, *op. cit.*, chap. iv., describes him as an active, irritable, fuming, vainglorious little man and elevated in his own opinion by being the proxy of Astor, and as a man of a thousand prospects, and great though somewhat irregular ambition. Alexander Ross, *op. cit.*, describes him as a man of but ordinary capacity, with an irritable, peevish temper; the most unfit man in the world to head an expedition or to command men. He was accused by Astor of betraying his interest; see letter from Mr. Astor to John Quincy Adams, January, 1823; Irving, *op. cit.*, chap. xxix; Franchere, *op. cit.*, appendix, 368; Horace Sumner Lyman, *History of Oregon*, ii, 298-301. His course in selling out to McTavish was defended by Hubert Howe Bancroft; *History of the Northwest Coast*, ii, 221-230; Alexander Ross, [*op. cit.*, 252-3] states that the transaction was at the time considered fair on both sides. The bill of sale published in appendix "M," 293, Gordon Charles Davidson, *The Northwest Company* (Berkeley, 1918), would seem to vindicate Mr. McDougal. See also Ross Cox, *op. cit.*, i, 190; Coues, *op. cit.* 747; Franchere, *op. cit.*, 166, 192. After the transfer of the Pacific Fur Company (Astor) property to the Northwest Company Duncan McDougal re-entered the service of the latter company as a wintering partner and remained on the Columbia until 1817, when he

1813, married [48] an elder daughter of his—a handsome
woman; of proud queenly mien; reminding me of
Egypt's Cleopatra, as pictured to us.   I distinctly remember her, living in   widowhood with her parents.
Though my aunt, she was no friend of mine; seeming
ever to have some pique against me, which however I
did not regard, as I did not   then   understand our relationship.   She was childless—if I mistake not—
while, I believe, I was not only the baby favorite, but
the heir presumptive of the old King, according to Chinook [49] and general Indian law.   Some old people of
the Columbia, after the old man's death, used to call
me, or speak of me, as Com-Comly, or shortly, Comly
MacDonald; but why, I never enquired, nor knew, nor

crossed the mountains.   He died at Bas de la Riviere, Winnipeg.   Franchere, *op. cit.*, appendix, 368.   Coues, *op. cit.*, 739, 759, 775, 779, 783.

[48] This marriage took place July 20, 1813.   For description of the
wooing and marriage see Irving, *op. cit.*, chap. lvi.   In Coues [*op. cit.*,
901] we find: "April 26—McDougal this afternoon completed the payment for his wife to Com-comly, whose daughter she was; he gave five
new guns, five blankets two and one-half feet wide, which makes fifteen
guns, fifteen blankets, besides a great deal of other property, as a total
cost of this precious lady."   See also Paul Kane, *Wanderings of an
Artist,* [London, 1859], 177, and for other taking of wives by the fur
traders at Astoria see Coues, *op. cit.*, 910-911.   McDougal deserted this
Indian wife when he left the Columbia district in 1817.   She afterwards
became the wife of Cazenove, (Townsend's Ke-ez-a-nos), who succeeded Com-comly as head chief of the Chinook nation, and she was
murdered in 1836 by Cazenove or some one of his retainers as a victim
or sacrifice on the death of his son. Samuel Parker, *op. cit.,* 251-252; J. K.
Townsend, *op. cit.,* 237-238.   Chief Cazenove was living at an advanced
age at Fort Vancouver in 1845 and was sketched by Paul Kane, *op. cit.,*
173-178.   See also article in The Portland (Ore.) *Oregonian,* Nov. 29,
1893.

[49] The Chinook tribe proper, resided on the North bank of the Columbia River from Gray's Harbor to Cape Disappointment, and on Shoal
Water Bay; the stock also embraced a number of closely related tribes
along both sides of the Columbia River from the Cascades to the sea and
some distance up the Willamette River; all speaking a common language
but in two dialects.   The name Chinook (Ts' inu' k) is that by which the
tribe was known to their northern neighbors, the Chehalis Indians, Prof.
Franz Boas, *Handbook of North American Indian Languages,* 563.   The
word also signifies a jargon trade-language used on the Northwest Coast,
composed largely of Chinook Indian words, still in use for intercourse
between the whites and the Indians of the Northwest.

cared to know. It was only in after life, that accidentally—as hereinafter stated—I learn't the esoteric of my birth and status in this Corona Borealis of our Northern Hemisphere; gone alas! to the limbo of all vanities —Vanitas Vanitatum! The monumental brass of Irving, in his immortal *Astoria*, alone bearing testimony to future generations, of this last of the Kings—of dynasty most ancient—of all America.

My father was the late Archibald McDonald,[50] a leading officer of the Hudson's Bay Company, and whose name, while in such service, is prominently associated with the establishment of the Red River Settlement, and of the Hudson's Bay Company's interests

[50] The elder MacDonald signed his name McDonald. His children, including our author, and their descendants, adhered to the original Scotch spelling. Clan Donald is the oldest and most famous of the Scottish clans. By local Highland tradition it is asserted that the MacDonalds are coeval with the family of Noah and at the time of the flood had a boat of their own on Lock Lomond, independent of the Ark. L. R. Masson, *Les Bourgeois de la campagnie du Nord-Ouest, etc.* (Quebec, 1890), ii, 3 and 4. Clan Donald claims immediate descent from Somerled of the Isles, who died in 1164, leaving three sons, Dugall, Reginald and Angus. From Donald, the son of Reginald, the clan takes its name. The MacDonalds are very proud of their descent and their clan history fills a two-volume work entitled *Clan Donald*. A Clan Donald society exists with headquarters at Glasgow, Scotland. Our author's family traced their descent back to the MacDonalds of Glencoe in the Fourteenth Century. Members of this family were prominently identified with both the Northwest Company and the Hudson's Bay Company. Archibald McDonald, as he wrote his name, was born at Leechkentium, Northern Argyllshire, Scotland, on February 3, 1790, and entered the employ of Lord Selkirk in 1812. Under the Deed Poll of 1821 he was named as a clerk and his name appears as Nos. 303, 230 and 147, respectively, on the Lists of Employees of the Hudson's Bay Company in America for the years 1821, 1822 and 1823. He came to the Columbia River district in 1823 and was one of the most capable and trusted officers in the Hudson's Bay Company's service. He was in a great measure responsible for the organization of the Puget Sound Agricultural Company, and first introduced to the Hudson's Bay Company the idea of raising of cattle herds and flocks of sheep on the Pacific Coast, as a business project. While at Fort Langley he first inaugurated the business of salting and curing the Pacific salmon for market. He died at St. Andrews, Quebec, January 15, 1853, and his gravestone bears the legend: "One of the Pioneers of Civilization in Oregon." For a brief biographical sketch of Archibald McDonald see *Washington Historical Quarterly,* ix, 93 *et seq.*

generally throughout the Red River region, extending
far southwards, into what is now Minnesota, and northwards to the McKenzie basin.   That was in 1813-1821.

In 1823, following his old friend and associate in
those troublous times of constant fight with the Northwest Company, Chief-trader John McLeod;[51] he was
in Astoria (then called Fort George) assisting in the
establishment of what had never existed, nor ever been
tried before, viz., a British-American Pacific Ocean and
Coast trade, on a basis to cope with its great natural
difficulties.   Amongst these difficulties, was the general character and conduct—truculent and ever hostile
—of the coast Indians—the men who, in spite of all
friendly approach and attempts at conciliation, seized
Astor's first ship there, the "Tonquin"—murdering her
crew, and causing her to be blown up by the despairing
hand of her last living man (wounded unto death) on
board.   That was in 1811.   From that time to this
(A. D. 1823) there had been no trade [52] with whites

---

[51] John McLeod, a sturdy Scotch highlander was a Northwesterner
clerk and trader.   He was named a Chief Trader by the Deed Poll of
1821.   His name appears as Nos. 48, 19 and 18 in the List of Employees
of the Hudson's Bay Company in North America for the years 1821,
1822 and 1823, respectively.   1822-1826 he was in charge of the Thompson's River district at Kamloops, being succeeded there by Archibald Mc-
Donald.   His family left Fort Colvile for Red River Sept. 25, 1825;
Washington Historical Quarterly, v, 165-166, and Mr. McLeod followed
them in April, 1826; Idem., 284.   In 1827-1828 he was engaged in re-
building Norway House, which had been burnt.   In 1831 he was granted
a leave of absence to England for his health, and was never thereafter
assigned as a wintering partner.   For further biography see Malcolm
McLeod's Peace River and Oregon Indemnity, 27-30.   McLeod's Lake
and Fort McLeod, the Hudson's Bay Company's post in New Caledonia,
now British Columbia, are named after him.

[52] Our author is in error in this statement.   The Northwest Company
made an effort to carry on a trade along the coast by means of coast-
ing vessels.   After a brief attempt the scheme was abandoned.   Alexander Ross [Fur Hunters of the Far West, i, 41] explains the cause of
the failure and says: "Even the coast trade itself was far from being
so productive as might be expected, owing to the great number of coast-
ing vessels which came from all parts of the States, especially Boston,

along those shores, except, in very desultory way by
the Americans, Russians, and others, chiefly with a few
specially friendly Chinooks at and about the mouth of
the Columbia, and Vancouver's Island.

___

all more or less connected with the Sandwich Islands and China trade.
Competition had therefore ruined the coast trade, and completely spoiled
the Indians." Most New England whale ships on the Pacific a century
ago were fitted out for trade, the captains conducting on their own account a lucrative "graft" known as "private trade."

The fact is that the American traders, "the Boston peddlers," as their
opponents called them, had, commencing with the "Columbia" and the
"Washington," outfitted in Boston for trade on the Northwest Coast under the respective commands of John Kendrick and Robert Gray in 1787,
from 1792 downwards been gradually absorbing this coast trade, and by
1810 or earlier, had completely monopolized it.   David Thompson, the
noted Northwesterner, in a letter published in *Report of the Provincial
Archives Department*, (B. C.) 1913, V115, states that 21 vessels engaged
in the northwest coast trade in 1792, of which about one-third were from
England, the rest from United States, mostly from Boston or New England.   See also list of vessels employed in commercial pursuits on the
northwest coast of America in the summer of 1792, in a report of Geo.
Vancouver, Friendly Cove, Nootka Sound, Sept. 26, 1792, published in
The Report of the Provincial Archives Department, op. cit., V28-29;
this gives the names of 11 English, 6 American, 1 Portuguese vessel,
and states that two shallops are then building in Nootka Cove for the
trade, and that seven Spanish vessels are then employed on the coast—
a total of 27 bottoms.

In Hubert Hugh Bancroft's *History of the Northwest Coast*, ii, 340,
appears a list of numerous vessels trading on the northwest coast before
the date mentioned by our author; see also list William Henry Gray,
History of Oregon, (Portland, Ore., and New York), 13-14.   In James G.
Swan's *The Northwest Coast*, (N. Y., 1857), appendix, 423-424, the names
of some 63 vessels are given as engaged in the trade of the northwest
coast of America for sea otter and other skins from 1787 to 1799, while
most of the Pacific whalers, as stated, carried with them the various
gewgaws which would please the savage eye for the purpose of trading
with the natives of the Pacific whenever occasion offered.   Alexander
Starbuck, *History of the American Whale Fishery*, (Waltham, Mass.,
1878), 97.   Iron and copper seem to have been among the most valued
articles of barter.   The great aim of Governor Simpson of the Hudson's
Bay Company, was to drive these itinerant traders from the field, a project which took many years.   In 1831 Archibald McDonald, our author's
father, writing from Fort Langley says [*Washingon Historical Quarterly*,
i, 258; also *Report of Provincial Archives Department*, (B. C.) *op. cit.*,
V82].   "In the face of two vessels our trade is not 150 skins less than
last year.   If the Americans are off this year I hope things will be better."   Two years later he writes again: "Here this year in the face of
three American vessels we collected 2,000 skins.   Nass, in opposition to
no less than seven, got as much besides 1,000 picked up by each of our

It was a matter of public policy, therefore—apart
from private considerations, in such remote isolation
from other female help—to allow, and even encourage,
the blood-bond of marriage by whites with the native
women. It was followed up, in other like cases, even as
to the men (mostly French Canadian, and some British) in the service of the company. All with excellent
effect; for the Chinook, though given to the singular—
unique, I believe—custom of *flattening*,[53] in infancy,
the cephalic region (forehead) of his intellectual faculties, is no "flat," in any sense, but has proved himself,

------

own vessels—but they cost dear, near two dollars for made beaver."
Washington Historical Quarterly, ii, 161.

Duncan Finlayson, writing from Fort Vancouver, March 12, 1832,
[*Idem.*, ii, 42], says: "And we have in view to extend our settlements
along the coast, the best and most judicious plan we can adopt for the
purpose of wresting that trade from the grasp of the Americans who
have so far monopolized it and no doubt derived considerable gain therefrom."

In a letter to the foreign office in February, 1837, [Hudson's Bay
Company's Correspondence, part 2, p. 24], Sir John H. Pelly, the Governor of the company, speaks of "The difficulties arising from an active
competition with the Americans"; and in the same volume, page 30,
James Douglas writes under the date Oct. 18, 1838: "The respite from
opposition we have enjoyed for the past and the present year induces a
hope that our American friends are withdrawing entirely from the business."

The story of the maritime trade during the period referred to has
never been written, and the references to the movement of these Boston
vessels are scattered through many volumes both printed and unprinted.

[53] This custom had an aristocratic significance and was a mark of
freedom; no slave was permitted to bestow this enviable deformity on
his child. Apparently the practice caused no impairment of the mental
faculties of the tribe. For contemporary descriptions of this practice of
flattening the heads of infants see David Thompson, *op. cit.*, 506; Alex.
Ross, *Oregon Settlers*, 113; Franchere, *op. cit.*, 324; Ross Cox, *op. cit.*,
i, 274-275; the Rev. Samuel Parker, *op. cit.*, 249; J. K. Townsend,
op. cit., 176; and for sketches of the appearance of these flattened heads,
see Captain Lewis's drawing, Thwaites, *Original Journals*, iv, 10; George
Catlin, *Letters and Notes on the Manners, Etc., of the North American
Indian*, ii, 125-126, cut 210, and Paul Kane [*op. cit.*, 205] where the picture of a Flathead child and mother is given. Corney [*op. cit.* 63] after
describing the Flathead custom, mentions a somewhat similar practice of
another tribe in binding the head with cords, until an equally grotesque
deformity was acquired.

Chinook Indian woman with infant undergoing the process of
head flattening
From Catlin's *North American Indian,* ii, 125.

in natural intelligence, and in general aptitude for civilization, morally as well as mentally, the most advanced on the American Pacific Coast.

The remark applies, with full force, to their women; who, marrying—for no other connection was, by the laws, there, then, or while the Hudson's Bay Company had sway, permissible—marrying, I say, with due solemnity, the employees of the company, proved in their Ruth-like fidelity to marital duty,[54] the gravitating element and factor of pioneer settlement throughout the great Columbia country—a region of about two hundred and fifty thousand square miles; the richest in the world; and of strongest healthful life.

The womanhood of that world—world beyond the distant, dimly seen, or fancied golden glaciered "Mountains" of *De La Verenderie*," and, after him, of Carver, to the "Great South Sea," was, in those early times, and until the arrival there, of my step and foster mother, Jane Klyne,[55] wholly native, as was that of the British

[54] Most of these Indian women proved capable and faithful wives to their white husbands, and, to their honor, many of the officers of the fur companies, who took to themselves wives from the women of the Columbia River tribes, displayed affection, loyalty and pride in their dusky partners and their offspring, and clung to them in their more mature and affluent years, after retiring from the company's service.

[55] The editors have been unable to ascertain the date or place of birth of Dame Jane Klyne. Archibald McDonald's autograph pedigree list places her at Fort Rae in 1813 a time and place which apparently preclude her birth in Switzerland. An article in the Portland (Ore.) *Oregonian*, Feb. 12, 1891, states that she was born at Jasper House. She was reputed to be a half or quarter breed Cree Indian. Deprived of any opportunities for early education, she studied with her children under her husband's tutorship, and is referred to by Elkanah Walker in his *diary* of date Sept. 17, 1838, as "quite an accomplished woman." She was through her husband's training a Protestant of deep religious convictions and a constant Bible student, and able to defend the tenets of her belief in religious discussion with the early missionaries. After the family removed to St. Andrews she became a member of Christ's Church and was known for her many acts of charity, and, in the words of a contemporary, "went about doing little acts of kindness." She was one of the last of the great native gentlewomen typified by the late Lady Strath-

when it became a Roman colony.[56] The Roman has
passed the way of all flesh; has dropped into his Nir-
vana, of ultimate nonentity. The Briton still lives!
Mother of Nations! Mother of these United States of
America; the grandest political brotherhood of Earth!

I say brotherhood, yet must confess, that it, sadly
lacks that, in its inherent hate of race; its castes; its
doom of black and Red, and Yellow, and Brown, and all
other shades of Heaven-painted humanity within its
borders. How, or why it is so, I leave to the framers,
rather, to the successors of the framers of the original
Declaration of the United States of America—the first
New England of America—to state. *Are* "all men
equal?"

For my part: proud, and with no reason to be
ashamed of my native "blue" blood of Ind[ian] in
America, I feel no contumely towards any of different
hue of humanity. At the same time, I must plead guilty
to the soft impeachment of being naturally quick to re-
sent an insult on this score; or on any score. However,
I have never had occasion to do so.

To return to my narrative. While thus a bachelor,[57]
in Astoria, with much need of a housekeeper in trade-
post duty elsewhere, to which, at any moment he might
be called, my father married the youngest daughter,

cona—fit consorts for the sturdy gentlemen of the fur trade. By her
will she left her foster child, Ranald, our author, a legacy of $400.00
as a token of her affection. She died at St. Andrews, Quebec, December 15, 1879, and her remains are buried in the church yard there besides
those of her husband.

[56] Our author overlooked Miss Jane Barnes, the buxom Portsmouth
bar maid, who arrived at Astoria, April 17, 1814, on the "Isaac Todd."
Ross Cox, *op. cit.,* i, 258-259.

[57] Archibald McDonald had, some years previous, formed an alliance
with another Indian woman, and a son of this union, then two years old,
was accidentally drowned in a mud hole at Norway House in 1816.
Archibald McDonald *pedigree list.*

then still in her teens, of "King Com-Comly"; the father and the maid, nothing loathe. Her personal name, in Chinook, signified Raven;[58] probably from the color of her hair, for black in complexion she was not, but like her sister (Mrs. MacDougall) was rather of Egyptian brown. For her change in life—following a custom in this regard of, I believe, the Japanese and other old Asian peoples, and probably, in mark of courtesy to the Whites—she was named Sunday—Princess Sunday.

The marriage ceremony, as described to me, many years afterwards by an eye-witness, Captain Thomas Butler[59] of Salem, Mass., would seem to have been a very imposing one; possibly the grandest, in its way, on the Pacific Slope of North America, up to that time.

At this time, Astoria (Fort George) had received a large accretion of goods and men, for trade, by the arrival of ships (two or three) from London under the new management by the Hudson's Bay Company, to which the interests of the Northwest Company had been transferred in partnership.[60] The gentleman in

---

58 The Chinook word for raven is "Koale' xoa."

59 The statement is repeated in our author's letter to Mr. McLeod Jan. 16, 1893, Provincial Library, Victoria, B. C. The name is not a Salem name, and does not appear in the list of vessels registered at the Salem Custom House, nor does it appear in the list of vessels and masters touching on the northwest coast 1819-1840. H. H. Bancroft, op. cit., ii, 340-342. Our author may have confused the name and meant Captain Seth Barker of the "Volunteer," owned by Barker & Sturges, Boston. These owners had several vessels on the coast about the time mentioned, and Captain Barker was undoubtedly familiar with the incidents stated. Otherwise, our author's Captain Butler was an out-of-town man, temporarily in command of some Salem vessel during a single voyage; his history and the name of the vessel are unknown to the editors.

60 The partnership was by consolidation in the Hudson's Bay Company, under its charter, by deed-poll of March 26, 1821, by which the Northwest Company (the larger, by far, say three to one, in trade stock) became absorbed, in nominally equal shares, in the smaller chartered body. The transaction was peculiar in many respects—giving rise to litigation and claims in Parliament unsettled to this day—as set forth in a recent pamphlet under the caption of Oregon Indemnity by Judge Malcolm McLeod, of Ottawa, Canada.—[Original.]

chief charge of the post was Doctor John McLoughlin,[61] chief factor—formerly a leading partner in chief
charge, on the Pacific Slope, of the interests of the
Northwest Company—himself married to an Indian
wife, and faithfully devoted to her as worthy of his
esteem; a man of deep religious feeling, and imbued
with highest respect for the canons of Christianity,
and particularly of his own creed, the Roman Catholic
—a very "Christ of the Pacific Slope," as Bancroft
(H. H.) in his *British Columbia* enthusiastically (but
with, perhaps, questionable propriety) calls him.

Under the provisions of the Company's charter and
license from the crown he held magisterial powers,[62]

---

[61] Dr. John McLoughlin did not come to the Columbia River district
until November, 1824. Describing Dr. McLoughlin, our author has said:
"He and my father were the only two persons that I was in any way in
fear of. Tall, with a venerable look, caused by his very gray hair, with
strong, powerful, commanding voice, to be short, with the air of a major-
general; with a strong if not obstinate will. The last I saw of him was
at Red River, Manitoba. Then he was very kind to me. Those who
knew him well say that he was of a very kind disposition—so was my
father—and why I should fear them was always a mystery to me." Letter July 25, 1892. Dr. McLouglin married the widow of Alexander McKay,
the Astor partner killed by the Indians in the attack on the Tonquin.
Several of his descendants reside in the Northwest. See Frederick V.
Holman, *Dr. John McLoughlin* (Cleveland, 1907), biography, 22-25.

[62] This is scarcely correct. The company's charter only gave the
power of appointment of magistrates for the vaguely described region
east of the Rocky Mountains, known as Rupert's Land. The license of
exclusive trade only applied to the lands west of the Rockies and gave
no such powers whatever. In Sir George Simpson's evidence before the
Committee of the House of Commons in 1859 occur the following questions and answers on this subject:

> 1191—(Mr. Lowe) Have you any magistrates, justices of the
> peace? We consider all our factors as magistrates.
> 1192—Do they hold any commission from the Crown or from
> the Governor? Their commission as factors is understood to
> answer the purpose of a commission as magistrates.
> 1193—Have they power to imprison and to decide any mat-
> ter? We have never had any case of imprisonment.

At Fort Vancouver Dr. McLoughlin caused his assistant to be appointed a justice of the peace. See hereon Frederick Holman, *op. cit.*,
38, 39.

and was, in all matters thereto appertaining, for peace and good government, governor in chief, with full consular authority—for the land, then, still, was as no man's land, except that of the King (Com-Comly) then there in primordial title. The native imposed its own laws as to this matter of marriage; a matter, with them, of ever rigorous social exigence; and, in some tribes— such as the Shuswhaps—with singular application, like that of the Jews as we have it in our Bible. I refer to the law, more particularly, which requires a brother to marry a deceased brother's widow. Not, I hold, that such custom and law—or others like those of the Jews of old, traceable in American Indian tribes, are assignable to such origin—for history and ethnic science, I think, preclude such conclusion—but are mere accidental similarities, arising from the nature of man with his inhering laws of social life, adapted and adapting to the varying circumstances of his case—his environment. Of many such, from Arctic to Antartic, the world over, I have been an observer; and, in this regard, have remarked, that as a general law, man, in every form of social life, is a law unto himself, and is not given to borrow or adopt that of another. In that is his Adam title of life on earth, with his co-ordinate responsibility to his Maker.

In this sense, in Chinook realm, Chinook law (custom sanctified) governed—the world over—as to any marriage, or any matter of personal contract, as marriage is. At the time in question, there was no law of any foreign country, not even of Britain, or England, or the United States, or any of such, of any force at the Gate of King Com-Comly; where, in fact his word was law.

Had there been any clergy there, and such service

had been required, it would, no doubt, have been allowed and had; but there were none; none within two or three thousand miles. No Christian or missionary,[63] Roman Catholic, nor Protestant, then, ever yet set foot in that region. Still, marriage there, was, and for ages had been, an institution—a sacred institution—a binding together by God (the "Great Spirit")[64] which, according to the people's own local law, no man could break asunder.

ROYAL MARRIAGE

The royal residence was, in the fashion of the country, a long, one-story, gothic-roofed, very large house of wood with doors and windows and other conveniences, and adornments outside, including a monumental totem pole by way of royal flagstaff. All about—quite a town—were houses on scarcely simpler scale, for accommodation of all the retinue—at least five hundred men—of the King. Add to that some of his subjects, about, settled there—for they were not of nomadic habit—a population, altogether of probably four or five thousand.

The locality was a striking one, and was the first se-

---

[63] Two Spanish priests made a trip into the Northwest from California about 1810. See letter from Wm. Davis Robinson to the Hon. J. H. Eaton printed in *National Intelligencer* Jan. 21, 1821, and re-printed in the *Niles Register,* March 10, 1821, reprinted in the *Washington Historical Quarterly*, x, 142-149. These friars reached the height of land at the sources of the Colorado, the Platte and the Snake River, but did not travel as far north as the Columbia River. Returning, they claim to have reached the coast of California about latitude 43:30; possibly via the Umpqua River on Coose Bay, State of Oregon. Spanish missionaries had also been sent to the settlement at Nootka prior to its evacuation under Signor Quadro, and had possibly touched at some point on the mainland. See Franchere, *op. cit.*, 180, note.

[64] All North American Indians, as well as my friends the Moes and Japanese, I consider to be essentially Monotheists.—[Original.]

Totem Poles of the Northwest Coast Indians
From photograph in Provincial Library, Victoria, B. C.

lected for Astoria; but for special considerations, amongst others, better anchorage, the south side— Gray's Harbor of 1792—was ultimately chosen, though itself far from being good for harbor purposes.

In the rear was the grand forest of densely fronded lofty Douglas pine and other such arborage. In front the gently sloping beach, tide laved, of golden sand and pebbled shingle.

From water marge to the King's court, where in open heaven, the ceremony[65] was to take place—a distance say of about three hundred yards—was a path of golden sheen, of richest *furs*,[66] viz. of prime beaver, otter (sea and land), nothing less!—not even seal fur, then of no account in the fur trade. Along this golden path way, as a guard of honor, were three hundred of the slaves, so-called, of the King.

On the arrival of the bridegroom and his party, headed by the chief of the whites, Doctor McLoughlin, at this landing, they walked the furried path; the yeomen of the guard (all warriors taken captive in battle), retaining their statue stand, arrived at the King's gate. With little preliminary of ceremony, the King, with royal grace and dignity, in silence, handed over the evidently not unwilling bride; not unwilling, for her true love in his young manhood was of the handsomest of

[65] This, according to Benjamin MacDonald, our author's half-brother, occurred Sept. 12, 1823.

[66] Though Washington Irving in describing the wedding of MacDougal and Com-comly's daughter, [*op. cit.*, London ed. 1838, iii, 189-193] does not mention any such great display as our author claims signalized the marriage of his mother and Archibald McDonald, yet Paul Kane, [*op. cit.*, 177] speaking of the former wedding, which occurred long before he came to Oregon says: "Com-comly, however, acted with unexpected liberality on the occasion, carpeting her path from the canoe to the Fort with sea-otter skins, at that time numerous and valuable, but now scarce, and presenting them as a dowry, in reality far exceeding in value the articles at which she has been estimated." See note 46, page 76, for de Smet's reference to Com-Comly's furs.

the sons of men—and *debonair;* eagle-eyed, and with
the thews and eclat of his mountain race; of most magnetic touch, and look, and tongue; a truly princely man.

Whether there was any ring, I cannot say. Probably there was. They, in any case, joined hands and
seemingly hearts; all with a patriarchal Godspeed from
his majesty of the Pacific.

And so, away from her home, away from her people;
as Ruth of old, did Naomi, did the princess of the Pacific, cleave unto my father, and become my mother—
mother in holiest wedlock; wedlock perfect in its simplicity, with no adventitious ceremony of man to mar
its sanctity; with no epithalamium to proclaim or bless
it—only the soughing of the breeze through the ever
harping trees, and, grander still, the deep organ bour-
den of the ever-sounding sea, by the shore, with "music
in its roar."

To crown the occasion, soon as the last foot of the
whites had retrod the fur path on their return, the whole
was picked up by the three hundred slaves in waiting,
and piled, at the boats on the river marge, and presented in *gift*, pure and spontaneous to the bride's
man.[67]   There was, of course, "cakes and ale"—Potlatch[68] in plenty for all—white and black—on both
sides of the river.

---

[67] None of this, however, went beneficially to him; for, by rule of
the company, no servant or officer of it, could take, even in gift, any fur;
all passed into their maw.   Such was the application of their motto,
"Pro-pelle-cutem,"   The pile was worth, probably, at least three thousand dollars.   It should have come to me as sole heir of the marriage.—[Original.]

[68] Chinook word for free feast with gifts.—[Original.]
The prevalent idea among the whites, that the potlatch was an
improvident act of profligacy on the part of the Indian, is erroneous.
The Indian potlatch was nothing less than an investment; the money
and property given away brought very large returns; as an insurance
scheme it surpassed anything yet devised by the white man. The Indian
who gave a potlatch expected every man who received a gift from him at

Thus ran out the merry chimes of the wedding of the last of the Royal House of Com-Comly, last King— regent—of the Pacific realm of the Chinooks—head of the nations of Flatheads—so-called—of the Pacific Slope.

How, with peerless bravery and persistence, they fought for their independence and ancient home hearths, against General Hearney and other United States military forces, till the final surrender, many years after, in all honor, for peace's sake, of noble Chief Joseph [69] is now matter of history—too recent and fresh for more than bare allusion.

To pass on!

the time of the potlatch, would give back to him at least double the value of that gift, and he must have been a terrible miser who would not return at least three times the value of the gift received. Age-old custom, backed by general approval of the Indians, was a guarantee for proper payment by the recipient of the gift; and no disgrace was greater than that following the Indian who, being able, failed to pay his potlatch obligations. Fully aware of the fickleness of fortune, the Indian who had amassed wealth arranged a potlatch and by giving away all his property made his own and the neighboring tribes his debtors. By instituting the potlatch the Indian thus not only insured himself against loss of property, but left something to his children; because it stands to reason that a potlatch could not be given every day, nor could the gifts be repaid immediately. If the Indian who gave a potlatch died, the gifts were repaid to his children. A man by giving a potlatch often insured to his children the possession of a great deal of wealth, and much of the wealth of the wealthier families among the Northwest Coast Indians was accumulated that way. Potlatch gifts were always "Indian gifts."

[69] This is scarcely correct. Aroused by the ill-advised and misunderstood efforts of Governor Stevens to confine them to small reservations of his own choosing, the Flathead or Salesh tribes commenced hostilities against the Americans shortly after the great Walla Walla Indian council of 1855. After the miscarriage of Chief Kamiaken's great plan for a concerted attack on the American settlements on the Coast and East of the Cascades, during the winter of 1855-1856, by the premature murder of Indian Agent A. J. Bolon and some miners in the summer of 1855, and the several defeats of the allied tribes of the Columbia River basin by the soldiers, culminating in Colonel Wright's campaign during the fall of 1858, the Salesh Indian tribes made permanent treaties with the Government and no further hostilities occurred. They refused to join Chief Joseph in the Nez Perce War of 1877. The Nez Perce (Shahaptin) tribe is an entirely distinct tribe, differing in language and history from the Salesh tribes to the north of them.

CHAPTER II

BIRTH AND INFANCY—LIFE IN BRITISH COLUMBIA

In due time, and it would seem without loss of time in this regard, I was born: Date, as per account, February 3, 1824—the very day on which a much better, more useful, and in every respect a greater man was born, viz., Horace Greely, of the New York *Tribune*, almost President of the United States.

As already stated, I was born under the British flag; in Fort George (formerly Astoria). In truth, I am and have ever felt myself to be a man of two flags; proper, in a way, to both. Yet, let me say, scarcely quite content with either. Of this, more anon!

My mother died a few days after my birth, [70] much to the sorrow of my father, who loved her sincerely, for her gentle ways and wifely devotion.

On her death my father marked his grief in every way of respect to her memory; and to this day, there may, for aught I know to the contrary, be some monumental mark of that sorrow, in the old cemetery by the old Fort. [71]

These facts are not, of course, to my personal knowledge, nor were they even mentioned to me by any of my family, but have been told by one who was a per-

---

[70] Ranald's half-brother, Mr. Benjamin MacDonald has given the date as "the salmon running time," which is usually in the months of May and June.

[71] The buildings of the Astor post were apparently abandoned by the Northwest Company in 1819 and new quarters erected. By 1834 the site of the Astor post was overgrown with grass and weeds and marked by a single chimney. J. K. Townsend, *op. cit.* All traces of the old Northwest Company and Hudson's Bay Company's post, Fort George, and of the cemetery were long ago obliterated. The site is now occupied by the City of Astoria. Our author's cousin, Christinia MacDonald Williams, had the chimney bottoms of this old post pointed out to her in 1865, *Washington Historical Quarterly*, xiii, 113.

sonal witness of them, and as a close family (cousin)
of the deceased—herself subsequently married to a
gentleman of historic fame as a scientist, [72] a chief factor of the Hudson's Bay Company, living here, at the
time—was cognizant of them. Herself, as fit companion for her husband, readily acquired, and ever
showed the refinement and intelligence, with sincere
piety, of the best of the purely white race—a lady in
every respect. I have not permission to give, thus pub-
licly, her name. [73]

On the death of my mother, I was, in course, committed to the nursing care [74] of the royal household
across the way; where, according to all accounts, I became the favorite, the "Toll, Toll" [75] (Chinook for the
(Boy! the Boy!) of Gran'pa.

———

[72] George Barnston, a contemporary of our author's father, was a
Scotchman born in Edinburgh—a man of good intellectual attainments
and universally respected and possessing great energy. His name appears as a clerk, Nos. 463, 357 and 291, respectively, on the Lists of Employees of the Hudson's Bay Company, in North America for the years
1821, 1822, 1823 and 1824. He was in charge of Fort Nez Perce (Walla
Walla) for some time up to the spring of 1831, and became a Chief
Trader in 1840. Like many of his contemporaries he espoused a woman
from the Columbia River tribes. Retiring from the service, he settled
at Montreal, where he took an active interest in public affairs, and became president of the Society of Natural History, which probably accounts for the reference to his "historic fame as a scientist."

[73] Have no objection to do so privately, on proper inquiry.—[Orig-
inal.]
    In a penciled note on the MSS. our author has written the name,
"Mrs. George Barnston." Mrs. Barnston and our author were distantly
related. Letter Ranald MacDonald to Malcolm McLeod Nov. 24, 1890.
Provincial Library, Victoria, B. C.

[74] According to Benjamin MacDonald, Ranald was committed to the
care of an aunt, his mother's sister, Car-Cumcum, and they occupied a
lodge at the fort at Astoria.

[75] The Chinook language is peculiar in its abundance of onomato-
poetic terms; these include the names of birds, a few other animals and
some miscellaneous terms. The term, "The Toll, The Toll," is doubtless
the result of an attempt to give an English equivalent for some such
Chinook name or term as "qoe' lqoel," meaning owl, or "Qul qul," meaning heron. See Boas, *Handbook of American Indian Languages,* 655.

Later on in 1824, the Hudson's Bay Company's establishment of Fort George was removed to a more suitable place then named Vancouver[76] (Fort and Post) about eighty miles further up the Columbia, on the north side, within tide water, with ample depth and accommodation for shipping.

There,[77] in 1825, after more than a year's widowhood, my father married a Swiss (German Swiss) young woman, or girl of 16 or 17—Jane, daughter (born in Switzerland)[78] of one Michael Klyne,[79] "Post-

---

The Chinook word for boy is Ekass-cas, Alex. Ross, *Oregon Settlers,* 323, or ik-qsks, Prof. Franz Boas, *op. cit.,* 597. It will be recalled that Ranald's mother's name was Raven; Toll, Toll, applied to the infant Ranald, is of the type of these bird names and probably signified some term like little "owl" or "heron" and applied to Ranald because of some infant characteristic. In a letter from our author's father to Edward Ermatinger dated Colvile, April 1, 1836, we find: "Ranald, or if you will have it *Toole,* was removed there from Pritchard's last summer."

[76] The removal of the Hudson's Bay Company's headquarters' from Fort George (Astoria) to the new post, Fort Vancouver, in April, 1825, is reported in the Oregon Historical Society's *Quarterly,* xx, 27. Sir J. H. Pelly, Governor of the Hudson's Bay Company, in a letter to George Canning, Foreign Secretary, dated December 9, 1825, gives the following explanation of the founding of Fort Vancouver:

"In compliance with a wish expressed by you at our last interview, Governor Simpson, when at Columbia, abandoned Fort George on the south side of the river and formed a new establishment on the north side about 75 miles from the mouth of the river at a place called by Lieutenant Broughton Bellevue point. Governor Simpson named the new establishment "Fort Vancouver" in order to identify our claim to the soil and trade with Lieutenant Broughton's discovery and survey."

[77] Mr. Benjamin MacDonald states that the marriage occurred Sept. 1, 1825. There was evidently some irregularity in the first ceremony or its record, and the parties, probably to avoid any complications for their heirs, such as arose in the Connolly case, afterwards went through the marriage ceremony again. This was performed June 9, 1835, at York Factory by the chaplain of that port, the Rev. Mr. Cochran. Letter Archibald McDonald to Ermatinger, Provincial Library, Victoria, B. C. The bride was but fifteen years old at the time of her marriage.

[78] This, *if correct,* would indicate that Michael Klyne and his family were among the Swiss emigrants of 1821, but see *contra* hereon notes 79 and 81 following.

[79] The name of Michael Klyne appears in the Lists of Employees of the Hudson's Bay Company in America for the years 1821, 1822 and

master" (as the office was then called) of Jasper House, [80] a trade outpost of the Hudson's Bay Company, situated on the east side of the Rocky Mountains,

---

1823 as Nos. 933, 749 and 545, respectively. He was probably identical with Michel Klein, one of the voyageurs attached to the Department of Athabasca in 1804 and mentioned in L. F. R. Masson's *Les bourgeois de la compagnie du Nord Ouest*, i, 396. Archibald McDonald's pedigree list mentions his wife, Jane Kline, daughter of Michael, as coming to Fort Rae in 1813, doubtless fixing Michael Klyne's service at that time and place. He is the Michael Klyne mentioned in the list of grantees from Lord Selkirk and the Hudson's Bay Company as the owner of Lot 227 in Register B of the Red River Colony; see Archer Martin, *op. cit.*, 147. He was in charge of Jasper House when Alexander Ross passed through in the spring of 1825, and is spoken of by him as "a man by the name of Klyne, a jolly old fellow, with a large family." He and his family then consisting of five children accompanied Edward Ermatinger from Edmonton to Jasper House in September, 1828. Ermatinger's Journal, *Transactions Royal Society of Canada*, vi, sec. ii, 81, 103-108. Being an outpost it would appear that Jasper House was only occupied during the winter. By Minutes of Council for years 1830-1833, inclusive, he was still assigned as Postmaster for Jasper House, E. H. Oliver, *op. cit.*, i, 645, 661, 678, 694. In the records of the Hudson's Bay Company at Winnipeg his name appears on a registered contract dated June 1, 1827, evidently for services as Clerk and Trader at Lesser Slave Lake. He probably retired to Fort Garry about 1834. Michael Klyne's mill is mentioned by Alexander Ross, *Red River Settlement*, 121. The name sometimes appears as Clyne and Michael Klyne's name is doubtless preserved in Cline's River at the headwaters of the North Saskatchewan, and in "Old Cline's Trail" north of Kootenai Plain leading towards Jasper house. John Palliser, *Papers Relative to the Exploration by Captain Palliser*, (1858-1859), 112. The old family homestead on Euclid Avenue, at Point Douglas, Fort Garry (Winnipeg), was abandoned at the time of the flood, when the family moved to Morris, Minnesota. Mrs. Klyne died at Fort Garry about 1855. There were a number of children besides Jane Klyne, including a daughter, Angelique, and four sons; Michael, Adam, who at one time carried mail from Minnesota; George, a member of the Provincial Parliament at Winnipeg in 1870 or 1872, and John. All were mentioned and remembered in the will of their sister, Jane Klein McDonald, and presumably were living at the date of the last codicil thereof, dated December 14, 1879.

[80] Jasper House—the last support east of the Rocky Mountains on the regular Hudson's Bay Company's route overland from the headwaters of the Athabasca to those of the Columbia River by way of Athabasca Pass—was situated at the outlet of Lake Jasper, an expansion of the Athabasca River, and so named after Jasper Hawes, a clerk of the Northwest Company, stationed in the Athabasca department, whose name appears in the list 1804 L. F. R. Masson, *op. cit.*, i, 396; ii, 26, note. Coues [*op. cit.*, 640], states that this house was built about 1800. It may be the post shown on David Thompson's map, "Northwest Company" at the headwaters of the Athabasca; if so, Thompson makes no

between the eastern ends of the Athabasca and Yellow
Head passes. This Mr. Klyne, a person of good education and of responsible integrity, was one of the colony
of Swiss, from Switzerland, whom the Earl of Selkirk
had induced to try their fortune in his Red River Settlement,[81] and who, on arrival there, finding the difficul-

mention of it when describing his journey to the Columbia River in 1810-
1811, though upon the return trip he speaks of arriving in this locality at
"the house of Mr. William Henry"; see David Thompson, *op. cit.,* 557.
This Henry's House was, however, evidently situated some distance
above Jasper House, as known in later years, and was one of the several small outposts in the vicinity known as "Rocky Mountain Houses."
See hereon, Coues, *op. cit.,* ii, 640, note: L. F. R. Masson, *op. cit.,* ii, 26.
According to David Douglas, [*op. cit.,* 261] on May 3, 1827, Rocky Mountain House "consisted merely of a small hut." These temporary houses
or forts were often known by different names, and in course of events
occasionally rebuilt. Ross Cox, who was at the post in 1817, speaks of it
[*op. cit.,* ii, 183] as "the melancholy hermitage of Mr. Jasper Hawes."
Further reference to this post will be found (inter alia) in Franchere,
op. cit., 296; Ross Cox, *op. cit.,* ii, 254; L. R. F. Masson, *op. cit.,* ii, 52;
John Palliser's *Further Papers, op. cit.,* ii, 25; de Smet, *Missions de
l' Oregon,* letters xiii and xiv; Paul Kane, *op. cit.,* 154, which contains
a wood-cut showing the appearance of Jasper House in 1846. As to the
appearance of the post when Michael Klyne was in charge, David Douglas, the botanist, who accompanied Edward Ermatinger across the mountains in 1827, in his *Journal,* [*op. cit.,* 262] under date of May 4, 1827,
says: "Arrived at Jasper House, three small hovels on the left side of
the river, at two o'clock, where we put up to refresh ourselves for the remainder of the day." In 1859 the place was described by Captain Palliser as "a little group of dwellings constructed in keeping with the pic-
turesque situation, with overhanging roofs and trellised porticos." These
were probably the work of Michael Klyne. Paul Kane was not so fa-
vorably impressed, describing the place in November, 1845 [*op. cit.,* 155],
as consisting of "three miserable log huts." The name Jasper House is
preserved in the name of a station on the Canadian National Railway
in the vicinity.

[81] In a memoranda of guidance to McDonell as agent for Selkirk's
Executors, under date 1821 under title Swiss Settlers, it is stated:
"There will be 250 or 260 persons of all ages, of whom 60 will be under
10 years of age or thereabouts." E. H. Oliver, *The Canadian North-
west,* 1, 211. These colonists were secured through the propaganda of
Colonel de May.

Archer Martin's *The Hudson's Bay Company's Land Tenures,* London, 1898, gives in Appendix "G," 194, a list of the Swiss who left their
native land in May, 1821, and late that year arrived at the Earl of Selkirk's colony. The list numbers one hundred and sixty-five in all—men,
women and children. Michael Klyne's name is not included. It must,
however, be noted that on page 29 Judge Martin states the number of
these Swiss settlers as one hundred and seventy-seven; no effort is made

ties of such a life, scattered[82]—some going to the western states then (A. D. 1820) approaching the higher reaches of the Mississippi, and some—as in Klyne's case—taking service with the Hudson's Bay Company.

After a year or so, I was placed under her care; at an age so young that I took to her as my veritable mother, and she, a woman of fine feeling, and true Swiss fidelity to her trust, ever, to the last moment of her long life, kept up, with tenderest care and solicitude, the kind deception.

She bore twelve sons and a daughter[83] to my father,

---

to account for this difference; it is possible that Klyne's family may have been included in the twelve not accounted for. The other Swiss settlers in the Red River colony were members of de Meuron's disbanded regiment engaged at Montreal and Kingston. The de Meurons originally belonged to two mercenary regiments recruited in Switzerland and under the pay of the British Government. They saw service in Continental Europe and in the American War of 1812, and the regiment was disbanded in Quebec, Canada, May, 1816. Four officers and a hundred men of these came with Lord Selkirk to Red River, arriving in the spring of 1817 and settling opposite Fort Douglas on the Seine. Another authority gives their number as three officers and eighty men—who left Montreal in 1816.

Michael Klyne's rank (postmaster) and place on the List of Employees of the Hudson's Bay Company, for 1821, after the coalition, *preclude* his having been a member of the Swiss colony of 1821, which did not arrive until November of that year, and would seem to identify him with the Michel Klyne of the Northwest Company list of 1804, and apparently preclude Jane Klyne's being born in Switzerland.

[82] The date given by our author for the departure of these Swiss is manifest error. The correct date is June, 1826. See hereon Alexander Ross's *Red River Settlement*, 57, *et seq.* In a letter from D. McKenzie to A. Colvile, dated Red River, Aug. 1826, [E. H. Oliver, *op. cit.*, 1, 261] we find: "Nothing important took place since he left us except the contemplated departure of Swiss and De Meuron's, with some Canadians who, like them, preferred to quit the country than submit to the labor of re-establishing their farms. The former to the number of 50, bent their course to the States, and of the latter 25 embarked for the Canadas, making a total of 180, big and small." A number of these settlers moved to the vicinity of Fort Snelling, near St. Paul. A few of these Swiss settlers appear to have left Red River as early as 1823; see hereon, E. H. Oliver, *op. cit.*, 1, 228-230.

[83] For genealogy and biography of our author's father and his family see Archibald McDonald, *Washington Historical Quarterly,* ix, 99-101 inclusive.

but, so it was said and I say, seemed to love me best of any. The love was certainly reciprocated.

Late in after life, when far from her, I learned, by accident, from strangers living at and about the place of my birth, the real state of our relations, the disillusion pained me beyond expression. However, it brought no reflections against my father, then in his grave, nor against my still beloved step-mother, then in the distant East (St. Andrews', Quebec), closing her lonely widowhood by the grave of her husband. In effect, the discovery made me, at the time, withdraw within myself, abandoning, at once, pursuits, in high honorable enterprise in British Columbia,[84] which in course might, I flattered myself, have placed me in a better—i. e., conventionally higher, and more comfortable position, as to wordly means, than is now mine to command. But now, with that philosophy incident to age, and further —being thereunto much advised, I creep out of my hermit shell and give, thus to the world, the little story of whence and how I came, thus to play my humble part in the drama of "Gates Ajar," of west and east, in the world of the Pacific.

To return to my narrative!

Again with my father, after my babyhood in the palace, I remained with him, his constant companion, save when out on expeditions of special danger—from trade post to trade post throughout the Columbia, and northward in the region now known as British Columbia. Much of that was in pioneer exploration and settlement, up to my twelfth year. The scenes and incidents of that life, up to my fourteenth year are, or at least most of them are, still distinct to memory. To give them

---

[84] Reference to enterprises in the Cariboo country in the early '60s in association with Sir James Douglas, Mr. Barnston and others.

tongue as I would wish, with full credit to those who took part in them, would fill volumes. Few of them are in any book; and then, only incidentally; generally wrongly; oft at second-hand; and sometimes with a distortion of facts and *suppressio veri* in larceny of merit.[85]

In 1823, the first post [86]—a large and well fortified fort, one hundred and thirty-five feet by one hundred and twenty, with high picket walls, two bastions with cannon, and a gallery four feet wide all round, was built on the Pacific Coast, north of the Columbia. It was chiefly for the coast trade, but for convenience, also, of the immediate land trade thereabout was situated about thirty miles up the Fraser, on its left or south bank, within schooner navigation. It was called Fort Langley, after a prominent stockholder of the Hudson's Bay Company of that name.

---

[85] While little credit has been given to many intrepid first explorers of Northwest, in the Provinces of Alberta and British Columbia, Canada, the names, if not the deeds, of such old Northwesterners as Alexander Mackenzie, Simon Fraser, Alexander Stuart, John Finlay and others are fittingly preserved in the names of their rivers, mountains and lakes.

[86] Our author is here in error. The site of Fort Langley was selected on June 29, 1827, on the left bank of the Fraser River some 30 miles above the Gulf of Georgia. Construction was commenced on July 30th by a party under the command of James McMillan, that had come from the Columbia River via Cowlitz portage. During the greater part of the work the men were lodged aboard the schooner "Cadboro," which had brought them from Puget Sound. By September 18th the post was sufficiently advanced to enable the "Cadboro" to discharge the trading goods and depart. On October 10, 1828, the post was inspected by Governor Simpson, when James McMillan accompanied the Governor to Vancouver, and the author's father, Archibald McDonald, was assigned to the post in his place. For description of the post at this time see Malcolm McLeod, *Peace River, Journal of Archibald McDonald*, 38-39, 118-119; H. H. Bancroft, *op. cit.*, ii., chap. 21; *Washington Historical Quarterly*, vi, 181, 186.

The fort was destroyed in April, 1840. So much had the northern posts begun to depend upon Langley for their salt provisions, that it was feared that they must be abandoned; in the end an agreement was made with the Russians whereby permission was obtained to purchase venison in their territory. When the fort was rebuilt the location was changed to a point some three or four miles further up the Fraser. Upon this site, at the present, two of the old fort buildings are still standing.

My father was placed in charge of it the same year, on the termination of his remarkable canoe voyage, with Governor Simpson from Hudson's Bay to that point as described from his manuscript journal of it in Judge McLeod's book, *Peace River*,[87] aboundingly cited in Bancroft's (H. H.) histories *British Columbia* and *The North West Coast of America*. The work, *Peace River*, published in 1872, covering, in its subjects (geodesy, climatology, agricultural and other economic resources) all the north and northwest of Canada, and the whole Pacific Slope north of Mexico, was, I have reason to know, a prime factor in the promotion of the present Canadian Pacific Railway.

On this subject, I could give much, of some public moment to the world; and might very properly do so, as one of the strongest arguments for that scheme, as advanced in press (papers and pamphlets [88] A. D. 1869-1874) by its first practical promoter, my old fellow Columbian, Judge Malcolm McLeod,[89] was the import-

---

[87] The person referred to as Judge McLeod is our author's friend and collaborator, Malcolm McLeod, Q. C., of Aylmer and later of Ottawa, Canada. So far as can be ascertained at present he never occupied the position of a judge; the title was one of courtesy. See note 89, post. The book referred to is really but the *Journal* of Archibald McDonald, our author's father, covering a canoe voyage from Hudson's Bay to the Pacific made by him in company with Sir George Simpson in 1828. Mr. McLeod has added many and voluminous notes. The volume was issued at the suggestion of Sanford Fleming as a part of the Canadian railroad propaganda; see McLeod's *Memorial*, 1899, 4. Five hundred copies were printed; some fifty were sold by the publishers, the remainder were bought from the publishers by Mr. McLeod and distributed by him gratuitously. In his *Memorial* Mr. McLeod describes his book as "a sort of blue-book with dry statistical details" and as "not calculated for general reading"; but this is merely the author's reticence; the book is delightfully interesting from cover to cover.

[88] A quantity of his notes, memoranda and manuscript papers are in Provincial Library at Victoria, B. C.

[89] Malcolm McLeod, the friend and collaborator of our author was the son of Chief Trader John McLeod and his wife, Charlotte, half-breed daughter of John P. Purden, a Chief Factor. He was born on October 22, 1821, at Fort Green Lake on Beaver River in the Northwest

ance of developing trade with Japan and China, as well as with Australia by such a railway; and in that connection was given by him in one of these pamphlets, and in the local leading newspaper press of the day, briefly, the story of my adventure in Japan as he had it, twenty years before, from my own lips, when a guest with him in Canada. In this way, my Japan of 1848-1849 with the C. P. R. of 1885. We, McLeod and I (I put him first, for such is his proper place in the matter) as in fact, our respective fathers, each again in the same

---

Territories. Until four years of age he lived with his parents at various trading posts, principally in the Okanogan district, and crossed the mountains with them in 1826. He left the West in 1830 for Scotland, there attending school under Dr. Boyd at Edinburgh and was in London for a short time in 1840. He was admitted to the Bar of the Province of Quebec in 1845, and practiced his profession for a while at St. Andrews in the County of Argenteuil; then moved to Aylmer, where he continued to practice his profession until about the year 1871, when he was appointed District Magistrate for the District of Ottawa. This position he held up to the year 1879, when he resigned and resumed practice at the bar of Aylmer, moving subsequently to Ottawa, where he died in 1897. The title Judge was given him colloquially only. He styled himself a Presbyterian, but was buried from the Church of England. Three sisters lived with him a number of years, one of them marrying a Mr. Pierce, a bookseller of Ottawa, and the two others dying about the same time as their brother, unmarried. A friend and contemporary fellow barrister has described him in the following words:

"He was a tall, spare, stern-looking man, but in conversation was one of the liveliest and most interesting men I ever met. His knowledge of the Northwest dated, as he was fond of telling, from the time he moved along the banks of the Mackenzie River on his mother's back; and all that we now know goes to show that he had nature on his side when he advocated crossing the Rocky Mountains by the Valley of the Peace River, when the railway to the Pacific Ocean was first mooted.

"He had an extensive knowledge of the law and had read even into the Laws of Scotland, which he was fond of quoting, but he seemed to lack the power to classify his knowledge and to make it applicable to the case at issue.

"Vices he had none, and on the whole was one whom it was a pleasure to know and an advantage to chat with. He never did an unkindness to anyone. As far as this world's goods were concerned he could not keep them with him, and when a wave of prosperity would come to him he was reckless as any Indian in squandering his money. He was quite an outstanding figure, and very much inclined to be very lengthy in his pleadings.

In 1869 he began the *Britannicus Letters* to the Ottawa and other provincial newspapers in favor of the proposed Canadian Pacific rail-

order [90] had, before that, A. D. 1822-28 practically prepared the way—were the first to solve that problem of a "North-west Passage".[91]

The fact is of standard record: but, in its esoteric, has been studiedly ignored, and, to the world, even denied by the millionaire beneficiaries thereof.   The subject is for other pages.

In 1834 or 1835,[92] my father was assigned to the

road.   He also wrote and published a number of pamphlets, in addition to "Peace River," i. e., Pacific Railway, Canada, Etc., 1875; Oregon Indemnity. Claim of Chief Factors and Chief Traders Hudson's Bay Company, 1892, etc.

[90] McLeod became a Chief Trader by the Deed Poll of 1821, while Archibald McDonald remained a clerk until 1828.

[91] In 1862, as the result of my own personal surveys of routes for transport of freight from the Ocean to the Cariboo mines in British Columbia, I obtained a charter to myself personally (in association with the late John Barnston, barrister, member of the legislature of British Columbia and other) from the Government of British Columbia for first a trail and then a wagon road from Bella Coola (Bentwick Arm) to the Cariboo mines with tollage.   Ultimately I took a prominent part in the alternate route through the gorge of the Fraser, canoed by my father in 1828.—[Original.]

The John Barnston, barrister, referred to is Mr. John G. Barnston, who was the second person to be admitted as a barrister in the Courts of Vancouver Island; then a separate colony from that of the mainland, known as British Columbia. Mr. Barnston appears to have been admitted to practice in Vancouver Island, sometime towards the end of 1858.   His application to practice at the Bar of British Columbia was made on December 9, 1861, to Governor Douglas.   He was not at that time a member of the legislature; indeed there was no semblance of a legislature on the mainland until 1864, and it did not become representative and responsible government until 1871.   Mr. Barnston was in 1873 elected, at a by-election, as one of the three members for the Cariboo District.   In May and June of 1861 our author, with Mr. Barnston and Messrs. Tompkins, Person and Ritchie, made a preliminary exploration from Alexandria to North Bentinck Arm on the Coast; report of which was made to Governor Douglas, July 24, 1861, and is on file in the Provincial Archives at Victoria, B. C.   The route was afterwards opened for pack-trains, which, for a short time were conducted over the route by our author and his associates.   The enterprise was never a financial success.

[92] Archibald McDonald left Fort Langley—where he had been stationed for some years—for Fort Vancouver in the spring of 1833, and after selecting the site and laying the foundations of Nisqually House in June of 1833 (Washington Historical Quarterly, vi, 179-188), he accompanied Mr. William Connolly of New Caledonia up the Columbia

charge of Fort Colvile, the highest trade post on the Columbia; the centre then of a very extensive Indian trade, including the great Kootenaye Country and the upper Columbia to the foot of the Rocky Mountains.   The location was just above the Kettle falls of the Columbia —then, as still, a central resort of Indians, from all around, for their salmon fishery; their chief food supply.

The site—a beautiful flat, of great extent, about ten square miles,[93] surrounded by mountains of moderate height, with (then) the celebrated "Buffalo grass and other finest herbage of cattle—was an admirable one for a farm in a large scale.

On its establishment in 1826,[94] it was at once stocked with three calves and three pigs,[95] brought, by boat, by

---

with supplies for the interior in July of 1833.   In 1834 and 1835 he was absent on leave, during which time he visited in Scotland.   See letter from himself dated Edinburgh, 20th January, 1835, set out *in extenso* in Oregon Historical Society's *Quarterly*, vi, 308-309.   From another of his letters appearing in *Washington Historical Quarterly*, ii, 254, it would appear that he did not take active charge at Fort Colvile until 1836.   He was in this position when John McLean, the author of *Twenty-five Years in the Hudson's Bay Company's Territory*, passed through.   McLean (*op. cit.* ii, 14) wrote: "We arrived at Colvile on the 12th (April, 1837) where we met with a most friendly reception from a warm-hearted Gael, Mr. Mcd——."   He was at Vancouver, May 30, 1836. Parker, *op. cit.* 293.

[93] The site of Fort Colvile contained about five square miles of land. For a contemporary description thereof (1848) see *inter alia Washington Historical Quarterly*, iii, 145.

[94] Fort Colvile was staked out by Governor Simpson on April 14th, 1825, and part of the timbers framed during the summer and fall of 1825. John Work's *Journal, Washington Historical Quarterly*, v, 105, 166, 169. For the abandonment of Spokane House on April 7, 1826, and removal of the employees and stores to Fort Colvile see John Work's *Journal, Idem.* v, 276-283.

[95] In John Work's *Journal* for April 11, 1826, we have the entry: "The express arrived in the evening, Messrs. McLeod, Ermatinger & Douglas. They brought three pigs and three young cows for the Fort,"—Colvile. *Washington Historical Quarterly*, v. 284.   In a letter from Archibald McDonald to John McLeod, dated from Colvile, January 25, 1837, reproduced in *Washington Historical Quarterly* ii, 255, McDonald says: "Your three calves are up to 55 and your three grunters would have

Chief Trader John McLeod, from Fort Vancouver, about 800 miles below.   The stock was from England; brought by the Hudson's Bay Company ships, round the Horn, from London.

From these three calves sprang, I believe, all the cat- tle—millions, since probably—literally on a "thousand hills"[96]—from California to Alaska, throughout the "Sea of Mountains", with valleys, of utmost fertility, innumerable, now constituting the States of Washing- ton, Montana, Idaho, Eastern part of Oregon and cen- tral and eastern British Columbia.

For gardening, the place, with a most favorable cli- mate, proved a very Eden.   Truly a lovely spot, of God's blessed Earth home for man!   The Fort, a fine one in the model of the times in the Indian Country, with high wooden walls (of squared tree trunks 12 to 18 feet in height) and bastions, with cannon, and gal- lery, inside, all round, was a veritable citadel of safety.

Here, in its cherished ruins; with the old bull dogs— cannon, three pounders[97]—of watch and ward, the rust-

---

swarmed the country if we did not make it a point to keep them down to 150." And see generally upon this subject Malcolm MacLeod's *Peace River*, 94, *et. seq.* Chickens, goats and pigs, brought from the Hawaiian Islands on the "Tonquin," had been introduced at Spokane House as early as 1814. See Ross Cox, *op. cit.*, i, 315-316.

[96] In a letter to the Kettle Falls (Wash.) *Pioneer*, dated August 31, 1891, our author says: "Sixty-five years have we the first pioneers of civilization in this wild of wilds in early days; by the sweat of our brows and enterprises, filled or at least largely covered every valley and plain with the fruits of our industry in herds and flocks and bands of horses for hundreds of miles in every direction. In this respect I could refer to an article or a series of articles in the New York *Century* under the heading: *The Bitter Root Valley and Montana,* where my uncle Angus of the Flat-head post, who died two years ago last February, was mentioned together with his noble family as being the first pioneers of the country and exceedingly rich in several thousand head of cattle and horses."

[97] This little cannon, now in the Museum of the Eastern Washington State Historical Society at Spokane, Wash., is reputed to have been one of two carried by the British to the Heights of Abraham in an attack

The Northwest bastion of the stockade surrounding the Hudson's
Bay Company's Fort Colvile

From a photograph by Frank Palmer, 1901.

ing "Woolwich infants" of England, with their "Tower mark" (the "broad arrow") still by me, I sit, Marius like,[98] in my father's veritable old arm chair; my battles over; save with the wolf; and the last,—last of all—when it may come—in ready welcome!

Here, during three or four years,[99] with younger half brothers, under the tenderest, and best, in every way, of parental care, I spent what I consider to have been the very happiest days of my life: in a world of our own; little; singularly isolated from the haunts of men; where only the occasional Indian, with silent step; with his furs for sale, and our (The Company's) own "Despatch"[100] to and from the East—in Spring and Fall—in hurrying way, with a single paddle boat (of eight for crew) with a passenger or two, broke the solitude. To that might be added the annual arrival from below, viz: Spokann [101] of the annual supplies ("outfit") for the Post: always a joyous occasion.

---

on Quebec during the French and Indian War. It is mentioned by our author's cousin, Angus MacDonald, in his *"A Few Items of the West,"* published in the *Washington Historical Quarterly*, víii, 188-229.

[98] The reference here undoubtedly is to the celebrated words of Caius Marius, whose struggle with Sulla is familiar to all students of Roman history. Driven into exile to Africa, Marius is said to have used these words: "Tell him that you saw Caius Marius sitting on the ruins of Carthage."

[99] Our author is in error. Young Ranald was at Thompson's River in 1826-1828, at Fort Langley much of the time between 1828 and the spring of 1833. He was at Ball's school at Fort Vancouver during the winter of 1832-1833 and left for Red River by the fall express of 1834. He could not have spent much time at Colvile.

[100] Some mention of the brigades carrying the company's dispatch appears herein. See pagees 55, 62, 63 hereof.

[101] Pronounced with accent of last syllable. It was the first trade post established by the Northwest Company, viz., in 1811, on the South Side of the Columbia River, after those (two) in the Kootenaye Country, by David Thompson in 1807-1808. Spokann was the first distributing centre of the whole Columbia fur trade and there its accounts were made up.—[Original.]
The correct date is 1810. David Thompson built his Kellyspell

In such life—where the good and evil in man were left to their own working and tendencies, unrestrained and unstimulated by external associations with humanity, individuality becomes emphasized—to put it metaphorically, man becomes, according to his bent and environment, saint, or devil.

Fortunately for our juvenile humanity (I speak of my brothers and self) we had guardian parents of highest Christian character [102] and life—my father a Scotch Episcopalian; my mother (step-mother) born and bred of Geneva—a thorough woman of her Bible.   Morn and eve, the Word! under their parental ministry, moulding the unalloyed clay of youth, for sterner virility—a harder life—in combat with the world.

After a home schooling [103] now calling for more advanced studies and special scholastic discipline, I was in (or about) 1838 [104] sent to the nearest school.   That

House on Pend d'Oreille lake in Sept. of 1809; Saleesh House in Oct. of 1809, and Spokane House was built by his clerk Jacques Raphael Finlay (possibly with Finan McDonald) in the summer of *1810*.

[102] Jane Klyne and her husband were Episcopalians and after retiring from the Indian Country became prominent members of the Christ's Church at St. Andrews, Province of Quebec.   While at Fort Colvile the Rev. Elkanah Walker and the Rev. Cushing Eells from the Tshimakain Mission were frequent visitors at Fort Colvile, and arguments were often had there on the different orthodoxic views of their respective churches; in the arguments Dame Jane Klyne, who was unusually well versed in the Bible and the creed of her church, is said to have held her own in religious argument with both of the missionaries.   See note 55, page 83 for further comment on Dame Jane Klyne's character as a Christian.

[103] Writing to his old friend, John McLeod, from Fort Langley on January 15, 1832 [*Washington Historical Quarterly*, ii, 265-266] our author's father, Archibald McDonald, says:—"What I regret is the condition of the boys—for there is nothing like early education—however, I keep them at it, mother and all.   My *Chinook* now reads pretty well and has commenced cyphering."   In addition to this home schooling our author attended John Ball's school at Fort Vancouver for a short time in the fall and winter of 1832-1833.

[104] In conversation in his later years our author stated that he went to the Red River school when nine years old.   In a letter dated Fort Langley, February 20, 1833, our author's father wrote: "I find it is high

was, then, in Red River (Selkirk) Settlement, on the
east side of "The Mountains"—an arduous voyage and
journey of about two thousand miles.   I went, in charge
of the late Chief Factor Duncan Finlayson, [105] then, in

time to get my little boys to school—God bless them—I have no less than
five of them, all in a promising way." (*Washington Historical Quarterly*,
ii, 163).   In another letter, dated Fort Colvile Jan. 25th, 1837 (*Washington Historical Quarterly*, ii, 254), the father writes: "We have as yet
but an only girl, who with our boy is all the family we have—the other
chaps are at R. R.—three with Mr. Jones, and one with the grandfather."
In another letter, addressed to Edward Ermatinger and in the archives
of the Provincial Library at Victoria, B. C., the father says:—"*Before he
went to Red River in '34,* I had him myself pretty well advanced in arithmetic, so that one would suppose he is now something of a scholar."   In
the Elkanah Walker journals under date Colvile, Sept. 27, 1838, we find:
"Some of his (McDonald's) sons are at Red River."   From the foregoing
it would appear that our author is mistaken in this date and that he left
Fort Colvile for Red River at least by the fall express of 1834.

    [105] Duncan Finlayson's name appears as Nos. 143, 114 and 91, re-
spectively, in the Lists of Employees of the Hudson's Bay Company in
America for the years 1821, 1822 and 1823.   He was promoted from
clerk to chief trader in 1828.   He was at Fort Garry, Red River, in
1830; at Fort Vancouver and elsewhere in the Columbia River district
during 1831-1837, having been promoted to Chief Factor in 1832.   He
was on furlough for the period 1837-1838, and was re-assigned to Fort
Garry from 1839 to 1844.   He was appointed Governor of Rupert's Land,
March 20, 1839, and served as such until June, 1844.   E. H. Oliver,
op cit. i, 48.   According to John Dunn [*History of the Oregon Territory*,
240] Finlayson in 1836 reconnoitered the northern coasts on the steamer
Beaver; this being her first appearance in those waters.   In 1837 he
was at the Columbia when W. A. Slacum arrived.
    As an incident of this trip across the mountains with Finalyson,
Ranald MacDonald writing for the Kettle Falls (Wash.) *Pioneer* of Nov.
13, 1890, says that camp was pitched on the shores of Arrow Lake, on a
beautiful sandy beach, at the back of which was a huge mountain of
perpendicular rocks hundreds of feet in height frowning down upon them,
and on the face of which were three cavities or holes about two or three
feet in diameter that were completely filled with arrows.   These holes
were up about thirty feet from the shore, the arrows having no doubt
been shot up from below, and were wedged in so tight that it was almost
impossible to dislodge them.   With his shotgun Finalyson at the request
of Ranald fired into the holes and brought down quite a number of
arrows in a broken condition.   The local Indians, themselves, according
to Ranald, could not account for the arrows being there.   Sixty years
later Ranald met Big Head Edwards, a chief of the Lake Indians, who
told him he had frequently seen the arrows but, Indian like, had very
little to say about them.   It was from these niches filled with arrows
that the Arrow Lakes derived their name, according to our author.
    Mr. A. D. Burnett, then editor of the *Pioneer* states that this
account of the origin of the name, Arrow Lakes, was afterwards con-

April, on his way to the East for annual general Council
Meeting at Norway House, held in early July, and
afterwards to assume, on appointment, the Governorship of Assiniboia, at the Settlement.

The route was by the Athabasca Pass, the highest of
the Rocky Mountain Range; since scientifically measured and reported in railway survey [106] as 6025 feet
above the sea, between the immediate heights of Mounts
Browne and Hooker, both reported as over 16,000 feet
above the sea.   The approach to the Pass, to a point
called "Boat Encampment", at the western end of it.[107]
This approach was through the canyon of the Selkirks.
This canyon—say from the "Big Eddy" just above
Revelstoke to the "Great Bend" at the foot of the Pass
—a distance, probably, of between fifty and sixty miles,
is the most formidable, and at the same time most interesting piece of travel I have ever went through: and
further, I never read of any like it.   He, truly, must
have been a brave man who first tried it, and lead such
way.   It was no native that did so; for none such had
the means; but it was that greatest of explorers and
mappers of northern North America DAVID THOMP-
SON, Astronomer of the North West Company of Canada; originally a "Blue-Coat Boy",[108] of London, Eng-

firmed to him by one of the pioneer steam-boat captains opperating on
the Arrow Lakes. The arrows were obliterated more than fifty years ago.

106 Fleming's Reprint of Survey 1874, for C. P. R.—[Original.]

107 So called from the fact of the boat used, on the Columbia, to that
point, arriving from below, generally at the end of April, being put into
campment there, while the party went on, on foot, to the East, and the
boat remained, where stored, till another party from the East, in October,
used it for descent to Port Vancouver.—[Original.]

108 This is a common error. In fact it was made by Mr. J. B. Tyrrell
himself, who is the recognized authority upon David Thompson. See
Mr. Tyrrell's article in *"Proceedings of the Canadian Institute," October,
1888.* Mr. Tyrrell has, however, pointed it out and corrected it. It should
read a "Grey Coat Boy." See Tyrrell's Introduction to *David Thompson's
Narrative,* xxviii.

land, engaged and brought by the Hudson's Bay Company. The story of the feat is in no book: probably not even in M. S.[109]—but I have it from an old intimate friend and family connexion of his [110] to whom, in familiar converse, in his old age—with no heed to future fame—the Grand Old Man—grand in stature, erect, and of Herculean mould [111] was in the habit, when thereunto drawn, to modestly murmur his such battles over again. He, in his exploration in that terrible region, in search for the Columbia River, was, for over a year, lost to the world [112]—even to his own people of the North West Company—in that "Inferno" of wild mountain rock. From the glacier sources of the Fraser,

---

[109] David Thompson's own *narrative* did exist in manuscript and through the efforts of Mr. J. B. Tyrrell of Toronto, Canada, has been brought to light and fittingly published. See David Thompson's *Narrative*, J. B. Tyrrell, vol. xii, *The Publications of the Champlain Society*, Toronto, Canada, 916. The history of the manuscript is given in the preface xvii, xviii. A very neat summary of Thompson's work will be found in Mr. T. C. Elliott's brochure *"David Thompson, Pathfinder."* Those who desire to go more deeply into the subject are referred to the published narrative with annotations by the two authorities, J. B. Tyrrell and T. C. Elliott.

[110] My friend, Judge Malcolm McLeod, of Ottawa, Canada.—[Original.]

[111] David Thompson's figure was short and compact. See David Thompson's *Narrative,* introduction ivi. He was evidently of strong physique, great endurance and tireless energy. Our author has possibly confused David Thompson with a contemporary associate—a gigantic Gael, Finan McDonald—and a distant relative of the author's.

[112] Thompson was never lost for a year or a day unless by "lost" is meant hidden from public view.

In a letter to Mr. Alex. Frazer, dated Dec. 21, 1810, Athabasca River, foot of the Mountain, among other things, David Thompson says: "I am always in such distant expeditions, that I cannot write my friends regularly. They think I slight them, but they are mistaken. It is my situation that prevents me, not negligence . . . . . If all goes well and it pleases good Providence to take care of me, I hope to see you and a civilized world in the autumn of 1812. I am getting tired of such constant hard journeys; *for the last twenty months* I have spent only bare two months under the shelter of a hut, all the rest has been in my tent, and there is little likelihood the next twelve months will be much otherwise." L. F. R. Masson, *op. cit.,* ii, 41, 42.

he had, following the suggestions of his own previous
explorations, further South, at last, late in the fall of
1810, struck the great river at the very spot where—
ten years before (*A. D.* 1800)—he had, via the Athabasca Pass, from the East, found it, but was driven
back by Indians.[113]

---

[113] These two sentences and those which succeed them represent
rather accurately our knowledge, or ignorance, of the explorations of
this truly wonderful man—David Thompson, until Mr. J. B. Tyrrell
began the work that placed the real facts before the world. Compare
herewith the statements in H. H. Bancroft, *op. cit.*, ii, 122-123.

David Thompson's *Narrative* apparently has one or more chapters
missing of the dates 1800 to 1807; also his geographical notes of 1801.
He says on page 375, "I have already related how the Peeagans watched
us to prevent our crossing the Mountains and arming the Natives on
that side, in which they succeeded." The *Narrative* does not contain anything on this subject; details of this expedition are entirely missing.
In a letter to Capt. Sir James Alexander, Montreal, reproduced in the
Report of the Provincial Archives Department, of British Columbia,
Victoria, B. C., 1914, V123, David Thompson says:—"In 1801 the Northwest Company determined to extend their Fur Trade to the west side
of the Rocky, and if possible to the Pacific Ocean; this expedition was
intrusted to me, and I crossed the Mountains to the head waters of
McGillivray's River (the present Kootenay branch of the Columbiba
named originally in honor of the N. W. Co. Agent, Mr. William McGillivray); but an overwhelming force of eastern Indians obliged me to
retreat a most desperate retreat of six days for they dreaded the western Indians being furnished with Arms and Ammunition. The report of
my attempt and defeat soon reached Washington and in 1804 the
Executive of the U. S. organized a plan of discovery to be conducted
by Captains Lewis and Clarke (the former a nephew of President Jef-
ferson) of the United States Army, with a company of picked soldiers.
. . . . . This expedition directed the attention of the Indians to the
head waters of the Missisourie, and in 1807 gave me an opportunity of
crossing the mountains and placing myself on the headwaters of the
Columbia River, and built a fortified Post of Stockades, etc,, etc., from
thence exploring the country, etc. . . . . ." His subsequent movements
west of the mountains are made familiar through his Narrative.

Thompson was driven back from Hawes' pass in 1810, which had
been used by him since 1807. He had had trouble with the Piegans
since 1808, occasioned by their resentment at his arming their enemies,
the Kootenais, with fire-arms. It is now well known that from Boat
Encampment, David Thompson in the spring of 1811, did not descend
but ascended the Columbia to his original Kootenai House, and did
not again reach the river until Kettle Falls, where he prepared a new
canoe and descended the river from that point. As noted, Thompson's
writings make little mention of finding a pass and crossing to the
Columbia River in the fall and winter of 1800-1801 when he was long
at Rocky Mountain House. There is reason to believe that a number
of the Northwestern half breeds and employees were across the moun-

Here, in 1810-1811, at the mouth of the mountain torrent which he had, in 1809-1810 been following from glacier heights of the Cariboo Mountains, afoot he wintered with his little band— a remnant, probably half a dozen or less—of faithful French Canadian voyageurs.[114] Here they made a canoe[115] (of cedar bark) wherewith to descend—if possible—the great mysterious river, to those greater waters which, according to Indian account, were "not good to drink" —the salt sea.

With such frail craft; without knowledge or guide of route; with certainty, however, of many dangers all along, Thompson, on the rising spring flood (April) committed himself, with his peerless crew of paddle men, to the plunge—a thousand miles of swift surging river course, with rapids, *dalles*, (some, most deadly!) cascades, Falls, and worst of all maelstrom eddies wherein no skill or force of man, as a rule, could prevail against the monster gulp.

On July 5, 1811—so the unquestionable record runs—he arrived, safe and sound, without the loss of a man, at *Astoria*, [116] then just established, in its primitive "huts".

---

tains into the upper Columbia River basin as early as 1800-1801. Thompson does not state the strength of his force on the west side of the mountains in 1801.

114 The names of these men are:—Michel Bourdeaux, Pierre Pareil, Joseph Cote, Michel Boulard, Francois Gregoire, and Charles and Ignace, two good Iroquois Indians: Charles Legasse and (Pierre?) Le Blanc, paddle men. Coues *New Light*, 704. Two Sanpoil (Thompson's *Simpoil*) Indians accompanied the party from Ilthkoyape (Kettle) Falls, July 3, 1811. David Thompson, *op. cit.*, 472, 473.

115 Hence the name *Canoe River* given to it by Thompson in his mapping (primal and still standard) of that region; so marked in the maps to this day. The river (a continuous mountain torrent) is not navigable, not even to an Indian canoe.—[Original.]

116 For David Thompson's own account of this trip, see his *Narrative*, 501. For other contemporary accounts see: Ross, *Adventures of First Settlers*, 85; Ross Cox, *op. cit.*, i, 77, 78; Gabriel Franchere, *op. cit.*, 120; Irving, *op. cit.*, Chapter x.

It was a peerless feat of travel! The same season he retraced it: back to his Pass of 1800; and thence home east to old Canada; a track, I— but under very different conditions—followed in all safety. Part of it, viz: from the "Big Eddy" just above the second crossing by C. P. R. of the Columbia, to the "Big Bend", and the Athabasca Pass itself, has been totally abandoned as a route of travel, since the Hudson's Bay Company, in sequence of the Oregon Treaty, gave it up.

From the Bend to the Big Eddy (foot of Lower or Smaller *Dalles* in the upper reach of the Columbia) is the Canyon of the Selkirks, with its deadly—most deadly—*Dalles aux Morts*,[117] with its pathetic little cemetery; churches, save by the towering rocks around, above, heaven roofed; its rude monumental wooden crosses, *"petits Calvraires"*, gaunt and weird, o'er the shallow graves, stone laid of cherished comrades, brave fellow voyageurs—many—there drowned!

There are no such men now-a-days! The "Old Nor'Westers"—masters and men—are all things of the past!—now, alas! little wot of: forgotten; unheeded, in the rush of the hour: over fields they so bravely won, and many died on.

They, really were the founders of the Greater Canada of today: and in Greater Canada, the so called "Great Britain" of Britain's pen prophets of the day.

Thompson—ever true to his "Blue-Coat" training —was ever, to his last hour, a man of highest principles,

---

117 This tragic spot is mentioned by most of the early writers; see Ermatingers *Journal, Transactions Royal Society of Canada, 1912,* vi., 107; David Douglas, *op. cit.,* 252; Alexander Ross, Fur Hunter's, ii, 180; Paul Kane's, *op. cit.,* 328, 333; also Father Blanchet, *Historical Sketches of the Catholic Church in Oregon,* and Angus McDonald's *"A Few Items of the West,"* in the *Washington Historical Quarterly.*

and purity and integrity of life; a goodman, and worthy of all esteem in the best sense.   In his old age (87), in the extreme poverty—pitiable distress (but from no fault of his own) he was left to die utterly unheeded by the Governments—Provincial and Imperial —he had so magnificently served.   His grave—unhonored and possibly unmarked—like that of others in like vicarious service—is as the dust of the highway to those now enriched by his work and that of his associates.   Pity! Shame! it should be so.   The world of Mammon heeds not such call.

In this connection there are many names and instances—some in like neglect and undeserved misery—that come to my mind, but it would be useless to mention them.   There is I suppose—I believe—a Providence in these as in all things; and that, ultimately, for good. So mote it be!

CHAPTER III

School at Red River—Bank Clerk, Canada—Aspirations

Arrived at Red River Settlement, I was there placed in the charge, as a board pupil, of the Rev. Mr. Cochran, [118] of the Church of England, who then, there, con-

---

[118] The Revd. Mr. William Cochran, who arrived at the Red River Colony in October, 1825, was soon made assistant chaplain under the Revd. Jones. He was much interested in educational matters and was the first clergyman of his church in Rupert's Land to undertake anything like aggressive missionary work among the Indians. See E. H. Oliver, *op. cit.*, i, 60. For further particulars of his life see Alex. Ross, *Red River Settlement*, 181-222. In 1846 he retired for a time to Toronto, but resumed chaplaincy of the Upper Church and settlement at Fort Garry in 1847. He was a Councillor of Assiniboia until 1853, and in 1855 he was appointed Archdeacon of Assiniboia. Captain Palliser, [*op. cit.*, 60], under date of March, 1857, says:—"Many young fellows, halfbreeds that were educated by him, bore testimony to his abilities as a missionary

ducted a school [119] for advanced as well as elementary education. The School was well endowed, and amply supported by the Hudson's Bay Company, principally

clergyman, for all agreed in testifying to the untiring zeal and energy of this estimable clergyman who, I was informed on all sides, was competent not only to teach school and preach fine sermons, but to teach his disciples to wield an axe and drive a plough." See also S. Tucker, *op. cit.* He died in 1865.

Writing to our author's father in the fall of 1838, the Rev. Mr. Cochran says: "I preached at the upper church last Sunday and saw the boys, they were all well then . . . . Ranald has certain indescribable qualities which lead me to imagine that he will make the man that is best adapted for the world." Mr. Colin Inkster, sheriff of Manitoba, Canada, is engaged in writing a life of the Rev. Mr. Cochran.

[119] The Minutes of Council of 1822 [E. H. Oliver, *op. cit.,* i, 638, 640] indicate that this school was commenced under the auspices of and was supported in part by the Hudson's Bay Company, and was first in charge of the Rev. John West who arrived on Oct. 14, 1820, as chaplain to the Company and took up his residence at Fort Douglas. Alex. Ross, *Red River Settlement,* 277; E. H. Oliver, *op. cit.,* i, 59. Mr. West's name appears on the lists of employees of the company in N. America for the years 1821 and 1822 as numbers 405 and 321 respectively. He left the colony on June 10, 1823. Governor Simpson in a letter to Andrew Colvile, May 31, 1824, says that the boys' school is kept by Harbridge who is "stupid, ignorant, consequential and illiterate," *Idem.,* 259; also that "Miss Allez is planning a school for females," *Idem.,* 259.

The Rev. David T. Jones came out in 1823 as successor to Mr. West, and was appointed chaplain to the company in 1825. Alex. Ross, *Red River Settlement,* 74, 128, 181, 222; George Bryce, *Remarkable History of the Hudson's Bay Company,* 300, 420. In the course of time several schools were developed. During the Rev. Mr. Jones' absence on a visit to England the boys' school appears to have been in charge of the Rev. Mr. William Cochran. The Rev. Mr. Jones returned from England in 1838. From correspondence of our author's father it appears that Ranald was first sent to Pritchard's school in 1834 and removed to Jones' in the summer of 1838, where he was a boarding scholar at £30 per year.

In the Minutes of Council for 1833 [E. H. Oliver, *op. cit.,* ii, 697] we find:—"The cause of education and religion is much advanced in Red River Settlement by the establishment of sundry schools under the superintendence of Rev. Mr. Jones and the Rev. Mr. Cochran, and Mr. Pritchard has rendered his valuable services gratuitously to that effect for several years past; moreover that gentleman has established a day school for education of the youth of both sexes in his neighborhood, which is attended by many children whose parents cannot afford to pay for their instruction."

In the Minutes of Council for 1837 [E. H. Oliver, *Idem.* ii, 769] we find:—"The Revd. Mr. Jones having by his letter of the 17th June, 1837, given notice of his intention to discontinue the management of the Red River Boarding school, and Mr. McCallum having expressed a willingness to undertake that charge provided the Company become the purby Chief Factors and Chief Traders of it having children there, of both sexes; for there was also a Mrs. Cochran (an English lady) to look after the female department. The School—open to all denominations—was admirably conducted, and proved satisfactory not only to parents but to the pupils themselves, both Mr. and Mrs. Cochran, in their kindliness, making it a home— or feel as a home—as well as a place of intellectual and moral discipline, to those in their charge.

After about four years here, I was sent,[120] by way of finish to my education, thence to Upper Canada, where, in the good Town of Saint Thomas, in the County of Elgin (an important commercial centre) I was installed in the comfortable mansion house of my father's old friend, of the Columbia, Mr. Edward Ermatinger,[121]

---

chasers of the buildings and will grant him a lease of the same for the term of five years at a rent of 10 P. cent per annum on the purchase money; and it being highly desirable that that institution should not be broken up, it is Resolved: &c. &c." Our author had a "high character for application and good behavior" from Mr. MacCallum. An out-of-print little volume: *The Rainbow in the North, A short account of the First Establishment of Christianity in Rupert's Land by the Church Missionary Society*, S. Tucker, 1861, deals with the history of these missionary schools in the Red River colony, and on page 75 thereof appears a cut showing the school our author attended.

[120] See biography pages 25-33, ante.
Our author's father gave each of his children the best educational advantages his circumstances and the times permitted. Other sons, John and Benjamin followed our outhor in apprenticeship at Mr. Ermatinger's after schooling at Red River.

[121] The Ermatinger family, founded by a Swiss merchant of that name, were among the first settlers in Canada after the conquest of the French. Members of the family were early connected with the fur trade. Fred'k W. Ermatinger, a son, was connected with the North-West Company and his name appears as a witness to the Agreement of November 5, 1804; Charles Oakes Ermatinger, another son, was also in the employ of the North-West Company. Lawrence Edward Ermatinger, another son, entered the Surveyor-General's Department and attained the rank of Assistant Commissary General. Edward Ermatinger and Francis (Frank) Ermatinger here mentioned were grandsons; children of Lawrence Edward Ermatinger.
On May 13, 1818, at London, England, the two boys were bound

formerly Chief accountant of the North West Company,[122] and afterwards on the coalition of the two companies, holding the same office in the Hudson's Bay Company's service in the Columbia.

Mr. Ermatinger having retired from the service with considerable means in hand, had opened a Bank there (in St. Thomas) under the name of the Bank of Elgin[123]—the region being one of the richest—if not the richest—in agricultural and other natural resources in the Canada of that day, and then much in need of local banking facilities.

At that time, there was, I think, only one other Bank

out to the Hudson's Bay Company as clerks for a period of five years, and they reached York Factory August 14th of that year. They remained in the company after the coalition of 1821.

Edward Ermatinger's name appears as Nos. 122, 94, and 83 respectively on the List of Employees of the Company in America for the years 1821, 1822 and 1823, respectively. He remained in the employee of the Company until the summer of 1828. In 1830 he settled at St. Thomas in the Upper Province, where for many years he carried on the business of merchant, banker and postmaster of the town, in which he spent the remainder of his days. He was a member for Middlesex in the Parliament of United Canada.

In the 30's he married a daughter of the Hon. Zaccheus Burnham of Coburg. Edward Ermatinger died in 1876 and his remains rest in the old churchyard at St. Thomas.

He was the author of *The Hudson's Bay Territories;* a series of Letters on this important Question, Maclear, Thomas & Co., Printers, King Street, Toronto, 1856. Also a *Life of Colonel Talbot and the Talbot Settlement.—Its rise and progress with sketches of the Public characters, and career of the most conspicuous men in Upper Canada.—* St. Thomas, 1859, VI 230. In 1912 his son, Judge C. O. Ermatinger of St. Thomas, Ontario, edited Edward Ermatinger's *York Factory Express Journal,* published in the *Transactions of the Royal Society of Canada,* vi, Section 2, 67-123, where a more comprehensive biography is given. See also brief biographical sketch of Francis Ermatinger, note 15, page 24.

122 Our author has confused Edward Ermatinger with his uncles, Frederick W. and Charles O. Ermatinger, both connected with the North West Company. Edward Ermatinger, himself, was a clerk and later an auditor or accountant for the Hudson's Bay Company.

123 It was probably the Bank of Montreal in which our author was employed, of which Mr. Ermatinger had a branch or agency in the same building in which the Bank of Elgin was afterwards organized in *1854.* Our author is also in error in stating that the Bank of Upper Canada was the only other bank then in Upper Canada.

in Upper Canada, viz: "The Bank of Upper Canada."
Mr. E. also occupied the very honorable position of
Member for the County of Elgin [124] in the first Parliament of Canada on the Union of the two Provinces in
1841.

A gentleman of fine culture and high public spirit,
with a practical ability in his special line of work and
study, viz: finance, he proved himself a very useful
member in such discussion. At the same time, like
most Nor'Westers, he was, by habit, unselfish and un-
obtrusive in his ambition—if such he had, beyond that
of simply doing his duty.

In his private life, and domestic, I ever found him
most estimable. To me he was ever considerately
kind: and in the manner of his kindness—marked,
ever, by a gentle reserve—there was nothing to hurt my
feelings in any way.

Done with schooling, the time had come to betake myself to preparation for some line of life.   As to a University education there was, in the first place, no facility, *then*, in Upper Canada, except perhaps—and
that in a very perfunctory way—in Toronto and Kingston.   For such, the habit of the time, in Canada, and
the North West, among Protestants, was to send youths
to England or Scotland.   But that was only for the
professions of Divinity, Medicine and Surgery, and literary and scientific professorships; in some of which,
native born Nor'Westers have made their mark, with
highest honor, even in London, England.

I had no inclination, however, in that way.   In fact,
had no inclination for any particular mode of life—for
bread.   Did not think of bread:but in vague, fatuous

---

[124] The County of Elgin was not set apart from Middlesex until
about 1850.

sort of way, had an abiding feeling that it would always, when needed, come to me—come, as did the quails and manna to the Israelites in the Wilderness. To me, in feeling—feeling as of the very web and woof of my nature—the world was a wilderness. Home, in the strict and ordinary sense, I had not. My father, with his family, was still a denizen of that, then, other world beyond the terrible—to me, all dividing—Mountains of the West; still in a service which, at any moment, might send him to its Dan and Beersheba—Alaska or Labrador, or anywhere else within its four million square miles of Siberian field work. To my mind's eye, and to that of the heart, there was no resting place, yet, in my moving world of waters; no olive branch yet, to the winged search.

Further than that: In spite of all my training for civilized life—so called: in spite of all magnetism of comfortable and endearing hospitality—sweets of a home, but which, still, is not home; and in spite of all possible influences and suggestions to win to such "higher life", I felt, ever, and uncontrollably in my blood, the wild strain for wandering freedom; *im primis* of my Highland father of Glencoe;[125] secondly, and possibly more so (though unconsciously) of my Indian mother, of the Pacific Shore, Pacific Seas, in boundless Dominion.

For a while, just before arriving at the age of majority, I was put, by way of trial, to a Bank stool. It was done kindly and from motives I was bound to re-

125 The ancestral home of our author's father—a deep valley in Northern Argyllshire, Scotland, commemorated in Scottish history as the scene of the "Massacre of Glencoe," where about forty MacDonalds were slaughtered by royal troops in February, 1692. On the tragic night our author's great grand father, John MacDonald, with his mother and a younger brother, Donald, escaped with difficulty from William's troops, *Washington Historical Quarterly*, ix, 94.

spect.   I made no resistance.   There was nothing better, before me; that I could ask for; and I submitted to
the ordeal as best I could.   The time had arrived for me
to cease from being a burden to my kind father, whose
large and increasing family—most of them in costly
educational institutions—had better claims on him.

But banking; or dealing with money in any way, was
not to my taste: I hated the—to me—"dirty thing" ! I
had no ambition for riches.   "Give us our daily
bread"! was prayer enough for me: It has—so far—
never failed me—the abiding faith in it having ever, in
God's own way, been bread and strength to me.

Thus situated: above; with no one to consult in confidence, I resolved to follow my own bent; [126] to go
forth,—out; to see the world; with no staff in hand, but
with the firm purpose of trying an adventure, long
thought of, and the evolution of which had deeply engaged me.   Like other youth, with the spirit of adventure which leads "forlorne hopes"—"*Excelsior!*"—in
battles of progress in the world, I panted to dare even
the impossible, or seeming impossible.

It was foolish, no doubt !   a mad scheme ! as the
world, in its smug common prudence, gauges such action.   Be it so, or not! I did it: Did it—not for, or from
any vainglory to myself that might arise from it, but
merely that some good to my fellowmen in general
might be the result.   As to self, *for self,* in all truth I
 can sincerely say it was not there: no more so than in
the case of many thousands of our race, who in thousands of ways, in peace, as in war, voluntarily breast
danger for something good in itself, and without hope

---

[126] From a letter of his father, Archibald McDonald, it appears that
in 1840 our author desired to secure a commission and enter the British
army.

of reward other than the consciousness of having done well: merit being, in such case, "its own best reward".

Such avowal may seem in itself vainglory, an incredible: but it is not so. My whole life since—much of it public record, official, and otherwise—my silence, since as to the matter—abstaining from claiming any reward or acclamation for such service, is some evidence, I think, of the fact that there was no thought of self in the matter. Standing now on the verge of my grave I solemnly say so.

And further: I declare in all truth, that my story, now, after many years, of what I did and went through in and about Japan, is literally true in every particular; without exaggeration, or coloring; and imperfect only in the fact, that in the nearly half century since the events occurred "Times effacing finger" has blotted out, more or less, many little incidents, which otherwise might have given body and life, in more perfect truth, to the picture of the story.

CHAPTER IV

First Suggestion as to Japan—Accounts of it—Wanderings in the United States—Voyage to Sandwich Islands—Incidents There

How I came to think of Japan was from the following circumstances:

When in the Columbia and northwards on the Pacific Coast, as above stated, Japan was our next neighbor across the way—only the placid sea, the Pacific, between us.

Then—as it had been for two hundred years or more—it was, by its own laws, barred to the world, except—and that with very close restrictions—to the Chinese and Dutch. It was death to any other foreigner, or even to any Japanese who had been, from any cause, absent in any foreign land, or ship, to touch its shores: even shipwrecked mariners, unless fortuitously speedily relieved by some foreign warship of sufficient force, had to pay the penalty of death, sooner or later.

This fact was well known to us of the Hudson's Bay Company in the Columbia. On one or two, if not more occasions the Company had to deal with Japanese cast, in shipwreck, upon their shores, there and northwards, they had been carried thither by the periodically prevailing winds, such as the South West Monsoon, and by the great "Gulf Stream", *Kuro Siwo* (the Great Black River, of Japanese nomenclature) of the Northern Pacific.

Amongst other instances was that of a Japanese Junk, a small, fish laden, or partially so, disabled, cast, with three of its crew still alive, on Queen Charlotte Island. That was in 1836.[127] The natives of the Island

---

[127] Should read 1834. In March of 1833 a Japanese junk laden with crockery of the flowerpot or willow-ware pattern, blown across the Pacific, was wrecked about 15 miles south of Cape Flattery (N. W. Coast of Washington), and all of the seventeen men on board lost except three who were seized and held as slaves by the local Indians. News of this disaster was conveyed to the Hudson's Bay officials at Fort Vancouver in the form of a piece of china-paper on which was a drawing showing the shipwrecked persons, the junk on the rocks and the Indians engaged in plundering it. Thomas McKay with thirty men was sent overland to Cape Flattery to rescue them, but got only as far as Point Grenville, when they gave up the task as impossible. These Japanese were subsequently rescued from the Indians in May, 1834, by Captain William McNeil—the Boston skipper—on board the Hudson's Bay Company ship "Llama" and taken to Fort Vancouver. Francis Heron in keeping the Journal of Occurances at Nesqualie House, under date June 9, 1834, mentions seeing Japanese on board the "Llama" at that date *Washington Historical Quarterly*, vii, 62. The Revd. Samuel Parker saw them at Fort Vancouver on Sept. 28, 1834; see *Journal of an Exploring Tour*, 152. These unfortunate Japanese were sent to England in October, 1834. For other accounts see: Sir Edward Belcher, *Narrative of a Voyage Around the World*, i, 304; Lee & Frost *History of Oregon*, 107-108, wherein Mr. Lee mentions securing from the wreck of some

had, in their fashion, made "slaves" of them; and in the
course of their peregrinations had brought them to Van-
couvers' Island. There they were redeemed and taken
in charge by the chief agent then in charge of Hudson's
Bay Company's interests in the Columbia and of the
Pacific Slope generally within British "influence," viz:

dishes and beautiful china tea cups; Charles Wilkes, *Narrative of the
United States Exploring Expedition*, iv, 315-316; Bancroft, *op. cit.*, ii,
341, 533. In a footnote on the latter page a list is given of numerous
Japanese junks wrecked on the Coast of Kamchatka and America.
Among the most noted of these vessels was the so-called "Japan beeswax
junk" reported to have been wrecked on point Adams [Bancroft, *Idem.*,
ii, 341] or according to James G. Swan, [*The Northwest Coast*, 206], on
the shores of Clatsop beach, south of the Columbia. Beeswax from this
vessel is still being washed up by the waves according to Lewis & Dryden [*Marine History of the Pacific Northwest*, E. W. Wright, ed.
Portland, Ore., 1895, 2, 14], who describe the vessel as not Japanese,
but one of Spain's Oriental fleet laden with beeswax and Chinese
bric-a-brac, blown northward and wrecked near the mouth of the
Columbia. We quote: "Most writers have given the location of the
wreck as being on the north side of the Columbia, but there is a strong
probability that the scene of the wreck was near the mouth of the
Nehalem River, at which place large quantities of beeswax have been
and are still being found. Aside from the presence of the beeswax, and
other traces of the wreck, the Tillamook Indians have had the story
handed down with considerable accuracy. Adam, a Tillamook chief who
died a few years ago, and who was a remarkably intelligent Indian, told
the writer that his father, when a young man had witnessed the wreck,
and that all the crew were drowned. (Other native accounts state that
the survivors were massacred by the natives.) As Adam was over one
hundred years old at the time of his death, there is no reason to doubt
that the Nehalem beeswax ship, of which so much has been written,
was identical with the one wrecked in 1772." Among blocks of beeswax
washed up, some are inscribed with the Latin abbreviations I. H. S.
and the wrecked vessel is supposed to have been the Spanish ship "Jan
Jose," which left La Paz, Lower California, June 16, 1769, with supplies
for the Catholic Mission at San Diego, Upper California, and was never
heard of again. See Mr. Smith's Address Portland (Ore.) *Oregonian*,
Dec. 18, 1899, 9; also The Wax of Nehalem Beach, *Oregonian*, January
26, 1908, reprinted *Oregon Historial Quarterly*, ix, 24-41. Another interesting wreck was that of the unknown Spanish vessel wrecked two
miles south of the mouth of the Columbia about 1725, of whom all of
the crew but four were massacred by the Indians, the latter married
native women. These were the first white men seen by the Chinooks
and ever since the Chinook name for all white people, without respect
to nationality, is "Tlo-hon-nipts"; that is, "of those who drifted ashore."
The names of two of these waifs have been preserved, "Doto" and
"Kanapee." See Franchere, *op. cit.*, 113; Mr. Smith's Address, Portland
(Ore.) *Oregonian*, Dec. 18, 1899, 9.

Doctor John McLoughlin already referred to.   Moved
by their distress, he, in sheer humanity—as was his
wont in such case—took every kindly care of them,
bringing them to his own hearth at Port Vancouver on
the Columbia; thence shipping them, by one of his
Company's ships, via the Horn, to London, England;
thence to Macao, China, where they were placed in
charge of the Reverend Mr. Gutzlaff,[128] the celebrated
English Missionary there, with instructions and means
for restoration to their country, soon as possible, by
Chinese or other vessel trading to Japan.[129]

[128] Karl Gutzlaff, a German missionary, was born at Pyritz, Pomer-
ania, Prussia, July 8, 1803, and went to Siam as a Christian missionary
in 1828.   He later settled in Macao, China, where he assisted in translating the Bible into Chinese, and where he later served as chief interpreter for the Superintendent of British Commerce.   He died at
Hong Kong, China, August 8, 1851.   See Frederick Wells Williams,
Life and Letters of S. Wells Williams, G. P. Putnams' Sons, New York,
1889.   He was the author of a *Sketch of Chinese History*, 2 vol., London,
1834, and *China Opened*, 2 vols., London, 1838.

[129] To Captain Mercator Cooper of Southampton belongs the honor
(in 1845) of flying the first American Flag in a Japanese port (see
Capt. Stewart note 263, page 234), from the whale ship Manhattan, 440
tons burden, owned by John Budd of Sag Harbor, N. Y.   Mr. Budd
bought her from New York in 1843, and Captain Cooper sailed on
November 8, that year, for the Northwest Coast, and in the course of his
cruise near Japan rescued eleven shipwrecked Japanese sailors from
St. Peters, an outlying island of Nippon, early in April, 1845, and
proceeded with them to the Japanese capitol, Yedo, although knowing
that foreigners were forbidden to enter any Japanese ports.   On the
way to Yedo (Tokyo) eleven more Japanese were rescued from a sinking junk.   The Manhattan entered the Bay of Kago-sima, in the principality of Satsuma.   Mrs. W. Buck, *Manners and Customs of the
Japanese*, 271.   At Yedo the twenty-two Japanese were taken ashore,
but neither the captain nor the crew of the Manhattan was allowed to
land, and during the time the ship remained in harbor it was surrounded
by a guard of Japanese boats.   The Manhattan remained in port four
days and was given necessary supplies without charge.   When she was
ready to sail, the natives towed the ship to sea with their boats.   Having
taken 3600 bbls. of oil, the Manhattan sailed for Amsterdam, Holland,
where her cargo was sold and a load of emigrants and freight loaded
for New York.   Arriving home on Oct. 14, 1846, the Manhattan discharged a valuable cargo and was withdrawn from the whale fishery in
1847.

Captain Cooper on his return was offered a mere trifle by the United
States Government for valuable charts of Japan owned by him.   Later
the Washington authorities paid a very large sum to the Dutch Govern-

All this was at the sole personal cost of the good Doctor; for the Company (H. B.) in its "money-bag" stock proprietary in London, formally repudiated all such, and such like outlay out of their resources, and every mouthful in such charity had to be paid by, and was rigidly charged, to the account of such agents, though by the terms of the bond of their partnership (Deed Poll of 1821) then still in force, they were partners—sole actual working and creative partners of the whole concern.

In this way it is a notable fact; and Bancroft, in his special chapters on the theme, in his "British Columbia", has glowingly, and with much credit for the noble candour of the avowal, given the details in proof—that this same Doctor John McLoughlin was the means of saving many—very many—destitute immigrants from the United States when, say up to 1848 there was no provision for them in that region.   He spent thousands of dollars, out of his own really far from abundant means in relief of such distress.   He actually gave away his store for his old age and family, in such charity, and died a poor man! saving other, regardless of creed or nationality, or race, from fatal distress,— Samaritan to the core!—it was in this sense, that, in truth, the historian (Bancroft, aforesaid) calls him "The very CHRIST of the Pacific Slope".[130] Exception

---

ment for similar charts. Mrs. Robert R. Kendrick of Southampton, N. Y.—a granddaughter of Captain Cooper—has in her possession the Japanese compass, charts and curios obtained by her grandfather from the shipwrecked Japanese and at the port of Yedo. An early account of the Manhattan's call at the Japanese port appeared in the *Seaman's Friend*, Honolulu, Oahu, S. I., February 2, 1846. For a full account see Entering a Forbidden Port, and The Manhattan's Log near Japan, in vol. i, no. i, of the *Southampton Magazine*, Southampton, N. Y., 1912. Also see Alexander Starbuck, *op. cit.*, 141, 406.

130 H. H. Bancroft, [*op. cit.*, ii, 704-707] pays a splendid tribute to the character of Dr. John McLoughlin; on page 705 he says:—"In

may be taken to such application of such Name, but, in light of the facts of the case, as given by Bancroft, the term—as designative of such abounding charity and practical love to fellowmen—is—intelligible.   In any other sense, the term is, of course, unacceptable to Christian sentiment.

While in Macao, in Mr. Gutzlaff's charge, four other Japanese, who had been wrecked on the Philippines, were, by an American vessel, brought to the same port, and were kindly taken in charge by Dr. Parker,[131] an American Missionary Physician, and also a partner of an American mercantile firm there.

With these seven pitiable castaways of Japan on their hands, these two worthy missionaries determined to do everything in their power to restore them to their country—hoping, at the same time, that some approach, if not ingress might be made, with their mission, to and into Japan.

Other considerations, of a mercantile nature, legitimate and even laudable, may have weighed with others in the venture.   A vessel (brig Morrison)[132] was chartered for the purpose; and in due course, with the two Missionaries Gutzlaff and Parker) on board, accompanied by Mr. S. W. Williams,[133] one of the editors of

writing any volume I have ever written I have encountered few characters which stand out in such grand and majestic proportions.   Few persons have done him justice.   His life should be written by the Recording Angel and pillared at the crossings of the two chief highways of the universe."

[131] Dr. Peter Parker.   A couple of pamphlets written by him on hospital conditions in China are familiar to us—one published in Canton,, 1839.

[132] The brig "Morrison" of Boston, King owner, named after the first Protestant English missionary to China, was chartered at Macao, China. The vessel was later sold and transferred to Spanish registry under the name of the "Carmine," and was in the oriental trade in 1859.

[133] Samuel Wells Williams of Utica, N. Y., who went to China in

the "*Chinese Repository*," Macao—a gentleman
thoroughly "up" in Chinese, an official Interpreter of
the language, proceeded to "Jeddo"[134] (now Tokio—
Capital of Japan), and there, in face of cannon mouth,
presented, with appeal in intelligible Chinese, the seven
unfortunates for restoration to their homes and people.
They were peremptorily refused, and driven back under
fire.[135]

The effort was repeated, about a month afterwards,
at a port further South, in the principality of Satsuma,
where, though received at first with more courtesy, they
were repulsed in like manner. Nagasaki was not tried,
because being neither Chinese nor Dutch, it was closed
against them, and moreover, some of the Japanese, on

1833 and studied the Chinese language, later publishing several dictionaries and vocabularies thereof. He was editor of the *China Mail* in
1849 and was engaged as interpreter by Commodore Perry for his
negotiations with the Japanese. Returning to the United States, he
was lecturer on Chinese at Yale University from 1876 to his death,
February 16, 1884. See *Life and Letters of S. Wells Williams* by his
son, Frederick Wells Williams, *cited supra*. His book on the Chinese
Empire, *The Middle Kingdom*, New York, 1848, passed through several
editions.

134 Yedo.

135 This voyage, to Uraga, bay of Yedo and Kagoshima in Satsuma,
which took place in the months of July and August, 1837, occupied 56
days and cost the missionaries about $2,000. The seven unfortunate
Japanese who were brought back to China were for some time employed about the mission at Macao. One of these, Sam Patch, joined
the Perry expedition in China and went to Japan where he was invited
by the Japanese Commissioners to remain in Japan and join his family,
and guaranteed safety, but, having full knowledge of the dire penalties
existing under the laws of the Empire, Sam Patch was afraid to leave
the protection afforded by the American vessels. He afterwards returned
to the United States in the "Mississippi" with another of the Morrison
waifs, named Dan Ketch by the sailors. Another of these waifs, Kiki-
mats, went to Nagasaki with Admiral Sterling as his interpreter in 1855.
See Frances L. Hawks, *op. cit.*, i, 340, 450, 342, 485, and Frederick Wells
Williams, *op. cit.*, 93-99, 226, 255, 258, 298. A prior Russian attempt to
return shipwrecked Japanese sailors, undertaken by Lt. Laxman in the
"Catherine" in the fall of 1792, resulted in a similar repulse. Mention of
this is made in Hawks, *op. cit.*, i, 45.

board emphatically declared that on no account would they land there.

I refer to this incident at fuller length than is perhaps proper to a mere introductiion, but being of direct bearing, and historical; and, moreover, being in evidence of the fact that there were others besides myself thus bent on effort to open the gates of Japan, I venture to present it.

However, I must admit, that when I started on my own mission, I had not heard, nor knew of this Morrison episode: but of the Queen Charlotte Island waifs I did know, being in the country at the time.

The following was the ultimate [136] Imperial Decree of expulsion of foreigners from Japan—date A. D. 1837 (or 1838, for accounts differ). [137]

JAPANESE DECREE OF EXCLUSION

The whole race of the Portuguese, with their mothers, nurses, and whatever belongs to them, shall be banished forever.

No Japanese ship or boat or any native of Japan shall henceforth presume to leave the country, under pain of forfeiture and death. Any Japanese returning from a foreign country shall be put to death. [138]

---

[136] There were others less rigorous, before, back about twenty years, from time to time.—[Original.]

[137] This edict is given in Richard Hildreth's *Japan As It Was and Is*, pages 191-192, and is taken from Dr. Engebrecht Kaempfer's *History of Japan*, book iv, chapter v. The order of the articles and the wording of some of the articles are somewhat different from what is given here. The decree was issued in June, 1636 (the 5th month of the 13th year of Kwauei (Qwanje as Kaempfer spells it). Hildreth is mistaken in saying that it was issued in 1638 and that all the Portuguese were then banished. It was the descendants of the Portuguese and Spaniards, called by the Japanese "Nambu Jim" (Southern Barbarians)—about 280 in number— and the Japanese parents who adopted such children, who were banished by this edict. Portuguese merchants, although comparatively few in number, were allowed to stay at Nagasaki on the Island of Deshima. The Portuguese trade was forbidden in 1639.

[138] Our author's high-minded and courageous effort to enter Japan was contemporary with several equally brave and self-sacrificing efforts

No nobleman or soldier shall be suffered to purchase anything from a foreigner.

Any person presuming to bring a letter from abroad, or to return to Japan after he had been banished, shall die; with all his family; and whosoever shall intercede for such offenders shall be put to death.

All persons who shall propagate the doctrines of the Christians, or bear that scandalous name, shall be seized and imprisoned in the common gaol.

A scale of rewards is then offered for the discovery of priests and natives of the condemned religion—the whole winding up with the terrible *anathema*:

"So long as the Sun shall warm the earth, let no Christian dare to come to Japan; and let all know, that the King of Spain himself,

---

by some Japanese themselves to leave their country or, having visited foreign lands, to return thereto. Among the outstanding characters of this class is Nakahama Manjiro. A boy of 14, he went fishing with four companions, sailing from Nishihama, in Takahama, in Tosa, on the 5th day of January, 1841, and was wrecked on a desert island off the southeast coast of Japan. On June 27, 1841, Captain Wm. H. Whitfield of the New Bedford whaler, "John Howland," in latitude 30°, 31', rescued the shipwrecked Japanese fishermen from their desert island. Finishing the whaling season, the "John Howland" touched at Honolulu, S. I., where the four Japanese fishermen were landed. The boy was brought home to Fairhaven by Captain Whitfield who had grown much attached to him, and he was given the American name of John Mung. He remained in Fairhaven about six years, going to school, receiving a good English education, and acquiring the customs and habits of American civilization, and learned navigation from his benefactor, Capt. Whitfield, whom he accompanied on whaling voyages. An overpowering desire to return to Japan and see his mother finally moved him to ship on a whaler for Honolulu where he found three of his countrymen—one having died— and he shipped with them on the whaler "Sarah Boyd," Whitmore captain, in 1850 for the Japanese fishing grounds. They purchased a whale-boat and left ship near the Loo-Choo Islands where they landed and remained six months, and finally made their way north to Japan in 1851. Immediately on landing in Japan they were imprisoned and held in confinement for thirty months. Shortly before Commodore Perry's expedition, Nakahama was released and he became one of the Japanese interpreters in the negotiations with Commodore Perry. See herein: *The Seaman's Friend,* Honolulu, S. I., October, 1884. In 1870 he went to Europe as a member of the Japanese commission to observe military maneuvers. He translated Bowditch's *Navigation* into the Japanese language and took an important part in the "New Era" in Japan. He an important manuscript narrative of Nakahama's experiences, written was made a Samurai. In 1912 Mr. Stewart Culver of the Brooklyn Institute Museum, Brooklyn, N. Y., procured at a book sale at Tokyo, Japan,

or the Christian's God, or . . . . .[139] if he violate this command,
shall pay for it with his head."

The only modification of this, up to my time there,
was the following—probably suggested by the incident
of the Morrison. The Edict bears date 1843; promul-

---

and illustrated by Kanata Koretazu, from drawings made by Nakahama
Manjiro. The manuscript has been translated into English by Genjiro
Kataoka, the Japanese painter, and is being prepared for publication by
Mr. Culver, to whom we are indebted for some of the facts stated. In
this narrative Manjiro gives an account of his rescue and an intimate
and lively picture of life in the New-England town; then tells of his
whaling voyages, of his adventures in California where he dug gold, and
then describes finally his return to Japan and the details of his reception
in his native country in 1851. His sane reflections upon conditions in
America seem to have made a deep impression on his countrymen, and
their influence is still felt in Japan. The simplicity of his character, his
reasonableness and his vigor are impressed on the reader of his narrative,
and it is pleasant to think that he took his place at last as a man in the
world, and does not occupy a neglected grave like the author of the
present narrative.

Nakahama Manjiro left five sons and a daughter, to honor his name.
On July 4, 1918, a celebration was held at Fairhaven, Mass., in honor
of Nakahama Manjiro at which Viscount Kikujiro Ishii, Imperial Japanese Ambassador at Washington, attended and presented the City of Fairhaven with a rare Samurai sword of the 14th century, the gift of Dr. T.
Nakahama, one of Nakahama's sons. Another son, Keisaburo Nakahama, is a paymaster in the Japanese Navy. Fairhaven (Mass.) *Star,*
Friday, July 5; 1918.

In this connection the editors feel constrained to mention the abortive
exploit of two adventurous and brave countrymen of Nakahama, referred to by Frances L. Hawks, *op. cit.,* i, 420-422.

The adventurers were Yoshida Torajiro, son of a hereditary military
instructor to the house of Choshu—himself a poet and learned in the
Chinese classics, then 24 years of age—and a common soldier, unim-
proved in learning but of enquiring mind, attracted equally by the adventure and by Yoshida's inspiring personality. With the sympathetic,
though secret, support of Sakuma Shozan—hereditary retainer of one of
the Shogun's counsellors, and armed with a letter in Chinese setting
forth their intentions signed by Yoshida as "Urinaka Manji" and by
the soldier as "Ichiki Kota," they attempted on April 25, 1854 to
board one of Commodore Perry's ships with the object of reaching
America and studying in foreign lands. Repulsed by the American
officers, who could not officially transgress the laws of the Empire, they
departed with great reluctance, and were last seen by the Americans
in a prison-cage and their subsequent fate unknown. The prisoners
were sent to Choshiu and after a long and miserable period of imprisonment, during which the soldier died, Yoshida, who, though in
prison, had gained some privileges, became involved, some six years
later, in a conspiracy against the Shogun's government and was executed
in Yedo January 31, 1859 at the age of 29, a martyr to the New Japan.

gated by agency of the Dutch, from their Factory (Dessima) at Nagasaki.

EDICT. A. D., 1843

"Shipwrecked persons of the Japanese nation must not be brought back to their country, except on board of Dutch or Chinese ships, for, in case these shipwrecked persons shall be brought back in the ship of other nation, they will not be received.

Considering the express prohibition, even to Japanese subjects, to explore or make examinations of the coasts or Islands of the Empire, this prohibition, for greater reason, is extended to foreigners." [140]

Such was the wall of fire around their own loved Isles, of this people.   People!—oldest of existing nations: most concrete: most potent in patriotic unity, Eminently a warrior race, they had signally repelled all powers on earth—from *Kublai Khan* (A. D. 1271-1292) to the present—from hostile touch.

These incidents are mentioned not for the individuals, but as representatives of an enquiring, heroic people whose vision and aggregate efforts and sacrifices and indomitable spirit have produced the Japan of today.   Read Robert Louis Stevenson's fine tribute to Yoshida in *Familiar Studies of Men and Books*.   In the language of the Chinese classic, quoted by a fellow prisoner of Yoshida's, when led to execution: "Better to be a crystal, though shattered, than lie as a tile unbroken on the housetop."

[139] Too blasphemous for expression.—[Original.]

[140] The intercourse of the leading European nations with Japan prior to 1849 may be briefly summarized as follows: The Portuguese, first landing 1543-5, were finally expelled in 1639.   The Dutch, arriving in 1600, were in 1641 sent to Deshima, and thenceforth continued to enjoy a limited commerce with Japan.   The English, arriving in 1613, were forced to leave Japan in 1623.   Attempts to renew trade relations were made in 1636, 1673, 1791 (Argonaut), 1803 (Frederick) 1808 (Phaeton's visit under Pellew), 1813-1814 (Sir S. Raffles, two attempts), 1818 (Gordon's attempt), 1849 (the "Mariner's" visit).   The Russian visit of Lt. Adams Laxmann in 1792 was followed by Resanoff's mission in 1804, the Descent on the Kuriles in 1807, and the captivity of Captain Golowin in 1811.   The French attempt under Admiral Cecile in 1846 was repulsed.

The repulse of the American boat "Morrison" in 1837 was followed by the visit of Captain Cooper of the "Manhattan" April 16-21, 1845; the repulse of the "Columbus" and "Vincennes" under Commodore Biddle in July, 1846; and the visit of Commander Glynn in April, 1849.

"Utopia" of the hoary East! : *"Wak-Wak"*—mythic—of old Arabian tale: most ancient, living of the families of Man: an "Easter-Isle" empire laved and sustained by lone teeming seas: Wonder in an ocean of wonders!—to us, on its opposite shore, gazing searchingly into the far, far offing, it was ever, an object of intense curiosity.   What, of such people?—What of their manner of life?—What of their unrivalled wealth with its gleam of gold and things most precious?—What of their life, social, municipal, and national?—What of their feelings and tendencies —if any—towards associatiion or friendly relations with other peoples, especially us, neighbors of their East?

These and such like questions and considerations ever recurring; the subject, oft, of talk amongst my elders —elders then the actual governors in administration of North American, as well as world wide larger interests on the Pacific Slope and Ocean—entering deeply into my young, and naturally receptive mind; breeding, in their own way, thoughts and aspirations which dominated me, as a soul possessed.

I resolved, within myself, to personally solve the mystery, if possible, at any cost of effort—yea life itself.

Mad! or not—I did so—at least in measure of my aim and power.

The present is the story of it.

Satisfied in my own conscience with my purpose, I never abandoned it.   That purpose was to learn of them; and, if occasion should offer, to instruct them of us.

My plan was to present myself as a castaway; and

with all seeming confidence—without seeming to court it—to rely on their humanity.

I could not believe them wholly lost to it.   It would have been cowardice to have done so.   "Have faith in one another" is a motto I early learnt, and have ever cherished.   Its application, of course, requires caution, and there is ever an element of risk in it: but in that is a very spice of life.

Man is born unto trouble, conflict, and danger in many ways; and in his mastery of them, in their risk and peril, when for good, is the merit of his life, humanly speaking.

My main difficulty—I assumed—would be to effectively disguise my motive, viz: to learn of them, and, if possible, to be their teacher as to things external to them, against which they had encased themselves, and as to which, especially the English, and all of that nationality, they had been studiedly prejudiced by the Dutch and Chinese, for their own ends.   I knew, moreover, that their condemnation of Christinanity was more particularly of that form of it known as Roman Catholic, which, previous to the decree first above cited, had shaken the Throne itself, in Japan, in treasonable conspiracy.

Keeping this in view, I limited the collection of books I had determined to take with me, to my simple English Bible, prayer book (Church of England), a dictionary, grammar, history (English) and geography &c—all in compact form.

I was not a man of learning, but always a lover of books: of these I was master enough for my purpose.

I knew that such freight—so strange for a mere castaway from a whaling ship—would naturally excite suspicion; but I had my story, ready, for the nonce. Themselves even of the middle and lower classes, being a people of literature and books, I thought I might pass on this score. The sequel proved so. In fact it was *that* that saved me: for seeing me ever reading, a man of books, they drew to me: the books [141] magnetized them: *and they* (books and Japanese) *made me their teacher!*

How the Design Was Carried Out

To carry out this design while sitting, like a Simon Stylites,[142] on my high stool in the Bank of Elgin, with little money or means of any kind to aid me; and with no friends or influence to appeal to in such endeavor, I felt as a stranger amongst strangers, with no hope—not the slightest—of sympathy from any quarter, in such a scheme. In the monomania of the project I had sagacity enough to keep it to myself. I had resolved on it; that was enough. For means to carry it out, I simply, with grip sack in hand, walked forth into the darkness of an unsympathetic world; alone, telling no one; with barely scrip for the hour.

That was in 1845, when I was just twenty one; in the freedom of manhood; with full vigour of youth; for for any honest work for the needs of the moment. I immediately went West to the Mississippi. Got occupation as a boat hand on one of its palace steamers. The work suited me: was apprenticeship for graver work, somewhat in the same line, before me. Thence, after much wandering, but ever holding my own, without fall or stumble; ever buoyed up with the hope of reaching my cynosure at some time, I made the port of New

---

[141] See Appendix II, pages 273, 277, for reference to the number of books taken into Japan by our author.

[142] A reference to the "pillar Saint"; a Syrian ascetic who passed the last thirty years of his life on a pillar near Antioch.

York, where vessels, to and from the world over, most do congregate.

Here, late in 1845,[143] I shipped before the mast on board the ship "Plymouth", Lawrence B. Edwards, Captain, for the Sandwich Islands, where I expected to find a favorable opportunity of shipping on board a "Whaler" for the Japan seas—a general resort for such service.[144]

---

[143] The whale ship, "Plymouth," 425 tons, of Sag Harbor, N. Y., Cook & Greene, owners, was bought from Boston in 1845 and sailed for the Northwest Coast on December 6, 1845, with Captain Laurence B. Edwards, Master. She returned on April 30, 1849, after an absence of over three years. This was the "Plymouth's" only whaling voyage from the port of Sag Harbor, which then had 63 vessels in the whaling fleet. The last whaler cleared from Sag Harbor in 1871. Captain Charles P. Cook of Sag Harbor, son of one of the owners of the "Plymouth"—then a boy ten years of age—still recalls visiting the ship with Capt. Edwards' wife, just before its departure, with our author on board, in December, 1845. See Alexander Starbuck, op. cit., 432; Walter S. Tower, op. cit., 69, 124, table II.

[144] The Pacific whale fisheries opened in 1780, and for sperm-whale fishing in 1787 by the "Amelia," Capt. Shields, an English-fitted ship manned by Nantucket whalemen. The "Beaver" of Nantucket, built in 1791 and sailing in August of that year under Captain Paul Worth, was the first American whaler in the Pacific. She was followed that same year by five Nantucket and one New-Bedford whaler. Alexander Starbuck, op. cit., 90, note, 186-187; Walter S. Towers History of the American Whaling Fishery, 53, 93.

American whaling boats now rapidly spread in their courses to all parts of the Pacific, and hundreds of islands received their first visit from white men from the New-England whalers. Much of the Pacific waters was then unknown and the existing charts were full of inaccuracies. Hundreds of small islands in the Pacific were first located on the charts and made known to civilization by American whalemen.

The Kadiak, Alaska, grounds were discovered in 1835 by the "Ganges" of Nantucket, Captain Folger; and the celebrated Kamchatka coast grounds, along the Siberian Coast and Kuriles, were discovered by the "Hercules" and "James," both of New Bedford, in 1843, Alexander Starbuck, op. cit., 98. By 1839 the majority of vessels on the Pacific were taking right and bow-head whales.

So large a portion of the American whaling fleet eventually visited the Pacific, that the United States was finally forced, after repeated petitions to Congress, to send an exploring expedition to these seas. Both Commodore Wilkes (1838) and Commodore Perry (1853) were indebted to these hardy mariners, and Maury in compiling his great work on Ocean Currents made constant use of the information supplied by them. Alexander Starbuck, op cit., 97.

The first vessel in the Bering sea grounds was the bark "Superior,"

In due time (five or six months) I arrived and landed there. The place was of special interest to me, as
during my life in the Columbia our (Hudson's Bay
Company) trade relations with the Islands were very
intimate, and many of the men in the Hudson's Bay
Company's service, as boatmen (and excellent they
were) were from there.[145]

---

275 tons, of Sag Harbor, Captain Royce, in 1848. The next year saw
154 ships whaling in that sea. Alexander Starbuck, *op. cit.*, 148.

The American whaling fleet reached its greatest tonnage in the
period of 1845-1850, when in one year 680 ships, 34 brigs and 22
schooners, aggregating some 235,000 tons, were in the fishery. The
fleet also reached its greatest production of whale-oil during this period,
when an annual production of 330,000 barrels was approximated. This
was worth, retail, about $2.50 a gallon. See Alexander Starbuck, *op.
cit.;* Walter S. Tower, *op. cit.*, 51-53, 67; Dr. J. Arthur Harris, *Graphics
of the American Whale Fishery, Popular Science Monthly,* July, 1914,
83-86.

The development of the petroleum industry sealed the fate of the
whaling industry by furnishing a cheaper and more satisfactory oil
for illuminating and general purposes. The decline of the whale fishing
was, however, hastened by other events: During the gold rush of '49
to California whalers offered an easy means of reaching California
and its gold-fields, and whole crews shipped apparently merely as a
cheap means of reaching the mines. Desertions from ships were so
numerous, as to leave them insufficiently manned and many whalers
were wholly abandoned by officers and crews; other whalers, chartered
to carry Argonauts to the promised land, rotted on the California beaches
after their arrival. Alexander Starbuck, *op. cit.*, 112; Walter S. Tower,
op. cit., 74.

During the American Civil War many New-England whalers fell a
prey to Confederate privateers. The "Shenandoah" alone captured and
burned 34 whaling ships and barks, besides bonding four others. Forty
ships from the Pacific whaling fleet were purchased by the United
States government and formed a large portion of the two famous stone
fleets, which, in 1861, were sunk off the harbors of Charleston and
Savannah to prevent the entrance of blockade runners and the ingress
and escape of privateers. Alexander Starbuck, *op. cit.*, 101.

Further serious disaster met the fleet ten years later. In the fall of
1871 a terrible fate overtook the Arctic fleet when 34 vessels were
caught in the ice and crushed off point Belcher. See account in
Harper's *Weekly,* December 2, 1871; also Alexander Starbuck, *op. cit.*,
101. A similar disaster met the fleet in 1876 when 12 ships and barks
were lost. Thus the glory of the American whale fishery passed.

[145] Many of these islanders had acquired a knowledge of English
from the crews of trading and whaling vessels visiting their shores.
Geo. H. von Langsdorff in 1806 [Voyages and Travels, 187] says of
them: "The Islanders are becoming very fond of a seafaring life, and

In the service they went by the general appellation of "Owhyees", from *Oawhu*, one of the principal islands of the group.

The place had also been always an objective point with me for immediate preparation for my contact with Japan.

Besides that, among other adventitious attractions to me, it had been the last field of work of my dearly loved friend and companion in the wild woods of the Columbia and Fraser, *David Douglas*, [146] botanist, of

they make excellent sailors. While on the Northwest coast of America, I saw and talked with several natives of Owyhee serving as sailors on board vessels from Boston." Archibald Campbell, writing in 1810, says: "He (King Tamaa-Hmaat) encourages them (his subjects) to make voyages in the ships that are constantly touching at the Islands, and many of them have been as far as China, the Northwest Coast of America and even the United States. In a very short time they become useful hands." Archibald Campbell, *A Voyage Around the World*, 213. The first of these Owyhees were brought to the Columbia River on the "Tonquin" in 1811. The first Owyhee to go into the interior was "Coxe," who was a member of Stuart's party from Astoria in the summer of 1811 and for whom David Thompson exchanged one of his voyageurs. Thompson took him to Spokane House. See hereon David Thompson, *op. cit.*, 510-511; Alexander Ross, *Fur Traders*, i, 114; Coues, *op. cit.*, 868. These Owyhees became an important part of the brigades west of the mountains and, intermarrying with local Indians, have left some of their physical traits impressed on their descendants among the Salesh tribes. Their name is commemorated in the Owyhee Mountains, Owyhee County, the town of Owyhee and Owyhee River in Eastern Oregon, where three of them, outfitted by Donald McKenzie for trapping upon that stream, were murdered by the Indians in 1819.

146 David Douglas first arrived on the Columbia River, near Astoria, April 9, 1825, and after a few days in the vicinity of that post, spent the next two years in the interior leaving the Columbia District May 2, 1827, for England via Hudson's Bay. He returned to the mouth of the Columbia River for a few months in the spring of 1830, and again in the fall of 1832 until his departure October 18, 1834. See his Journal published a few years ago. It is probable that young MacDonald—then an active boy between nine and ten years of age—may have been a youthful "friend and companion" of the great botanist while in and about the trading posts at Astoria (Fort George) and Fort Vancouver. In any other sense, our author's statement is misleading. Our author's father writing to his friend John McLeod on Feb. 20, 1833, says: "I was at Vancouver last fall (1832). Mr. David Douglas just returned from California, via. Sandwich Islands." *Washington Historical Quarterly*, ii, 161-162. Our author's recollections of Mr. Douglas were probably from being with him 1832-1833.

"Douglas Pine" fame.   After his wanderings for many years—six or seven if I remember right—on the Pacific Slope of the mainland, he came here; where, while gathering specimens on the edge of a "cattle hole", he slipped into it, and was gored to death, in it by a wild bull.

That was in 1833.   Everybody who had known him lamented him; for with all his enthusiasm in his pursuit, he was ever the most sociable, kindly, and endearing of men.   A sturdy little Scot; handsome rather; with head and face of fine Grecian mould; of winning address, genial, and with all, the most sincerely pious of men. He walked the terrible wilds of the West, generally *alone!* from the Pacific shore to the Rocky Mountains, midst wild beasts, and savages fiercer: in danger oft; but ever equal to the occasion.   He, literally, feared no evil.   The Lion in the man awed all.

The heroism of his work has not—that I am aware of—been made known to the world.   Hence these few words in such reference.

Ready and eager to go on, I looked out for a Whaler bound for the northern seas of Japan.   I found one before long; and therewith my story, proper begins.

CHAPTER V

NARRATIVE

Ship on Board Whaler for Japan Seas — Sandwich
    Islands— Ladrones— Castaway Settlers —Treasure
    Trove—China and Japan Seas—Whale Fishery—
    Adrift

At the Port of Sahina in Mowhu (one of the Sandwich Islands) after a sojourn of a few days throughout the group,[147] I looked out for a vessel wherein to ship for my purpose.

Accidentally meeting, in port, my old Captain of the "Plymouth", which had lain over in Kalakakna Bay to repair, I applied to him for reshipment, again before the mast, on the ordinary partnership terms of whalers— of payment on share profit—but with the special stipulation on my part, that I was to be free to leave the ship off the coast of Japan wherever and whenever I should desire, when the ship would be full, or be on the eve of returning or going elsewhere, and that in the meantime he was to teach me to make observations for latitude and longitude in navigation. I had provided myself with Hadley's quadrant and nautical almanac for the purposes. The captain objected at first to such a condition, but finally agreed to it, on terms which will hereafter appear in the narrative. I believe he thought the condition would never be exacted; and certainly he never manifested any desire that it should be.

We left the Sandwich Islands, for Hong Kong, in company with the Whaler "David Paddock"[148] of Nantucket.

On our voyage we sighted some small islands, and

---

147 The Sandwich Islands became the general rendezvous of all the whale ships employed in the North Pacific Ocean. As early as 1825 Capt. F. W. Beechey stated that in the spring time whaling vessels to the number of fifty or sixty sails assembled in the harbour of Honoruru (Honolulu) at one time. These vessels made repairs and took on board large supplies of vegetables and fruit, as sea stock, to enable them to remain upon their fishing ground until autumn, when many of them returned to the port. Capt. F. W. Beechey, *Narrative of a Voyage to the Pacific*, ii, 117. See also note 157, page 150.

148 "David Paddock" of Nantucket, 352 tons was built at Rochester in 1841 and sailed on its first voyage Oct. 7, 1841, Chas. B. Swain 2nd., Master; David Jones, owner. Returning October 17, 1845, the ship again sailed from Nantucket for the Pacific whaling grounds on December 8, 1845, and accompanied our author's ship, the "Plymouth," from Honolulu to the Japanese coast. She separated from the "Plymouth" in June, 1847, and was later wrecked at La Perouse Straits off the Jap-

touched at Gregan and Pegan, two of the Ladrones,[149]
where we got wood and a large number of hogs. Gregan is the most northern of the group.

We here met with an adventure which I thought very
little of at the time, but since in hearing, or rather reading of the report of vast buried treasure in the old Spanish times, it has recurred to me, with a passing thought
of what might have been done, with such like trover, by

---

anese coast. Alexander Starbuck, *op. cit.*, 276, 426. We quote from the
Nantucket (Mass.) *Inquirer,* February 2, 1849:
  Wreck of the Ship "David Paddock" of Nantucket. "On the 20th
of July at half past 9 o'clock in the evening this vessel being full,
and bound out of the Japan Sea, in North Latitude 45, 28, and East
Longitude 141, 5, struck on a sunken rock not laid down on any chart.
The ship's company took to the boats and lay under the lee of the
vessel until the morning, when she had six inches of water on the
cabin floor, but she could not get off, although the spars were cut away.
Land was discovered about 15 miles off, which proved to be Feeshee
Island. They landed upon the southwest cape of Saghalen, and remained
there three days. The inhabitants treated them with great kindness,
but would not allow them to go back into the country. A house and
food were furnished gratuitously, and when they left they were presented with four or five hundred pounds of rice. The inhabitants, who
were few, appeared to be Tartars under a Japanese governor. After
three days residence they all left in their boats to cross the Matsmai
Straights, but fell in with the "Globe," Dagett, of New Bedford, in
the passage. All hands were saved. The following ships succeeded
in obtaining a portion of the "David Paddock's" cargo; "Caravan" of Fall
River, "Bridgeport" and "Neva" of Greenport. Reuben Andrews, first
officer of the "David Paddock" reached Honolulu on the "Samuel Robert-
son," Turner, Captain, at the time the barque "Don Quixote" arrived
from San Francisco with the news of the discovery of gold. He joined
the "stampede" for California, and was one of the 60 passengers
arriving in San Francisco in October, 1848, on the schooner "Sagada-
hock." His daughter resides at Nestor, California.

  [149] This course from the Hawaiian Islands—westward to the Ladrones
—was the usual one to keep within the limits of the trade winds which
are more variable in a higher altitude.
  The Marianne, Ladrones or Thieves' Islands—so named by the crew
of Magalhaes' fleet on account of the thieving propensity of the inhabitants—comprise a group of 16 islands lying north of the Caroline
Islands in the North Pacific Ocean. They were discovered and named
by Fernao de Magalhaes in 1521. Guagan or Guam, the largest of the
islands, is a station of the Pacific Cable, and interesting as ceded to
the United States by Spain in 1898. The chief inhabitants of the Islands are descendants from settlers from Mexico and the Philippines.
Pagon and Guagan mentioned by our author are among the northern
islands of the group.

myself as well as others with me at the time and who
were personally cognizant of the facts.   The story,
briefly, is this:

GREGAN AND PEGAN WITH THEIR "ROBINSON CRUSOES" AND TREASURE

On our way to the Ladrones, we approched, unconsciously, a rock in mid-ocean known as "French—Frigute—Shoals".   Here we experienced the severest gale
during the entire voyage, blowing our mainsail and
some of our fore and aft sails clean out of the bolt ropes,
but by bending new ones, and good management, we
weathered all danger.   It was touch and go with us, for
we have found ourselves in the bight of the shoals.   We
calculated the shoal to be from ten to fifteen miles in
length.

When the weather moderated we shaped our course
for the Island of Gregan, for wood and water.   On arriving at the Island with our consort the "David Paddock", we came to, under the lee of the Island, by backing our main yard.   Each Captain went ashore in his
own boat.   I was one of the party.

The Island was fringed with cocoa nut trees near the
beach.   On landing we discovered—Robinson Crusoe
like—human foot prints on the sand.   We were surprised; having been assured that the Island was not,
and never had been inhabited.   On ascending the beach
we saw a naked man dodging from tree to tree.   By
following him we came to a clearing, with a yard, and
three or four thatched cottages, and eight other men,
with several women, and a few children.   Before arriving at the place, we were met by the mysterious dodger; but now in full dress, wearing a shirt—just a
shirt—nothing more!—He introduced himself as

"Liverpool Jack".[150]   He told us that there was another white man, living about a mile north of him, named by him "Spider Jack", living with a sickly wife.   He gave

[150] First Officer Andrews of the "David Paddock" also makes mention of these two English sailors.

Many British and American sailors who had deserted or been discharged from their ships were eventually to be found upon the various Pacific Islands.   Some of these, scoundrels under any circumstances, became leaders of the natives in their attacks upon trading and whaling vessels; some of them became influential men upon the islands, both by reason of their superior civilization and through marriage with dusky maidens—daughters of the chief men of the islands.   One of the most marked cases of this latter kind was that of David Whippey, who left a Nantucket whaling vessel while at the Fiji Islands about the year 1824 and, making himself friendly and useful to the chiefs, soon became a most important man among them.   According to the custom there he acquired several wives (albeit he is said to have left one behind him in Nantucket) and became the father of a numerous family. He was appointed one of the United States vice-consuls, and for many years was of great service to our government.

Alexander Starbuck, *op. cit.*, 98 note.   The editors have found two accounts of Whimpey: William S. Cary of Nantucket, sole survivor of the ship "Oeno," wrecked on Turtle Island, one of the Fiji, April, 1825, in his log book published in the Nantucket (Mass.) *Journal* in 1887, after giving an account of the shipwreck and massacre of the rest of the crew of "Oeno" by the natives, tells of meeting Mr. David Whippey whom he saw while he (Cary) was on the island of Motosick, coming in a canoe from Ambow, about fifteen miles away.   On landing Whippey reached out his hand, addressed Cary by name and asked him if he didn't know David Whippey.   Mr. Cary answered that he formerly knew Dave Whimpey and that he was a fellow townsman and an old playmate of his.   "Well," said Whimpey, "I am David Whippey."   As it was about a year since Cary had seen a white man, this meeting must have been in 1826.   David Whippey told Cary that he had left the brig "Calder" some thirteen months before, bearing presents from the captain to the king of Ambow, together with a request that he would collect all the turtle shell he could; the captain promising to return in a few months and trade with him for it.   But now the time was so long that Whimpey had given up all hope of seeing the brig again.   In fact, he stated that he had no desire to leave the island, as he was a particular favorite with the king and chiefs and was a chief himself.   He informed Cary that there were two other white men who lived with him; one of whom had come in the Manilla brig, while the other had lived at the Fijis ten or twelve years.   The king of Ambow valued the white men highly, as his people had previously been troubled very much by the mountaineers coming down and committing depredations on their sea-coast villages.   These mountaineers were very much afraid of the white men's muskets, however, and had not troubled the king since the white men had been with him.   Cary visited Whippey on his island quite a number of times, and finally got away from the islands in a ship which chanced to stop there.

There is another account of David Whimpey in the Charles Wilkes,

me to understand that they had a falling out about a child they both claimed.

Their wealth consisted of pigs and chickens: the more wives they had, the more pigs and chickens they could attend to.

From Liverpool Jack's account of himself, he had been fourteen or fifteen years on the Island; and that Spider Jack had been about four years longer.   The Spider, after hoisting the Spanish flag—for he supposed we were Spanish men of war—soon joined us. From an account I afterwards learnt of them, it seems:—

That twenty one years previous to our visit, a whale ship, the "Peruvian"[151] of New London, Connecticut, cruising in those seas for sperm whale, had picked up a large canoe with twenty one living souls on board, in a

---

Narrative of the United States Exploring Expedition during years 1838, 1839, 1840, 1841, 1842, published in five volumes in 1845.   In volume iii, page 48, appears an account of meeting David Whippey in 1840.   He told Capt. Wilkes that he went out there in his brother's ship, but left the ship on account of ill treatment.   He also told him that he had then been on the island eighteen years, and, when first seen by the Wilkes party, was arriving in a canoe with some of his children.   David Whimpey was of great aid to the American officers, acting as interpreter, and they mention him at intervals all through the volume. There is a foot-note saying that after the expedition left the islands he was made an American vice-consul.

[151] The ship "Peruvian" of New London, Conn., 388 tons, appears on the New Bedford whaling lists for the first time as sailing for the Crozette Island fisheries Oct. 15, 1841, Brown Captain, Fitch & Leonard, owners, returning in July, 1843.   It continued in the fishery until 1849 when it was broken up.   Alexander Starbuck, *op. cit.,* 378, 564.
   There was an earlier whale ship of the same name: The "Peruvian" of Nantucket, Mass., a ship of 334 tons, built at Scituate, N. Y. in 1818; sailed from Nantucket for the Pacific Whale Fisheries on Sept. 25 of that year, returning Sept. 15, 1820.   It was under the command of Capt. Edward Clark Jan. 9, 1822, to April 2, 1824; under Capt. Alex. Macy June 8, 1825, to Dec. 14, 1827, and from June 8, 1828, to Oct. 21, 1831, and owned by C. Mitchell & Co.   Its last voyage was under Capt. Edward B. Hussey, Jr., to the Indian Ocean whale grounds Dec. 6, 1852, to Oct. 19, 1856, and the ship was broken up at New Bedford in 1857.   Alexander Starbuck, *op. cit.,* 226, 242, 254, 266, 498-499.

destitute condition.   Out of pure humanity the Captain took them on board and supplied them with necessaries.

In giving an explanation of their condition it seems that they were blown out of sight of land in going from one island to another in the Kingsmill Group, so that they were left to the mercy of the winds and waves.

Not wishing to encumber his decks the Captain landed them on Gregan, after seeing that it was fit for habitation, giving them a sow with pig, a cock and a couple of hens.   They had then a vast number of each kind. We were not long in getting a supply on leaving the Island.

I conversed with both Jacks.   Neither of their stories could I trust.   In making the observation that I thought it strange that the pigs and chickens had increased, while the men and women had not—for they were little more than the original number—they both agreed about having plenty of arms, and of having had a larger community of white men and negroes among them at one time.   That they manufactured a kind of whiskey from the cocoa nut with a tea kettle and a gun barrel.   That they had several fights; and murders had taken place among them.   Then peace would be declared each party would make a show that he had destroyed the only weapon he owned, but on the next occasion of a carouse out would come the weapons.   Both told me no one would trust another.   No doubt the poor Kingsmill Islanders were the greatest sufferers.

Both spoke confidently of a large amount of treasure buried in the Island of Pegan, near Gregan: that they knew the exact spot; and to corroborate this, one of our men who had time to accept Spider Jack's invitation to visit his hut or house reported seeing there half a chestful of silver dollars: and that Jack tried to persuade him to desert the ship.   He declined; from fear of being murdered.   At that time, I had no cause to doubt the man.   What puzzled me was, that there being no trade, how he (Jack) came to have so much money.   We were the only visitors they had had since they were on the Island: so they said.

THE STORY OF THE BURIED TREASURE

At the time of one of the great revolutions in South America, the wealthy, to escape, had chartered a vessel, and put on board, their money and valuables, church plate and pictures &c; in fact she was loaded with wealth.   In an unguarded moment she was taken possession of by a desperate gang; who escaped, and made for the Ladrones; where they buried the treasure, after appropriating enough for their present need.

That, in time, they separated: some died; or all may have died except *three*.   That, in time, these three visited the treasure.   That the Captain or Chief called one of the party aside as if for consultation, but instead of consulting, murdered him: then turning to his surviving companion murdered him also.   That, alone, he returned to Manilla, where, after a while, he, in remorse gave himself up to the authorities, telling the story. That on his representations, the Manilla Government sent to the place, a man-of-war with the man on board to show the spot.

That on arrival at Pegan, the boat was along side of the ship ready for the passenger.   That on going over the side to embark in the boat, to land, he fell between the ship and the boat, never to rise again!   The two Jack's pointed to the side of the mount where the man-of-war sailors had turned up the ground in a fruitless search for the buried treasure.   Our informants told us that we were nearer to the spot than they (the man-of-war's men) had been, for—said they—"we are within a quarter of a mile of the place".

They might as well have told us that we were less than a hundred miles, for we never had a thought of losing a moment for it.   It may be there yet!

This conversation occurred on the Island of Pegan (uninhabited) where we were for wood.   We made the best of our way back to Gregan to get our pigs and fowls.

From there we steered generally West, keeping a little North some-times, so as to sight the Bonin Islands, thinking we might find sperm whale.

From there we went to the Bashee Islands, Spanish Possessions, South of the Island of Formosa.

In the Straits of Formosa we landed on the two principal Islands of the Bashee Group.[152] One of these, viz: Battan, was apparantly under fair cultivation, and possessed a good though small harbor.   Its Capital consisted of very miserable huts, but the "Governor's Palace" and a place of worship—both in a state of ruin —were built of stone.   Here we got some yams, a few onions, and some beef.

Late in the afternoon of the day on which we left the Bashees, we fell in with the first school of whales— sperm whales—and killed a great many.

We experienced very heavy gales in the China Sea, and they were heavier at this time than at any other.

---

[152] The Bashee, Bashi or Batan Islands are a small group in the China Sea, lying north of the Philippines, and discovered by Dampier in 1687.   They came under American control in 1900.   They were frequently visited by American whalers.   First Officer Andrews of the "David Paddock" mentions both visits to the island of Battan, and adds in his log book that "the Governor gave a grand dinner" for them; that "each captain and mate received a present of a ton of black ebony," and that at the Governor's request each of the captains took away a young native boy, about 10 years of age, as a servant.

While cruising about the Bashees we fell in with a
French Ship, the first we had seen since our departure
from the Sandwich slands.   We thence steered for
Hong Kong, where, arrived, we stript, and laid over for
a month, fitting out for a cruise in the *Japan Sea* further North.

From Hong Kong we returned to Battan to get some
vegetables, but, unfortunately, were too early.   On our
first visit there, we gave the natives potatoes for seed:
they had not had any for some years.   We also furnished them with some beans and Indian corn,
though they had plenty of each, but our grain was larger than theirs and they preferred it.

Leaving the Bashees we sailed by the Loo-Choo Islands [153] to the Tonghai Sea, and thence by Quelpert Island,[154] to the Sea of Japan.

QUELPERT ISLAND

Quelpert is a beautiful Island; situated near the
Straits of Corea, about 120 miles from Nagasaki in Kin
Sin, one of the Japanese Group, in the South, about
250 miles from Shanghai; about 300 miles from Nan-
kin; about 400 miles from Pekin; in the direct line of

---

[153] The Ryu-kyu or, variously spelled, Riu-kiu, Liu-kiu, Lu-chu or
Loo-choo Islands are a chain of 37 small islands extending southwesterly
from Kiu-shiu (the most southerly of the larger Japanese Islands)
toward Formosa.   They were then, as now, under Japanese control, but
owing to their remoteness the Japanese Government was not able to
strictly enforce there its decree forbidding intercourse with foreigners.
American and other whaling vessels occasionally touched at the Loo Choo
Islands when distressed for provisions, vegetables or fruit.   Capt.
Beechey (1825) states that relations between the natives and the sailors
had ever been estranged.   Commander Glynn who touched at Napa
Keang in the Islands on his way to Nagasaki in the spring of 1849 says:
"Foreigners there mingle with natives, because there are no means to
prevent it."

[154] This island, now under Japanese control, lies some 60 miles off
the southern extremity of Korea.

communication with the Capital of China and the Pacific; and within about 250 miles from the mouths of the Hoangho and Yang-tzse Rivers, streams draining upwards of fifteen hundred thousand square miles of land teeming with almost every staple of food for man, cultivated, to the utmost, by upwards of three hundred millions of the industrious—most industrious it might be said—the cradle, home, and cemetery of nearly one fourth of our fellowmen on earth: a people of a high civilization; with aptitudes moral, intellectual, and physical requiring but the sympathetic touch of our more utilitarian dynamies of life to win them to a closer comity in the family of nations. On this theme, my ideas may seem wild, but to myself, they are the conclusions of personal observation. What the future, under the Providence of the Great Father of all, may have in store for us in this score, I undertake not to say, but leave to the logic of events to develop. As a traveller bye the way, within the area defined, I note the abounding economic resources on which men and nations live, move, and have their social being. These resources—many of them scarcely touched—such as coal, iron, and other economic skill and machinery for the improvement of the material welfare of our brethren beyond the sea—our Western neighbors of the Asian East.

We sailed about the Island, fishing, for about a week, off and on, in a summer sea, in good view of it.   I would say that it is about twenty five miles in length, and, on average, about half that in breadth.   I have little doubt but that it has good natural harbours: we, however, neither sought nor saw any.

Its position is a commanding one for a naval depot. It is Lat. 33 deg. 30 min. N. Its temperature is moderate: cooler, and healthier much than Hong Kong, and evidently, with abundant vegetation—forest clad throughout, so far as we saw; and with every resource and facility for ship supplies. Fortified, and held by a naval Power it might be made the *Malta* of the great Eastern Asiatic Archipelago, and even of the vaster Northern Pacific—the Greater Atlantic of these latter times. Russia may take it. That rising power has, grasped all it dare of the Kurile Chain,[155] but that, nor even her Vladivostok (ice bound in winter) does not, and cannot secure her anchorage in the Junk thronged seas of China and Japan.[156]

The Trident of the Pacific has yet to be raised. God forbid! that it should be so by other hands than such as may, under Providence be missionary of a Christianity at one with us: a Christianity whose natural fruits will be peace on earth and happiness to man in the widest and highest sense.

During our cruise about this "Isle of Beauty" we saw many whales, and captured some.

At length we left it, and on March 6th entered the Japan Sea.

Here we had fine weather; seas comparatively calm. During our stay in the Japan Sea proper, between the Islands of Japan and the Mainland—which lasted about three months—we had, invariably, calms or very light breezes, scarcely enough to fill our top sails; we, however, experienced a good deal of fogs, especially while in the Channel of Tartary or western part of Sagalhien,

---

155 So named from the Russian word "Kuril," meaning "to smoke," on account of the smoking volcanoes on the Kurile Islands.   Charles Peter Thurnberg, *Travels in Europe, Africa and Asia,* iii, 240.

156 An early appreciation of Russia's need for the later developed outlet through Manchuria to the Yellow Sea at Port Arthur—lost to Japan in the Russian Japanese War 1904-1905.

where we took our last whale. The wind—when we had any—was variable; blowing from different directions, but never with any force while we were in this sea: currents and tides it must have, but I did not remark them sufficiently—nor could—to be able to give a correct account of them. There was no difficulty in the navigation of that sea during the months we were there: Yet, I would say; that at the Equinoxes, it may be dangerous from want of sea-room, if a vessel was not fortunate enough to make a harbour of refuge; and there are few such.

We had no monsoons, though to the south (the Yellow Sea) they have them. The China traders take advantage of these winds to go to Nagusaki in their largest junks, and with the exchange to return to their country. Monsoons are winds that blow six months from the North East (April to October) and six months (October to April) from the South West.

Whaling was so easy in the Japan Sea; the fish were so numerous that we had no occasion to chase them with our ship: we had nothing to do but to lower our boats, harpoon them, and bring them alongside for stripping. In the forepart of the season we took several whales. Towards the latter part of it—the fish having run north—we sailed into the Channel of Tartary, where we captured four whales.

LEAVE SHIP

The ship being now nearly full, I asked the Captain to go back towards Japan, where, on the Island of Timoshee, off its northern coast, I intended to land. On our way, we captured more whales; some of the fish were very small, while others were as large as large North

Western ones.   On the last ground of fishing we sighted from 25 to 30 whaleships. [157]

At length on June 27th, 1848, the ship being then full
and lying off the coast of Japan, about five miles from
the nearest Island, I asked the Captain to let me leave
the ship.   With much reluctance, he consented—according to our bargain.   I then bought from him a small
boat, specially made for himself, rigged for sailing, a
quadrant—for I could take an "Observation" for lat-
titude and longitude—provisions for thirty six days &c.
I also assigned to him, in trust, the balance of my share
in the whaling adventure, say about six hundred dollars.

Against the strong and earnest remonstrances of
the Captain and crew, I stepped into my boat, taking
with me my box of books and stationery, a few clothes,
quadrant, &c, but I had no chart.   My comrades refused to unloose the knot which bound me to them.
One of them (McKay) offered to accompany me.   I
refused him.   A sailor's feelings are ever warm and
true.   The companionship of peril forges a masonic

---

[157] The discovery of the Japanese whaling grounds has been attributed to Captain Joseph Allen of the Nantucket whale ship "Maro" in
1820.

Dr. P. F. Von Siebold (1822-1830) states that 68 square rigged ships
were then counted by the Japanese as passing Hakodate and Matsmae in
one year, most of them engaged in the whale fishery.   By 1829 one
hundred whalers annually   visited   the   Sandwich Islands, the great
rendezvous of the Pacific whale fleet.   Charles S. Stewart, *A Visit
to the South Seas, etc.* (*1833*), 365.   The year 1848 was near the height
of the whaling boom.   *The Seaman's Friend,* of Honolulu, Oahu, S. I.,
under date of December 1, 1848, says: "During the last season for
ships to cruise in the Japanese seas, not scores, but hundreds of vessels
spread their canvas within full view of the coast."   Starbuck (p. 98)
gives the total American whale fleet in 1848 as 678 ships and barks,
37 brigs, and 22 schooners, a total of 737 vessels with an aggregate
capacity of 233,189 tons, and valued at $21,075,000.00.   Of this great
fleet nearly 600 vessels were cruising on the different whaling grounds
in the North and South Pacific.   The foreign whaling fleet at this
time numbered but 230 vessels.   See ante note 144, p. 134, 135; also
Walter S. Tower, *op. cit.,* 52-53, 121.

bond stronger than the tinsel chain of mere worldly interest.   Life for life is the motto of his comrade heart.
"Happy to meet; sorry to part", is ever truth with him.
I sorrowed for their sorrow, expected not to meet them
again!—A sailor, in his manhood, has tears!—Myself,
with averted face, had to cut the rope by which I hung
to all them.   I felt in the cord the strong electric sympathy bursting from the true friendly hearts of my comrades.   With a quivering "God bless you, Mac !" they
bade me a long, and, as they thought, a last adieu!—
It may have been so, for I have seen none of them since,
save one, the Captain.[158]

----

[158] While in San Francisco in 1859 (eleven years after the above
incident) I accidently met my old Captain (Lawrence B. Edwards) of
the "Plymouth." He recognized me first; and was overjoyed to see me;
took me to his elegantly furnished mansion, and introduced me to his
young wife (his first had died), and to his family. He insisted on giving me fifty dollars on our account. I told him I did not need it then
and refused it. He told me he had never had a settlement about that
voyage with the owners on his return home—for he left, as soon as possible, for California, where the gold excitement was then at its height.
He told me there was some kind of litigation going on with regard to
the ship and cargo, etc. The cargo was a rich one; estimated by us at
about five thousand barrels of oil—say worth about $150,000—and even
my share was quite a little sum, say about $750. He said that as soon
as it was settled, he would let me know. I never, however, had a word
about it since, from any quarter. To me it is lost.

I cast no reflection, in this matter, on the good Captain; and none is
called for; for I never applied for the thing and my address was ever unknown to him and the parties with whom such settlement rested.—[Orig-
inal.]

Owners and outfitters were, during these years, in almost constant litigation with captains, shareholders, creditors, etc., over the
partnership returns from these whaling voyages. During this cruise
the "Plymouth" sent home 13,000 lbs. of whale-bone, and returned home
April 30, 1849, with 4,873 bbls, of whale-oil and 16,000 lbs. of whale-
bone. This catch was worth, at prices then prevailing, $71,000.00.
This was among the largest returns of any vessel for that year and one
of the most profitable voyages in the entire history of the American
whaling fleet. See Alexander Starbuck, op. cit., 147, 432-433.

On the 28th of August, 1849, Captain Edwards sailed from Sag
Harbor for San Francisco on the "Sierra Nevada," a schooner built in Sag
Harbor, N. Y., and the first vessel of that name afloat. She is reputed
to have been one of the fastest vessels of her class ever afloat. The
"Sierra Nevada" made the voyage from Shanghai to San Francisco in
thirty-three (33) days, the shortest on record by a sailing vessel. She

We parted!   They "Homeward bound!"   I, for the
mysterious dread Japan!   But my mind was fixed; as
the needle to the pole; and my hot heart, full of its purpose of years, rose in swell in unison with the Pacific
billow.   There I floated!—like a bird on the ocean of
fathomless chance: wild and free as the roving sea gull:
at home on its heaving bosom.

CHAPTER VI

Dropped on Ocean Out of Sight of Land—Situation—
Landmarks—Night in Boat—Nights (Two) on Island—Upset—Afloat—Rescue — Ashore — Treatment.

When I left the ship, it was in a dense fog; with no
land in view.   The Captain, however, gave me the bearing for the nearest Island,[159] which, he said, was about
five miles distant; course Northeast.   After bidding
adieu to my shipmates, the ship went one way, and I
the other; she hoisted the Stars and Stripes, dipping in
several times, which I answered by dipping a little white
flag which I had provided.[160]

---

was later sold to the Government for revenue purposes.   Captain
Edwards settled in California.   From *The Corrector*, Sag Harbor, March
7, 1874.   Our author probably met the Captain in 1859 when he stopped
at San Francisco on his way to the Cariboo gold fields in British
Columbia.

[159] Rishiri Island.

[160] "All hands gathered aft to see the last of the bold adventurer.
He took off his hat and waved it, but in silence.   The same was returned by the ship's company.   Soon the order was given to brace the
main yard, and the gallant ship was going in an opposite direction.
From our ship's mast he was viewed with the naked eye as long as he
could be seen; then the spy-glass was passed from one to another that
they might have a last look at the little vessel.   He was watched from
our masthead until he was gone from our sight forever."   Statement of
a shipmate in the *Seaman's Friend*, Honolulu, S. I., issue of December
1, 1848.

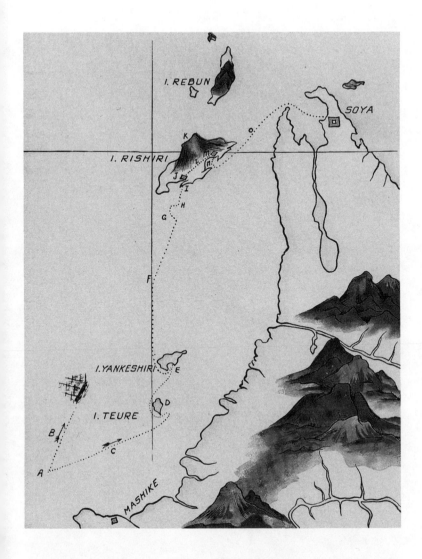

Map of northern Yezo, showing MacDonald's route on leaving ship and landing on the island of Yankeshiri, off Yezo, Japan, June 27-30, 1848, compiled from Mr. MacDonald's original sketch, imposed on a map of Yezo of 1854

Legend.

A leave ship
B ship's course in parting
C my course towards nearest land
E first land seen, where I slept in
    boat and spent two days
F course thence, and my first view
    of Tomashee
G where I overturned my boat

H where I met Ainu boat
I where landed
J village
K snow-capped mountain
L line of march to Tootoomari
M Tootomari
N Junk's anchorage
O course thence to Soya

The nearest land was an uninhabited Island called, in our maps Timoshee, but by the natives of the neighborhood, Dessery or Desserai, [161] in, or near, the Straits of *La Perouse*, off the coast of Yesso. The wind was light.

When I had gone about half the distance, I saw a reef and breakers—then changed my course to East to avoid the breakers, when the southernmost of two Islands loomed up out of the fog. I was afterwards, if I recollect right, told that it was called Tootoomari. [162] I did not land in it, but steered for an Island South of these two. [163] In attempting to get the weather-gage of the Island I fell in with rocks and surf, and in trying to tack, missed stays, and was drifting on a lee shore. I succeeded, however, in getting to the leeward of the Island by wearing round my boat and setting the aft sail all square. Here I fell in with a herd of sea lions, making a great noise. Their call—wo! wo!—was a compound of the bark of a large deep-mouthed dog and the bellow of a bull. I shot one with a pistol. These animals were somewhat like overgrown seals, about twelve feet in length; weighing probably about ten or twelve hundredweight. There I left my spoil, and steered for the bight of the bay of an Island, where I landed.

Ascending a neighboring height for a view, I found the Island to be uninhabited; about five miles in circumference. I was "Lord of all I surveyed," but, after all,

---

161 Reibun Island lies about 10 miles northwest from Rishiri Island.

162 Pontomari, a village on the northern coast of Rishiri Island. In a map of Yezo of 1868, the village is called Kotontomari.

163 To the south of Richiri Island lies Yankeshiri Island, about 6 miles in circumferance. The sea near the island is said to abound in sea lions. "Shiri" in Yanke-shira and Ri-shiri means "island" in Aino, but in use by the Japanese is usually followed by "Jima," the Japanese word for island.

poor indeed. Naught was there to welcome the stranger, My boat on the strand; my ship out of sight, save the tip of her mainmast pointing heavenward out of a distant fog bank; the lonely Isle!; the ceaseless sullen dash of waves on the beach; the looming realm of dread Japan!—all, in the reaction, weighed like lead upon my soul. But the die was cast; and I felt that even then, if at the gangway of a homeward bound, I would not turn from my purpose.

Unable to find a suitable resting place on the Island, I slept in the cuddy of my boat. Next morning (June 28th) I awoke refreshed, and after a breakfast on beef, biscuit and chocolate, I started on an exploration of my new dominion, which, so far as I could see, was contested only by innumerable ducks, geese and other water fowl.

I found the Island covered with small trees and bushes (of names unknown to me), cane brake, and sward, the whole picturesquely dotted with lakelets and ponds, full of ducks, geese and other water birds.

On it I spent a Robinson Crusoe life for two days, (28th and 29th); maturing, during that time, my plan of invasion, which will appear in the sequel.

My object in this delay, was to allow sufficient time to elapse between the departure of the ship and my contact with the Japanese, to obviate the suspicion of my having voluntarily sought their shores. I thought that the vessel might have been seen by the natives; and expected a rigid inquiry as to the how and why of my leaving the ship.

At the distance of about ten miles in a northerly direction, I perceived another Island,[164] with a snow-

---

[164] This must be Rishiri Island with Rishiri Mountain, "the Fuji of Yezo," but the distance from Yankeshiri Island is about 45 miles.

capped mountain, rising as if from the centre of the Island. The snow rested from the crown to a short distance down; it was old snow; I am not prepared to say how long it remained, whether the year round or not; I should say it might disappear in July or August. Roughly guessing I should say the mountain was fifteen hundred to two thousand feet high. [165]

Before going further on my voyage, I landed my cargo,and then, intentionally capsized my boat, to ascertain whether I could right her again. My design in this was to present myself in distress; for, with all their reputed cruelty to foreigners, I assumed, or half believed, that even Japanese would have some compassion on such of their fellowmen as storm or uncontrollable circumstances should cast upon their shores. Misfortune, if not a passport in all cases, is certainly so in some; with it, or its counterfeit, I determined to try the brazen gates of Japan.

After clearing the small bay which had served me for a harbor, and when I was in deep water between the two Islands, I shook out the reefs, and purposely capsized my craft, with sail set. I then cast adrift the back stays, and unstepped the mast, making, the sheet fast to the painter, then taking hold of the centre board, I righted, and then bailed her. When righted, the only things in the boat were two barrels of water, a small keg of provisions, and my bed; my chest, oars and rudder were afloat; my chest and an oar I recovered with some difficulty—the latter for steering as I had to let the rudder go. Satisfied with the result, I returned to, and spent another night (June 30th) on my island.

Next morning (July 1st), early, I started for the

---

[165] Rishiri Mountain is 5637 feet high; viewed from a distance of 45 miles it naturally appeared much lower.

large Island already referred to, and being in high spirits hoisted my little flag. Supposing the Island to be inhabited, I designedly upset my boat about five or six miles to the leeward of it, and lost nearly all my clothing, some books, and all my bedding, pistols and bailer; my chest had been heedlessly left unlocked. After much work, I righted my boat.

During this time a ship, which, years afterwards, I learned was called the "Uncas",[166] approached within about eight miles of me, and according to the account of the incident which I read in an American paper, picked up, or merely saw—I forgot which—my lost "tiny rudder" as the account called it. The trover gave rise to a report in the newspapers by or through the Rev. Mr. Damon,[167] then of the Sandwich Islands, of my adventure, and to the surmise of my having been lost at sea. In time, some way or other, this came to

---

[166] The "Uncas," a ship of 410 tons built at Falmouth, Mass., in 1828 and first owned by Elija Swift of Falmouth, was one of the famous vessels of the American whale fishery. Sailing for the Pacific grounds on November 17, 1828, under Capt. Henry C. Bunker, she returned July 15, 1831, after an absence of two years and eight months with a cargo of 3468 bbls. valued at $88,000.00—one of the largest returns in the history of the fishery. She was sold to New Bedford in 1843 and was owned by A. H. Howland, C. W. Gelett, Captain, at the time here mentioned, having sailed from New Bedford August 27, 1846. She returned May 11, 1849, and was sold for the merchant service in 1862. Alexander Starbuck, op. cit., 268, 146, 436, 550. The incident of the "Uncas" picking up the rudder of MacDonald's boat was reported in The Seaman's Friend, under date Dec. 1, 1848; see appendix II-A, page 273. This was copied by American newspapers of the day.

[167] The Revd. Samuel C. Damon, Seaman's Chaplain, publisher and editor of The Seaman's Friend, a semi-monthly journal (4to) devoted to Temperance, Seaman, Marine and General Intelligence, published at Honolulu, Oahu, S. I., 1843-1878. He is not to be confounded with Joseph Damien—known as Father Damien—born in Belgium on January 3, 1840, and admitted to holy orders at the age of nineteen. In 1873 Father Damien voluntarily sought the leper colony at Kalowao, Molokai, Hawaiian Islands, and for 12 years was a general aid to the unfortunates. Attacked himself by the disease he died on April 14, 1889, after a life of remarkable self-sacrifices. Read Robert Louis Stevenson's fine tribute to him, or C. W. Stoddard's South Sea Idyls and Lepers of Molokai.

the knowledge of my father, then in Canada, who believed it.

Thus to my family and friends I was, for a while—two or three years—as one dead. I refer to this story of me, as further corroboration of this narrative.

To proceed!

Now drifting from ashore, I stepped my mast, set sail, and steered with a scull—the recovered oar.

While standing at the stern I accidentally fell overboard. With difficulty I swam up to the boat, which quickly heaved to, in the wind. Before striking for the boat, however, I captured my chest which (pitched out by the same heave, of wave, which upset me) was afloat—so was my bread (a barrel of biscuit), but, it I had to abandon; my chest being, carelessly again, still unlocked and unfastened, was partially emptied, my compass was gone, but the quadrant, books and writing materials, etc., were to the fore. I then tacked towards the large Island, but stood off all night; not sleeping a wink, from fear of rocks ahead, indicated by breakers.

At dawn next morning (July 2nd) I saw smoke on the Island, and men launch a boat like a rather large skiff, and row it towards me. On their approach, I raised the plug of my boat and nearly half filled it with water. When about a hundred yards from me they hove up and began to salaam me, throwing out their arms, palms up,[168] bowing, stroking their great beards, and uttering a gutteral sound in respectful salutation, as indicated by their look and manner. There were

---

[168] "They saluted us by rubbing the palms of their hands together and then raising the hand slowly several times towards heaven; after which they stroked their beards from chin to breast, and then threw themselves on their knees exactly in Japanese fashion, repeating a compliment in like manner," George H. van Langdorff, *op. cit.*, 328.

four in the boat. When near enough I accosted them
with a "How do you do?" with a salute with the right
arm. They seemed to take it in compliment, in response.

Soon as they reached me, I fastened my boat to theirs,
and jumping on board signified to them that I wished
them to bail my boat, and also to row me ashore. While
one of them set to bail (with my cap, or little sailor
hat, my only bailer now) the rest continued their salutation. They did not seem to be afraid of me; but to
be wonder struck as to who or what I was. Becoming
impatient of their mummery, to make them desist, I
took hold of the pair of sculls which had been used by
the man now bailing my boat (now in tow) and pulled
about a ship's length. They immediately followed my
example, but from sheer inability to keep stroke with
them (though fairly smart at the oar) [169] I gave up.
They also, with one accord, dropped their oars and
looked earnestly in my face, as if asking further orders. I again pointed to the shore, and directed them,
by sign, to row thither.

One of them, inquiringly, pointed to one side of the
Cove, and another to the other. In reply to their respectful question, I pointed to the village [170] which I
had seen them start from. The village (a large wooden
house surrounded by a few miserable huts) was situated at the foot of a very high mountain.

On landing, I was greeted as I had been by the boat-

---

[169] Their oars were peculiar with hardly any blade [Orig.] Hawks,
Narrative of the Expedition of an American Squadron, etc., i, 450, gives
a description of these boats and the Japanese manner of rowing with
these oars, and a lithograph thereof appears opposite the page cited.
Oars ordinarily used by the Ainus, shown in contemporary drawings,
had a *broad* blade.

[170] The village was called Notsuka. It is on Oshitomari Bay at the
Northeastern part of the island.

man—the people—about a hundred men, women and children—being seated cross-legged on the beach. Two of the boatsmen got me a pair of sandals from one of the women, and put them on my feet.

They then took me, gently by the wrists and helped me to ascend the steep rocky bank.

I found that what, at a distance, I had supposed was a farm, with farm house and well cultivated country, was in fact, a barren waste of coarse rank grass and ferns. In proceeding through it my feet came several times in contact with the stumps of brushwood, and not being accustomed to the use of sandals, I very often stumbled. When about halfway to the large house, I spoke sharply to my conductors for hurrying me over the ground. Perceiving from my gestures and countenance that I was dissatisfied with something, they commenced rubbing their hands together as if imploring pardon. To avoid further hurting their feelings, I stooped as if to adjust my sandals, but they would not allow me to do so—doing it themselves and appearing to be glad of an opportunity of performing an act of kindness to me; the rest of the way they adjusted their pace to mine.

On approaching the house—the large one above alluded to—we were met by a Japanese whose exterior denoted consequence. The front part of his head was shaved, and the hair was gathered into a top or queue which projected slightly over the forehead. His dress consisted of a long cotton clerical looking gown, kept round the body by a wide belt. Thinking that he might be a priest I touched my hat to him. He gave some orders to the men. My conductors thereupon took hold of me by the hand, while the rest scampered off. I was followed to the house by the priestly looking personage.

In entering the house—which was of one story, with paper windows—we had to walk about twenty feet on bare ground, we then ascended two steps, each about one foot in height, and found ourselves on a flooring of boards about twenty feet in length; further on was another flooring about a foot higher; to this, the supposed priest conducted me. He then busied himself in spreading out mats, stirring the fire and giving orders. He, by signs, requested me to put off my sandals.[171] I, for the first time, then perceived that he had none on. Placing mine in a particular spot, he gave me to understand that I would always find them there. He then led me to a bedroom, offering me a gown, and advising me to change my clothes—then still wet—then left me.

Seeing several books in the room, I opened some of them and found amongst them an almanac, on the last page of which (beginning of book according to Japanese) was a mariner's compass, with twelve points, but with the needle headed to the *South*.

All the points, except the South, were marked in black; the South being in red characters, which, I subsequently learned, constituted the Japanese word for a horse, one of their signs of the zodiac. The Japanese word for a horse is Ma or Doura, both signifying that animal.

Here I may give—as I afterwards learned them—the Japanese signs of the zodiac: 1, *Ne*, a rat; 2, *Ouss*, an ox; 3, *Torad*, a tiger; 4, *Ov*, a hare; 5, *Tatz*, a dragon; 6, *Mie* (Mn), a serpent; 7, *Ma* (or Doura), a horse; 8,

---

[171] "The Japanese never enter their houses with their shoes on, but leave them in the entry or place them on a bench near the door, and are thus always barefooted in their houses, so as not to dirty their neat mats."   Charles Peter Thunberg, *op. cit.*, iii, 273-274.

Tsitzuse, a sheep; 9, *Sar*, an ape; 10, *Torri*, a hen; 11, *In* (or *Yeagan*), a dog; 12, *I* (ie), a boar.[172]

I give the words according to the sound as I best could catch it from my informant Tangaro,[173] further on referred to.

To resume the narrative!

After a short interval, my host invited me to partake of a repast which he kindly provided. It consisted of boiled rice,[174] some good fish (broiled), ginger, preserved shell fish, and a variety of pickles. Before, and during the meal, mine host several times offered me a bottle of something which he called "grog-yes."

On smelling it—for being then a temperance man (a teetotaller) I did not taste it—I found it very like whiskey. The liquor is a distillation from rice, called by the Japanese saki. The name "grog-yes" puzzled me; but on inquiry afterwards, I learned that it arose from the fact of the crew of the "Lawrence",[175] who had been in

---

172 The Japanese compass is divided into twelve points named according to the twelve signs of the zodiac. Charles Peter Thunberg, *op. cit.*, iii, 122-123.

The signs are 1Ne, 2 Ushi, 3 Tora, 4 U, 5 Tatsu, 6 Mi, 7 Uma, 8 Hitsuji, 9 Saru, 0 Tori, 11 Inu, 12 I. Mn, Doura and Yeagan, mentioned by Mac Donald, are neither Japanese nor Ainu words. Compare with Charles Peter Thunberg, *op. cit.*, iii, 90, 122.

173 Nasal pronunciation. Taguro? Takuro? Takaro?

174 Among Japanese dishes mentioned by Golownin are; stewed rice, pickled radishes, fresh and salt fish, boiled or fried in oil of poppies and seasoned with grated radish and soya; soups with herbs or macaroni, also white fish and mussel broth; barley meal fish patties, etc. Captain Vasilu Mikhaiforich Golownin, *Memories of a Captivity in Japan*, i, 206.

175 The "Lawrence" of Poughkeepsie, New York, under command of Captain Baker, sailed on July 10, 1845, for the Pacific whaling grounds. On May 27, 1846, in latitude 44 degrees 30 min, north, longitude 153 degrees east, in the vicinity of the Japanese coast, the vessel encountered a heavy gale, and late in the evening struck on some rocks. Captain Baker, First Mate Meyers, and part of the crew were lost in taking to the boats. George Howe, Second Mate, and seven of the crew succeeded in getting off safely, but one of the men, Hiram Yates, died before reaching land. George Howe and the remaining six men landed at

that quarter, answering "Grog? Yes! fetch it on." when it was offered to them.

(I may here mention, that when in China, on my way to Japan, I was told that one of the men of this same "Lawrence" was killed by the Japanese for attempting to escape while a captive with them. I never knew the particulars[176] of the case. It did not frighten me.)

After breakfast I took a short walk out of doors— the only freedom I had in Japan; and that under close watch. On my return I found that my kind host had provided me with a bed and a good mosquito bar. There was no bedstead. I saw none in the country. The bed clothes consisted entirely of a large cotton gown, thickly wadded with cotton wool.

Not having slept the night before, I turned in and now did so most comfortably.

In the meantime they brought up my sail, anchor, kegs and chest to the house. At my request, my clothes were washed in fresh water, and dried. All communication so far was by sign language.

Etrofu Island, Japan, on June 2, 1846, and were detained on the island by the Japanese from June 4, 1846 to May 31, 1847, when they went on board a Japanese junk and were taken first to Hokadate, and thence to Nagasaki, where they arrived on August 20, 1847. At Nagasaki one of the men, who tried to escape, was killed by the Japanese. The experiences of these men were similar, in many respects, to those of our author, and the crew of the "Lagoda." The Dutch ship, "Hertogenbosch," took them on board and left Nagasaki in the beginning of December, 1847. The Dutch ship delivered the men to the United States consul at Batavia. A contemporary statement by George Howe in the *Singapore Free Press,* January 6, 1848, is reprinted in U. S. Senate, *Executive Doc't.* 59, 32nd. Congress, 1st Session, 70-73. Their experiences are also noted in Alexander Starbuck, *op. cit.,* 141-142. See also hereon, note 219, pages 196-197.

176 The particulars are given in George Howe's statement U. S. Senate, *Executive Doc't* No. 59, 32nd Congress, 1st. Session, 70-73.

CHAPTER VII

Examination of My Outfit—Inoes Tributary to Japan—Japanese Officers—Worship—Religious Ceremony of Inoes at Meals—Drink Habits—Writing—Map—Inoes Character, Origin, Etc.—Nootska—Tootoomari—Arrival of Junks.

On the following day, two Oyakata (Ketchinza and Kemon, the former an aged man) chiefs or overseers of the Island, visited me. They took a minute inventory of everything brought ashore. Everything seemed to excite their curiosity—especially my books and letters. They looked intensely at every article, first one way then another, and then would talk about it. Last of all, they opened my keg of provisions. Being religiously abstainers from meat, they were horror struck in finding the beef and pork. After a long consultation they examined the pieces with a long fork.

I spent the afternoon in writing Ino words on my slate; an occupation which seemed to amuse the onlookers.

The people I was now among were not Japanese proper, but Inoes [177] pronounced (Eye-nose) who are tributary to the former.

---

[177] Francis L. Hawks [*op. cit.* i, 454-455] describes the Ainu or "Hairy Kuriles" as the indigenous race on the island of Yesso and a wild, dirty people whose chief occupation was fishing. Dr. P. F. von Siebold remarks on the analogy between the Japanese and Koreans and those Kurilians who occupy the islands of Yesso and Tarakai or Karafto.

In Golownin's time the boundry between the Kurile and the Japanese villages on the Island of Yezo lay 150 or 200 versts (between 100 and 134 miles) distant from Chokodade. Capt. V. M. Golownin, *op. cit.*, i, 122.

The Japanese called the other part of the island Ainu-Kfumi or country of the Ainu. Also Einzo-zi or Einso—this in time became the Es-so or Yezo of today. Capt. V. M. Golownin, *op. cit.*, iii, 237-238.

G. H. von Langsdorff, [*op. cit.*, i, 333] says: "The proper name of the island, is Jesso, and the inhabitants are called Ainu. It is very probable that in ancient times Jesso was the name given to the whole

The two Oyakatas, on leaving, gave me a present of preserved ginger.

In the evening I reconnoitered the outbuildings, and amongst them, remarked a small one, which I was told, was a place of worship.

There was nothing in it; and I never saw anyone enter it. The only acts of worship I witnessed here were performed, morning and evening, by the Japanese, at an altar in the dwelling house. The altar was somewhat like a small book case, placed against the wall, and decorated with very hideous images of fantastic shape. The ceremonies were simple:

Before saying prayers, saki was placed on the altar; a bell was then rung to call the attention of the god or gods; the worshippers, kneeling then clapped their hands, and with the fingers up-turned, assumed the attitude and look of devotion. Sometimes, however, I remarked that the hands were clasped and the thumbs crossed. They appeared to be very particular as to the manner of holding their hands in the act of prayer.

---

island; but since the Japanese have driven the Ainu to the north and possessed themselves completely of the southern part of the island, the northern part only has retained its original appellation." "In the language of all the people who belong to the Kurilian tribes, Aino or Ainu signifies *Man,* and is the name they give themselves. According to my investigations as a linguist, the Kurilian tribes seem to be spread from the southernmost point of Kamchatka to Japan, over all of this range of, and the whole coast of what is falsely called Chinese Tartary below the Amur, to the place where the Ussuri-Uka falls into the sea." G. H. von Langsdorff, *op cit.,* 328, note by von Klaproth. "The expression of their countenance was friendly and benevolent; they had tolerably large eyes, rather high cheek bones, a somewhat broad and compressed nose, and among most the cheeks and chin were overgrown with long black beards. They had a language of their own, but understood some Japanese words, and, as far as we could comprehend them, seemed to disavow being Japanese or belonging to Japan." G. H. von Langsdorff, *op. cit.,* i, 328.

Ainu (plural Ainues), used by Von Langsdorff, is now the accepted spelling rather than Ino, Inoes and Ainos, as used by our author.

Only the Matsmai people, [178] so far as I saw, go through this form. I never saw the Inoes worship at any altar; but before commencing their meals (consisting generally of rice, fish and saki) they pour the liquor into a bowl, and, with chop stick, sprinkle it in four directions —first, towards heaven, as an offering to the sun; then to the right, to the god of the Sea; then to the left, to the god of the Earth; and forwards, to the god of Fire. This explanation was given me by the—I believe—ever veracious Tangaro; of whom, more anon.

Inoes—I may observe—are very fond of saki, and their employers are not backward in supplying them with it, so long as there are wages out of which it can be paid. However, I must say that I never saw any of them intoxicated.

On the third day after my arrival, Kechinza, accompanied by a number of men, returned, and told me that he was going to *Soya*, [179] the nearest military station—about twenty miles off—to report me. Before his departure he went to the altar; rang the bell,

---

[178] Matsumai is the name of the principal town on the Island of Jesso; it signifies the "Town of Firs," Von Langsdorff, *op. cit.*, 323, note. Capt. V. M. Golownin stated that it was named from one of the titles of the Japanese prince who originally bought the site and a part of the Southwest coast of the island from the Ainu. Golownin, *op. cit.*, iii, 236-237. Matsumai now appears on the map as "Fukuyama." Yezo (Mac Donald's Jesso) in Japanese now signifies "uncivilized" or "barbarous" from the Ainus or "hairy Kuriles," who originally inhabited the entire island. Yezo is now called Hokkaido on recent maps of Japan.

[179] Soya is on the main Island of Yezo near the northernmost cape of the same name. The distance from the Island of Rishiri is about 30 miles.

"At Soya, the most western point of land, some Japanese are established under a civil officer. They are here by order of the Japanese government to watch the coast; and the officer, with two sabres at his side, came in virtue of his office on board our ship to enquire who we were . . . . he appeared to be a sensible man, and, as far as we could judge, well informed; he showed a great deal of geographical knowledge . . . . . He knew the name and situation of Kamschatka, and talked about Ochotsk and *America*." G. H. von Langsdorff, *op. cit.*, i, 332.

clasped his hands, remained some time in the attitude of prayer, and then bade us farewell.

I remained here, when I first landed, about ten days; under what I may call hospitable restraint, with the privilege of rambling in the immediate vicinity.

There was nought in or about the place of man's work or of nature to delight the eye or please the taste. The two villages, already alluded to, consisted each, of a poor looking one story house, of wood, and poorer huts. The inhabitants—Inoes—were nearly all, by occupation, fishermen. The large house was occupied by the Japanese in charge.

Tangaro, a very intelligent Japanese, one of the staff in charge, in duty, and apparantly *con amore*, was my constant companion. His desire to learn English seemed to be intense. If ever man could be compared to a point of interrogation he certainly could. Pointing to objects, with eye, and mouth and ear open, and intent, he would ask the names in English, which he received with avidity, and seemed, in a way, to deeply impress upon the tablet of his memory. I could not impose upon him: there was too much of that child like credulity and faith in him that averts the shafts of even idle ridicule. I was perhaps equally anxious to learn his language. On the principle of fair reciprocity, I insisted on his giving me Japanese, or whatever was his vernacular, for my English. He did so.

Making—to the surprise of all; for we had company at all times—a pen of a crow quill, I commenced a phonographic vocabulary of his words and common colloquial expressions, Japanese. I continued this afterwards, at intervals, during my imprisonment in the country.

I was soon given to understand that it was contrary to rule and desire for me to do so. Still I managed to keep up my notes, and the habit.

Tangaro wrote with a brush, Japanese fashion, in vertical columns, from top downwards, the columns ranged from right to left.

The characters of his writing I would take for Chinese, mainly, with others (their own) of simpler form. However, I don't know Chinese, but when I see it, recognize it, or think so.

During my stay at this place, after Kechinza had started for Soya, this Tangaro (or Tankaro—it is difficult to express in letters, the precise pronunciation of the consonants, though not so of the vowels, which are all broadly Roman—this colloquial attendant let me call him) one day led me into a field of long coarse standing grass near the sea shore, some distance from the village. Squatting down he invited me to do the same; which I did. He then pulled from its concealment in his dress, a map of Japan, coloured, and apparently well executed, but lacking the lines of latitude and longitude. Before proceeding to the examination of it, or rather of me on it, he cautiously rose a little and peered over the friendly grass. Why he did so, I will explain hereafter when speaking of the secretiveness and system of espionage of the Japanese.

Directing my attention to the map, he asked me to point out where my ship was when I left her or last saw her. He also enquired whether I had been at the Southern ports of Japan. We were now at or rather beyond the extreme North of Japan proper. Yesso— the homeland of the Inoes—being (as before said or intimated) merely tributary to Japan, with a certainly distinctive people in physique and mental and moral characteristics—stronger in body on the whole; heavily bearded and very hairy generally—which the Japanese are not, in general—but morally inferior, in the sense of being a subject race; but in that way only, so far as I know, for I had no opportunity of judging of their domestic life. To me they seemed a simple kindly people;[180] and I shall ever gratefully remember their Samaritan kindness to me.

ORIGIN, ETC. OF INOES

I have been asked as to my idea of the origin and racial features of these Inoes or Ainoes as the word is also spelt in the books. I have never read up, specially, on the subject of human races, but have seen a great many of them in the course of my travels through, I may say, every habitable zone of the globe, in both hemispheres. I am specially familiar with the inhabitants—natives and other—of the west and northwest coasts of North America from San Francisco to Sitka. Amongst these, especially the *Hydras* and *Bella Coola* coast Indians [181] of British Columbia, I remark a striking similarity of physical type with my sturdy friends of Yesso; but in disposition they differ much:

---

180 "They were extremely free and sociable in their behavior." G. H. von Langsdorff, *op. cit.*, i, 32.

181 The Bel-houla (Mayne, 1862), or Bellaghchoolas (Dunn, 1846) are a branch of the great Hydra or Haidah Indian stock or family inhabiting Queen Charlotte's Island and the adjacent coast from Prince of Wales Archipelago south to Bentnick Arm; a territory three hundred miles long by one hundred fifty broad, including many separate tribes or nations. They were great rovers and the vikings of the Northwest Coast. Mackenzie named the Indian village at the mouth of the river "Rascals' Village" on account of the hostile manner in which his party was received. They were exceedingly warlike and made frequent raids on the more peaceful Indians to the south of them. Vessels trading among them had to exercise extreme vigilence to protect both life and property. This resemblance is merely superficial; see note 257, page 227.

Female Ainu

Headman Ainu   Male Ainu

From a picture of 1854 in the "Tour of Yezo by Muragaki, Awajinokami."

The North West Coast Indians being all more or less warlike, and of an independence of spirit which neither force nor kindness can subdue. Not that they are unsusceptible of kindness or amity from the Whites, but they will bend to no man, and are exceedingly lordly, in their own, to all comers.[182]

As to the origin—whence they came—of these Inoes, my idea is that they came from the mainland of Asia, by way of the peninsula of Sagalhien—the Tartar Country.

When I got amongst them first my feeling was that I had got into a nest of pirates of Tartars, with their heavy beards, uncombed long hair, and unwashed faces; they looked uncouth and wild, both in person and dress, comparing very unfavorably in this respect, with the clean, refined, and cultivated Japanese.

To return to the map.

The map, as one of Japan, was fuller and more elaborate than any I had, or, in fact have ever seen. Distances on it were indicated by marks of a day's journey from the great bridge of Jeddo—or "Bas" (Japanese for bridge) of Nipon[183]—the theoretical centre of the country. What "a day's journey" of Japan is, I cannot say, but from the general slowness of Japanese movement, including travel, I would suppose it

---

[182] Alexander Ross, an early Astorian and North West Company fur trader, for nearly fifteen years in the Columbia River district, says: "From Chili to Athabasca, and from Nootka to the Labrador, there is an indescribable coldness about an American savage that checks familiarity. He is a stranger to our fears, our joys or our sorrows; his eyes are seldom moistened by a tear or his features relaxed by a smile; and whether he basks beneath a vertical sun on the burning plains of Amazonia, or freezes in eternal snow on the ice bound shores of the Arctic Ocean; the same piercing black eyes and stern immobility of countenance equally set at naught the skill of the physiognomist."

[183] Nippon-bashi; our author's "Bas" is the short form for bashi-bridge.

to be about ten or twelve of their miles—*ri*—which
are about two and a quarter of our miles—say about
twenty five of our miles, for a day.

In the location of the principal cities, and the general coast line, the map seemed to correspond with
ours of that part of the world.   I remarked, however, that in this Japanese map, what in our maps is
laid down as the Island of Yesso (large) is divided
into two islands [184] by a narrow strait.   The parts rel-
atively North Eastern and South Western.   In the
latter is the City and port of Matsmai, the capital of
these and other neighbouring Ino Islands.   This capital is the residence of a Governor Vice-roy (Tajo) [185]
in Japanese government.

The Inoes, so far as I saw and could learn, have no
Government of their own, but seem to be simply scattered individualities, in families, without any ostensible
communal organization; though there seems to have
been such, from the uniformity of their manner of life,
and subordination to their distinctive customs and religion and to their Chief, so called; but how so constituted, or being, I cannot say.

I may here state that this was the only purely Japanese map I ever saw.

The others which subsequently fell within my notice
appeared to me to be merely copies of European ones.

About the tenth day of my sojourn in this village—
which I now knew to bear the name of Nootska—

---

[184] The reality is that Yezo and Saghalin are divided by the Straits
of Tsugaru.   In some early maps published during Behring's absence
Russian Kamchatka was delineated with so long an extension towards
the south that this peninsula was shown connected with Yezo.

[185] The Daimyo of Matsumae.   "Tajo" is, correctly pronounced,
"Taisho," meaning a general.   In the bulgar language "taisho" is frequently used in the sense of "chief."

while standing at the window of my quarters, two Junks passed Nootska Cove, and sailing round towards Tootoomari, anchored at a considerable distance from the village. (See sketch)

In the evening, the officers of the Junks came over to Nootska. Like true Jacks ashore, they were jolly, and, as shown by a present of sweet meats to myself, were also generous.

CHAPTER VIII

Examination—Departure for Tootoomari—Residence
    Confinement—Interpreters—Stay—Start, in Open
    Boat, for Matsmai—Return to Soya.

On the following morning, my hosts told me to keep within doors; and by way of impressing me with a due sense of my position, they placed mats before my window: a proceeding which rendered my then present and future dark indeed.

Soon afterwards, half a dozen officers from the Junks, with some soldiers visited me. These officials were seated on the highest floor. I was provided with a stool made for the occasion. To their questions as to my name, and the whereabouts of my ship, etc., I answered, as I had done before to Tangaro, to the effect, that the Captain and I did not agree; that I left his ship; and that it had started for its port home.

My stores were again minutely examined, and inventoried, and a sketch made of every article of interest, such as my quadrant boat, kegs, and anchor. They measured everything, even the thickness of the chest. They scrutinized most particularly my woolens, and took the height and dimensions of my person. Being five feet eight inches in height, and very broad

shouldered and large chested—even stout in propor-
tion, and muscular, I was something of a giant amongst
them, their average height being, I would say, about
five feet four inches or even less.[186]

The examination being ended, we proceeded, on foot,
from Nootska to Tootoomari, by an apparently new
way.

My place in the march was between two officers
and two lines of Inoes. The chief of these Inoes was
dressed in a plain faded silk gown. As to myself, I
felt that I was then in an awful state. I wore a cotton gown, which being too short by several inches was
a poor make shift for a dress of ceremony. One carried my pipe, another my tobacco pouch, and others
my mat and brazier with live coal for smoking. They
had no matches, nor flint and steel or anything of the
kind.

The Japanese are great smokers, and pride themselves on the quality and variety of their tobacco. It
is a stock subject of conversation with them.

But to return to our march.

Ever and anon I was respectfully asked if I was
tired. Notwithstanding my response in the negative,
they stopped at about two miles from our starting point;
and spreading mats, squatted and smoked. More, of
course, was thought than said. Conversation by signs
—our only means of conversation then, in our unbliss-
ful ignorance of each other's language—was incon-
venient to the dignity of our smoking: but if looks did
not belie, we were as one in the friendly calumet—
the magic weed giving forth its incense of peace and

---

186 Golownin records that he and his companions were like-wise
carefully measured by the Japanese. Capt. V. M. Golownin, *op. cit.*, i,
255. See appendix II-B, page 275, for Japanese record.

soothing solace on the motley crowd of the prisoner and his keepers.

At about five miles from Nootska we arrived at Toot-oomari.[187] Here we were met by a band of Inoes. On approaching the village they took off my hat. They all went bareheaded except the two officers. Curtains of cotton, striped, of various colours,[188] were put up along each side of the street or way on our line of march. Why these curtains were so used I never could find out.[189] If intended for concealment from my view they certainly did not answer the purpose, for I could see over them.

The colours on the curtains were principally black, red, and blue, according—so I afterwards learnt to the insignia of the different feudal families.

I was led into the principal house, and into a room about twelve feet square, with a grating of wooden bars about four inches in thickness, and the same apart.

The place—an ordinary dwelling—was clean. Being well fed, kindly attended, and amply supplied with all conveniences, with the luxuries of tea and tobacco *ad libitum*, I had no reason to complain of my quarters.

---

187 Pontomari is about 3½ miles from Notsuka.

188 The stripes are usually red and white, black and white, or blue and white, put alternately and the number of stripes five. These curtains are hung in order to conceal from sight ugly things on the wayside. See next note, also Capt. V. M. Golownin, *op. cit.,* i, 47, 125, 179, 275; also Charles Peter Thunberg, *op. cit.,* iii, 122.

189 "The houses, as well by the water-side as all along the place, with the fortresses and guard houses, were covered with hangings, on which were the imperial arms and those of Fisi, so that we could see nothing of the houses or the people, nor could they see anything of us . . . . . The reason of this, the interpreters told us, was, that the common people might be kept off, since they were not worthy to see so Great a Man as the ambassador face to face." G. H. von Langsdorff, *op. cit.,* i, 303-305. This curtaining of the house, etc., was the mark of authority—government—civil or military and an old and universal custom. The common name of the Yedo Government was Bakufu—that is General's Court. The vulgar were not supposed to know—only obey.

A day or two after our arrival at Tootoomari, the
officers left me, with the exception of Meyanzima,[190]
a young man about twenty-two years of age. He and
Tangaro were then my special guardians. I remained
in this prison about thirty days, during which I quit-
ted the room or cage only thrice, and then solely for
a bath in the house.

It was a beautiful day in the forepart of August that
I left Tootoomari: without regret; with high hopes
that in a month or two, I would be released, and be at
liberty.

On leaving the house, I went to my friend *Kemon*
who was kneeling on a mat by the door, where it was
for the occasion. He rose up, and I gave him my
right hand, using the word (which I had picked up)
Sionara ![191] (farewell).

He appeared to be much affected. Our conversation did not last long, for the officers appeared to be
anxious to see me on board the Junk. I was escorted
by two officers and six soldiers. The road leading
down to the water was lined on each side by a great
many Inoes—men, women, and children, who saluted
us as we passed them on our way to the Junk. The
procession was led by two Inoe chiefs; then Kechinza
and Kemon; next a soldier, then myself with two attendants behind me; then followed the rest of the soldiers, the officers bringinig up the rear. It might have
been about ten o'clock in the forenoon when the two
Junks left the little bay.

One of the Junks having a small covering was alloted to the guard and me: the other had our baggage;
it also had my boat, for the Japanese would not suf-

---

190 Shonosuke Miyajima, a foot Samurai.

191 Sayonara.

fer it to touch the water. Our crew consisted of an Oyakata from Soya who acted as Captain, a Chief of the Inoes whose dress consisted of a faded silk frock trimmed with gold, distinguishing him from the rest— and nineteen men. Twelve of these had oars, using them as we do, but with a dip action rather than a pull: six used sculling oars, aft, two men to each. These sculling oars were peculiar, large, broad in the blade—blade and shaft not in line, but the former, at an angle, downwards, in the water, where worked by a lateral alternate movement—true sculling — with great power; on the principle of our ship screw propellor; the blade slightly concave. On the way, the crew, when at work, were constantly singing or uttering some refrain to time their movements: the scullers, with their quicker action, did not sing, but exclaimed, rapidly, something like "I see you, I see you !" or "Yos in yo ! Yes in yo !—those in forward, rowing, sang a great variety of songs—pretty much as we do—one singing a piece, then all joining in chorus. They all had fine, pleasant voices.

About one o'clock, dinner was served. The Inoes collected round their noon meal.

In eating and drinking they observed the same ceremony, on board, as they did on shore.

About two o'clock the officers' dinner was served, and I was invited to share it with them.

It consisted of boiled rice, fish cooked in different ways, and a variety of pickles. Everything was served in beautifully japanned wooden bowls on wooden trays which were also japanned.

At the time of my embarkation at Tootoomari, I was desired by the Officers to occupy the covered part of the Junk. I entered it, crawling on my hands and knees. It was with great difficulty that I could sit straight although sitting cross legged. I told the officers about it; and asked them to give me permission to go out; but they objected to this, so that I had to make myself contented. During the time I was in, I suffered a great deal of pain, so it was with joy that I saw the table laid outside, for then I knew I would have an opportunity to get out, and be able to stretch my legs. However, after dinner, I was told by the officers I could go out and in as I pleased.

On the passage we had very light and variable winds —the sails sometimes set, and sometimes not—but by incessantly applying the oars we entered the Bay of Soya about 6 P. M. On approaching the coast we saw but few boats. When any were seen, the officers would direct my attention towards them and say "American Ship!" but on looking I could easily distinguish them from such and would answer "No! No!" with a shake of the head.

As soon as we were observed entering the Bay, a number of boats, manned by men and women, came off and towed us in. We were received on the landing by a number of soldiers dressed, not in uniform, as I expected, but in mantles,[192] generally of black silk, with their coat -of-arms figured on the back and on each sleeve;[193] they also had on a pair of wide trousers.[194] The officers were armed with two swords,[195] and the privates with one.

---

192 The "haori."

193 The Japanese always have their coat of arms put on their cloaks. Charles Peter Thunberg, *op. cit.,* iii, 277.

194 The "hakama."

195 To the lower orders, a sword was strictly prohibited. The next in rank, tjonen, were permitted to wear one sword. The higher orders— Samurai—wore two swords—on the same side, one above the other—

Officers and Foot-soldiers—Captain, on horseback
From a picture of 1853.

Before we left the Junk, Omibia Shegune [196] came on board, and appeared to be very glad to see me. He inquired after my health, by pointing to the head and making use of the word "sick", which he had learnt when with me in Dessery. After being assured of my good health, he arranged the order of procession.

On marching up to my prison I remarked the order or march: first, went eight men, two abreast; then Simeza, [197] then myself, next followed by two attendants, then a number of soldiers; the rear brought up by the Officers.

The sides of the streets through which we passed were all curtained off. I also saw some, at a short distance, painted in imitation of forts. On the landing, the Inoes were seated on each side of the road, and bending to the passers bye with their accustomed civility. In the Square where the Government House is situated, were a number of Officers with their men holding their flags and lances, to whom each person bent, in passing, so as to touch the feet with the fingers. Not wishing to follow their manner, I only touched my hat. The officers seeing this, sent word to Tangaroo to tell me to take off my cap, which I did.

I was then taken to the door of Government House,, where I saw the Commandant [198] seated on the mats,

these were never, by any chance, laid aside. See Mrs. W. Buck, *op. cit.*, 21; also Charles Peter Thunberg, *op. cit.*, iii, 123.

[196] Oba was one of the superintendents of foot-Samurai, stationed at Soya in 1848 and his name appears among the escort of MacDonald and frequently in the following pages of this book.

[197] Teikichi Shimizu, a soldier who was also stationed at Soya in 1848 and became a member of MacDonald's escort.

[198] Captain Toyoshichi Sato who commanded the Soya military station in 1848. His name appears in the "Memoranda of the foreigners forewarded to Nagasaki and their escort."

with an officer on each side of him. No word, nor salutation passed between us. I was told by Ombia to enter the house; which I did, and was conducted to a newly built prison: it was slightly put together, as if built in a hurry. According to appearances, I thought it was not their intention to keep me there long. It had two apartments; one for the guard, and one for me. Both rooms were carpeted with clean mats. They wished to know whether I was satisfied.

I told Tangaro to tell them that a prison was not good for me: that I would not make compliments to any body with the bars and gratings between us. The officers told me to seat myself on a bench which they kindly provided for me. They then asked me whether I did not suffer from the heat, that if I did, they would make alterations to suit me. I told them I wanted room to walk, the room allotted to me being only about twelve feet long and eight wide, with a wash room &c. They told me that whenever I wished to walk I could also use the other room, so that by having my door open I could have a range of about twenty feet. I also told them that I wanted more air. They —through the interpretation of Tangaro — informed me, that they would, on the morrow, have the windows open during the evening.

A great many officers came into my prison: no doubt from curiosity. After they left me, Tangaro came in with a small box containing sweetmeats, which he offered me in the name of the *Oyakata*:[199] nothing was sent or offered in the name of Saddo,[200] the Commandant.

The next day, an inventory of my goods and chat-

---

[199] The Daimyo of Matsumae.

[200] T. Sato of the previous note.

tels was taken in the presence of *Saddo, (Saddo Sama* as his proper title was)[201] in the guard room; most of his officers were there: they were mostly young men.

He himself was a person of seventy-four years of age (as I was informed), but has the appearance of only fifty.

On his entering the guard room, all the officers— who had ranged themselves round the room and my prison—bowed their faces to the ground.

Bars being between us, I kept my seat on the bench, silent and still. Nothing was said to me. Everything was closely inspected. My Quadrant, some India rubber, and my slate appeared to excite their special curiosity.

At this place, the Officers very often cautioned me against drinking too much water, and, instead, gave my keepers tea for my use. I also got from the soldiers parched rice boiled in water.

By Meanzima and other officers who were one day collected in my prison to hear the wonders of the world, from me, I was told that there were five cannon in Soya, and about a hundred officers and soldiers, but that in case of need they could be reinforced from other stations.

They told me that there was only one doctor in the place; attached to the military force there; that he was at the time visiting in the neighborhood, and would not return for some days.

They also told me that the second in command had left, but that I would see him, for he was expected daily. Shortly after, one afternoon, while looking out of the window, Meanzima touched me lightly on the

---

[201] Sama is a mere honorific address, corresponding with our Mr. (Mon Siuer), or "Esquire" in its common application, or even "Lord" in its lower and purely complimentary sense.—[Original.]

shoulder, which made me turn round, and see a figure before me, whereupon I turned to Meanzima for an explanation. In answer he pronounced the word (in English) "Doctor!"[202] I then guessed he was the person expected. His head was thoroughly shaved. Noticing me, he was in the act of saluting me in his own (Japanese) fashion, but not seeing me go on my knees like him, but standing, giving only a formal bow, he also bowed,[203] but only when on his knees. He brought me some sweet-meats. Asked where I had come from: what was my name, and age. I told him. Before leaving, he wished to know whether I was sick. I answered him, No!—but he would not be satisfied till he felt my pulse. I put out my tongue, but that frightened him. Japanese don't regard the tongue in such case.

He, and several other officers also asked me whether America, England, and France were larger than Yesso. Being answered that they were larger, one of them replied that he could not believe it; but that, in any case

---

202 The doctor was called Yoseki Kakizake. In those times priests and physicians of the higher class shaved the head quite bald, while surgeons retained all their hair gathered into a knot at the top of the head. Capt. V. M. Golownin, *op. cit.*, iii, 122; Charles Peter Thunberg, *op. cit.*, iii, 175-179. Mrs. W. Buck, *op. cit.*, 21.

203 The Japanese are very rigid in requiring the same (equal) attitude, courtesies, salutations. "In their intercourse with each other, the Japanese, of every rank, are extremely polite; their mutual obligingness and polished behavior, attest the real civilization of the people. Capt. V. M. Golownin, *op. cit.*, iii, 35. "With respect to courtesy and submission to their superiors, few can be compared to the Japanese. Their equals they always salute with great politeness both at meeting and parting." Charles Peter Thunberg, *op. cit.*, iii, 254-255. Their behavior, from the meanest peasant up to the greatest prince and lord, is such as the whole Empire might be called a school of civility and good manners." Capt. V. M. Golownin, *op. cit.*, iii, 110, 111. We found the people of distinction here uniformly polite and courteous in their manners, but for their language and costume, we might have supposed ourselves among the most polished Europeans. A. H. von Langsdorff, *op. cit.*, i, 241. Hawks, [*op. cit.*, i, 247, 249] mentions their studied politeness.

Japan was larger—his words being "Tevan toghin tchnsin and datur were",[204] or something like that. Understanding very little Japanese, yet, the conversation was, mainly, through the interpreter.

One day—a week before I left—I noticed the Officers were all dressed in their holiday clothes.

I enquired the cause of it. They informed me it was *Sunday* (*Tsitase or Ositats*). I said I thought they had no Sunday. They told me they had two every month, viz: on the first and fourteenth of every month.[205] They told me also, at the same time, that I was to go away in a few days: that they were going to pray for fair and prosperous winds.

The same afternoon, *Saddo-Sama* attended with officers, paying me a visit. He inquired after my health.

He also formally told me that I would leave, soon as the wind was fair, in a small Junk which he had provided: that he would not detain me any longer, because he was aware that I would like to go away; but he hoped that the large Junk would arrive while we were waiting for a fair wind. Before leaving, he came up to the bars (of my cage) and made me a formal bow, which I returned, with my thanks for their trouble. From these officers, I received every attention; tea, sugar, pipe, tobacco, all such luxuries being supplied by them without my asking. I was allowed to

---

204 These words are so corrupted that little meaning can be made out of them. The Japanese name for Formosa Island is Taiwan, and the probable sense of the remark was that Japan with Formosa and other Islands, whose names are corrupted beyond recognition, was certainly larger than America, England and France.

205 The first and the fifteenth, not the fourteenth, were ceremonial holidays. See Charles Peter Thunberg, *op. cit.*, iii, 88. The first day is called "tsuitachi," but as MacDonald left Soya on the 26th of the 7th month "Ositats" a week before that day, cannot be the first day of the month.

read my books, but they did not allow me to keep my own key.

Their reason was that the common people should not see anything I had, but whenever I wanted any clothes or books out, all I had to do was to mention it, and I got them. On such occasion, Ombia, who kept the key, and four or five others used to be present to see what I took out, and what I returned into the chest.

The following day, Tangaro left me, to return to Dessery or Desserai. There were tears in his eyes while he was saying he was sorry he would never see me again. We shook hands warmly, at parting. ("Sionara.") His place, as interpreter, was taken by the person who had been keeper of Inoes over George Howe[206] and his party. He was so appointed on account of his slight knowledge of English. *Musko,*[207] the boy attendant, often expressed his wish to go to Matsmai and Nagasaki with me. Liking the bright boy, I spoke to Ombia to get permission from Saddo to allow him to go, which he did and succeeded, so far as Matsmai.

The next day, at dawn, I was called up by the boy. There was a fair wind. The baggage was all taken on board. After breakfast the officers came into my prison to bid me farewell. Each shook hands with me on parting. Meanzima stayed with me till the last. He said that he also was going to Matsmai, as well as the rest of the soldiers. I asked him at what time they would leave. He told me in about fifteen days, but that they were going overland, and that it would take them

---

[206] George Howe was the second mate of the whaler "Lawrence," shipwrecked May 27, 1846, see note 175, page 161.

[207] Mus(moos)ko means "son" and sometimes "young boy"; musume means "daughter" or "girl."

thirty days, whereas as I was going by water in the Junk, if we had a fair wind I would reach Matsmai in eight or ten days; if contrary winds, in fifteen or twenty days.

All the soldiers were dressed in uniform, and marched down to the jetty. Along side of it was the Junk—another similar to the one I had come in from Dessery. They made me go on board of her first, then followed *Ombia*, the Doctor, and five other officers besides a number of private soldiers. All of those remaining testified their regret, by one after another coming to me to bid me *"sionara"* (farewell!).

At about one o'clock we arrived at a small fishing village called after my second keeper—I forget his name —who, I believe, was the owner of the fishery, and probably of the Junk we had.

While at dinner on shore a large Junk was observed to pass. It was the long expected Junk. Every one of the party appeared to be pleased, except myself; for by continuing the voyage in the small Junk I would have had an opportunity of seeing towns and other places on the way, it being impossible to sleep in the little open Junk—one of about twelve or fifteen tons, open for rowers, of whom there were twelve or fifteen—with no accomodation for sleeping on board. We would have had to put ashore every night, to sleep; even for meals we had to do so.

After dinner we returned to *Soya*, there to await the sailing of the large Junk, as she had to take a cargo of fish. The following day the Captain of the Junk came to see me. He told me I would be pleased with the cabin and be comfortable; that I would have plenty of room. He had learned how I was discommoded in the other.

CHAPTER IX

Embark on Junk for Matsmai—Description of Junk
Voyage—Stop on Way—Arrival at Matsmai—Re-
ception—Display on Vessel—Harbor—Crowd of
Boats—Crowd of People—English Terms, Etc.—
Informed of Transport to Nagasaki—Asked to Stay
—Refused—Kindly Treated on Board

After a week spent in discharging and reloading the
Junk, I was shipped on board of her with a number of
officers and soldiers. The streets, as before were curtained along my line of march. Some of the curtains,
this time, were pure white, with the coat of arms of the
Prince of Matsmai and Yesso, and some were painted
with port holes in black.[208] I was told again there were
some cannon in Soya; but I saw none.

The Junk, now ready, was covered with white curtains (cotton sheeting) with painted port holes representing the grin of war—the false teeth[209] of a people
who have long and happily chewed the cud of a fancied
and certainly traditional invincibility, who cannot yet
be said—so far as I know—to have felt the touch of
any naval power, ancient or modern.

They have never yet been conquered. Arrived where
they are, in the van of the movement of our scattered
humanity from its traditional cradle in Mesopotamia,
by wanderings beyond records, and with scarce trace,
they have ever remained *there,* in their impregnable
fortress of a well-guarded *Ultima Thule.*

On the quarter deck of the vessel, for banners, along

---

[208] This notion—so common among foreigners—of portholes is a misconception of the crests or heraldic patterns on the curtains.

[209] Our author did not know the facts as indicated in the preceeding
note.

the guards, was a forest of spears, upright, with glittering steel heads, shining shafts, ornamented with gold and silver and mother of pearl, and appended were elaborate sheaths, of finest fur, for the spear heads; and —strangest of all—suspended from the high prow of the vessel, almost to the water, was an enormous swab, apparently of hair or fibre, or fine strips like such, a veritable Neptune's shaving brush.

I am not imaginative—at least not abnormally so— but I must confess that that huge black swab of hair, etc.—large as a tar barrel—did puzzle me not a little. There was no other figure head. Painted port holes for imaginary cannon, and uncovered spear heads were plain enough, and spoke for themselves; but an enormous ugly dangling "what you may call it," swinging and dipping with the motion of the waves, into the limpid sea, was beyond my comprehension. Utility condemned it—called not for it; unless, indeed, it were an offering to Yebis, the Neptune of Japan.

Left to myself, oft and long to meditation free, I often, idly, thought of it, when lying in my cabin, cribbed and thought-weary, in the solitude of my prison on the ever-rocking sea. To ask about it I knew, from experience, would be useless—so, there, I left it, hanging, like Mahomet's coffin, between sea and sky—intangible to my fancy's utmost stretch.

We embarked by crawling through a port hole about three feet in height, opening directly into a main saloon, where I found a number of officers seated, Japanese fashion, on mats. The highest military officer seemed to have supreme command on board.

Tea and refreshments were served, in compliment, to such as were to return to shore.

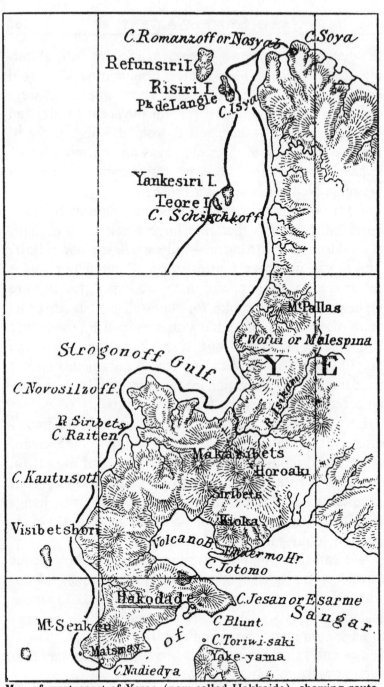

Map of west coast of Yesso (now called Hokkaido), showing route
by which MacDonald reached Matsmae (now
called Fukuyama)
From Perry's map of 1855, compiled from Von Siebold's

Ombia, who on my first landing acted as director, now rejoined us, and was my welcomed guard.

They put me into a small cabin towards the stern of the vessel. Pointing to the lines hanging up, and to an iron rod over a foot in length and an inch and a half in diameter, they gave me to understand that prisoners attempting to escape are knocked with the latter and bound with the former.

Though a prisoner, they gave me the run of the deck. As a Japanese Junk is not a thing of every-day sight to foreigners, I shall try to give a description of this one.

DESCRIPTION OF JUNK

It was of about two hundred tons burden; a size above the ordinary. The bow was high and sharp; poop still higher; the general longitudinal section an ellipse; deck not flush, but with a rise amidship, for cargo; stern, square above water; probably rounded with due water lines, below—I could not see on this point; rudder, large and heavy, with tiller about twenty feet in length; no rudder chains nor wheel for steering.

Generally, there was only one man at the tiller, steering, in the day time by compass, in view, and at night according to the watch, the calls being made from below by the watch at the compass there.

There was only one mast, about forty feet in height; one yard; a square and a lug sail, of course, canvas. Sometimes a temporary mast was rigged.

The sails were reefed from below by securing the points to transverse bars on deck. The crew consisted of about twenty-four sailors. The anchor was a grappling iron with four flukes, not sharp but square. The hawser was in no respect extraordinary. The operations of weighing anchor and hoisting the main sail were per-

formed with a sort of Spanish windlass or capstan between the lower and upper decks, fixed to each, the
beam being perforated with two holes through which
the working poles were put; they had no pauls or
ketches. The haulyards were rove through the upper
deck, and secured on the lower to bitts for the purpose.

With such a rig, in such a vessel, freighted with fish
salted and dried, and with kelp, did I enjoy a lubberly
voyage from one prison to another.

Our general course was from point to point. Some
of the bays were so large and deep that land was out
of sight for ten or twelve hours at a time. Having run
short of provisions and water, we dropped anchor off
a village of about forty houses. They refused to tell
me its name, and also to allow me to land.

The Oyakata (Mayor or Chief) of the place came
on board. He kindly gave me a present of some fruit.

About noon of the fifteenth day of our voyage (September 7th) we entered the port of Matsmai. Its distance from Soya, as we sailed, I estimated at about
three hundred and fifty miles. We were much re-
tarded by calms.

Before entering port I was summoned into my cabin.
In the main cabin—I should have stated—there was an
altar, of wood like cedar, about three feet in length and
four in height, two feet of this being like a box, the
other two feet draped with silk curtains.

It was adorned with pictures of man with heads
shaven, and surrounded with a circle of glory. Devo-
tional services were performed before this altar, at rise
and set of the sun, by the Captain and cabin passengers. They did so by kneeling before the altar, at opening the door of it, clapping hands to summon to prayer,

and calling out *"Namma noa-soe, Namma noos!"* [210]
All then joined in prayer, telling their pea-sized black
beads, in a mumbling tone for about twenty minutes.
The sailors went into a place like an alcove, with chec-
quered board over head, and there prayed, in the same
way. Such was the *Japanese* manner of prayer which,
as at Nootska, came under my observation.

I have described what I saw in this way at Nootska.
On all these occasions the worshippers seemed earnestly devout.

But to return to our voyage! It was in the beginning
of September that we arrived at Matsmai. We passed
a number of small Islands on the Southern part of the
Island of Matsmai.

The vessel on arrival was dressed out with a number
of small flags and the Government flag of Matsmai;
the lances of the officers planted as before described,
at regular distances round the poop. We seemed to excite the surprise of a number of fishing boats.

On entering the Bay—a magnificent one—we lost
the wind and nearly lay becalmed. Previous to this, I
was told by the officers to keep below, and was confined in the officers' apartment; but I could hear the
sail flap and the noise cease. Soon afterwards I heard
the sound of boats, and was told that they came to tow
our Junk into harbor.

During the afternoon I could hear the noise of several boats around us and the voices of many strangers.
Through a chink in the partition I could see a number
of strange sailors who had come to assist, but no officers besides our own. I saw one of our own make his

---

[210] Namu Amida Butsu—Sacred Eternal Buddha—the usual petition
and ejaculatory response. Namy miyo ho henge kyo—another petition
or ascription of the Nichiren sect. See Wm. Elliott Griffis' *The Mikado's
Empire,* chapter XVI.

exit through a port hole into a boat and direct its head
towards the shore. I was told that he had gone to report our arrival to the chief. I saw him return shortly,
and not long after he was followed by a great many
boats full of Japanese officers. Two of them appeared
to have excited a great deal of confusion among our
officers. They appeared to be superior. For their reception, mats were spread on the steps and all around
the cabin.

Then all were silent; not a whisper could be heard,
nothing but the noise of the water occasioned by the
arrival of the boats struck the ear. They first passed
up a couple of camp stools, and then followed, these
two distinguished officers who exchanged compliments
with the military officers of the Junk. Then followed,
some thirty or forty inferior officers and soldiers who
made their compliments in coming in and took their
seats on the mats provided for them.

I now noticed all eyes turned in the direction of my
door, and saw two men rise to go to it, no doubt to remove—as I supposed—the sliding doors, for my presentation. I moved myself from my place of observation, and waited for them to call me out. But I was mistaken. The partition was removed, and I was at once
in their presence. The manner of such exhibition—so
dramatic—annoyed me. I felt, however, I had to do
something; though no one spoke, nor moved, in the
way of formal presentation or direction to me. Rising
with as much dignity as I could command to one knee,
I made my compliments on one knee, with wave of
ˌhand and with dignified respect to the assemblage generally. It was received stoically.

The officer on my left appeared to be the Chief—a
person about five feet six inches in height with remark-

ably large eyes, plump, and with healthy countenance. His first exclamation was *"Nipongin!"* [211]—whatever that was. He was dressed in a pair of wide silk trousers, of large pattern, with garters below the knees, the bottoms inserted in the tops of his white linen mocassins, and a mantle of black silk with the coat of arms or *"Mondogro"* [212] of the Government of Matsmai. After a little while, of silent regard of me, he turned towards and he nodded in the direction of the other officers and said *"Nagasaki"* (pronounced Nangasaki) "go away Tajo!"—(or Tasho—pronounced with a slight sibilation).

From that I inferred that the officer thus addressed was to be the chief of the party that was to take me to Nagasaki. The first officer then spoke to one of the inferior officers, who slid on the mats, on his knees, and took a position along side of me. He, by odd words of English and signs made himself understood to me, and interpreted to his superior what he said to me in English and what I said. He commenced this way:

Pronounced the word "Carpenter"; then made a sign, namely the act of hitting with a hammer with the right hand, and bringing the left thumb and forefinger together, as if holding a nail, said "Ship." By which, I understood that they would repair a ship for my conveyance to Nagasaki—at the other end, almost extreme south of Japan, about a thousand miles away, by sea.

I then asked—"Why take all that trouble? Why not allow me to remain among you?"

Anxious to have the answer of the Chief man to this,

---

[211] "Nipponjin" (nippon jin) means a Japanese. The officer struck by MacDonald's resemblance to the Japanese, used the word with an exclamatory inflection—"A Japanese!"

[212] Mondokoro.

I asked the interpreter to interpret to him what I said. Which he did. The only result was a loud laugh, and answer of "No! No!—Nagaski!—go away!"

The Chief again spoke to the interpreter, who interpreted to me, but very obscurely. The purport, as I gathered was, that I should not sleep on board, but on shore in a house provided by the chief.

They left me with the assurance that they would come for me as soon as they had every thing prepared. The sliding doors were again closed; but after they had left the ship one of the doors was removed for the admission of air. I whiled away the time by smoking my Japanese pipe and tobacco, talking to Musko; pacing my room; and sipping tea giving Musko employment to supply me. It was a close room; and the weather sultry. In regard to creature comforts I certainly had no reason to complain, but on the contrary, they were, all, aboundingly kind and ever kindly to me.

CHAPTER X

Crowd on Disembarkment—Carried in Palanquin— Arrive at a Small Town—Singular, but Kindly Reception—Signs of Former Occupants, Prisoners— McCoy and Others, Crew of Ladoga—Fate—Ermaetz, Sea Port—Departure in Larger Junk— Friendly Farewell—Kind Treatment—Manner of Eating—All Writers and Readers—Paper, Etc.— Writing—Books.

At about half past six in the evening, the officers who had come with me, came to me, all dressed, and told me that the boats were ready to take us ashore. On getting to the gangway, I saw the harbor—a large bay—literally covered with boats—junks and boats covered with flags and lights (paper lanterns).

A sign was made to me by Ombia to enter a boat next the vessel, and to occupy the centre, where a number of clean mats were spread. The six officers followed me, forming a circle around me. It was with great difficulty we could extricate ourselves from the junks and boats. We several times came in contact and got entangled with other boats; but happily no accident occurred.

We all landed safely on shore, where a line of soldiers were drawn up for our reception.

Ombia and another officer conducted me to a sedan chair (or palanquin)—in Japanese, norimon.[213] The whole neighborhood was crowded with human beings to catch a glimpse of me. I really believe that every person had a lantern; it looked so. They gazed at me as if I were a wild beast, I could not stand it. I made good my retreat into the palanquin, which I made to answer a double purpose—for what the Japanese had provided in order that I should not see the country I made use of that I should not be stared at.

After taking the precaution to lash the palanquin with cords, the bearers and soldiers marched forward at a rapid pace; street after street was passed; soon the city of Matsmai was left behind; but onwards the soldiers (bearers, etc.) marched; hills, valley and streams were passed; this I knew from the movement of the conveyance, boxed up though it was without even a peep hole. Occasionally, at different villages, there was a halt, to exchange the bearers of the palanquin, and to take some refreshments.

At such times the officers would gather round me,

---

[213] The "kago."

and try to converse. Eatables were brought to me, but I was not inclined to eat anything. The march then would continue. It was sometime after midnight that they came to a halt in a small town. The palanquin was gently put to the ground. It was unlashed, and an officer opened it, and beckoned me out. He and another then conducted me through a file of soldiers into a large room; but not before I got sight of a dead wall topped with sharpened spikes of iron and bamboo.

We entered a building by a gate in the wall; went through a long passage into a room where we found a personage who was represented to me as the Governor of Matsmai;[214] all alone. My conductors retired. The Governor (so called) took me by the hand in a friendly manner, and led me to the other end of the room. It seemed to be an apartment for dwelling, without anything to give it a prison look. Its floor was covered with mats; it had two fireplaces, one in the centre, and one at the end to which the Governor conducted me, and where a glowing fire, tea kettle, cup, saucer, etc., offered a cheerful welcome. The room was large, with partitions of paper on sliding frames. The Governor requested me, by signs, to be seated; the seat offered was something between a form and a table—a short board bench.

On the wall, I perceived two English letters, J and C—J on one side and C on the other, evidently written with charcoal.

At the sight, a long train of conjectures flashed through my brain.

On looking round for some more, and casting my eyes overhead, I saw a patch of new boarding over a

---

214 This must be Gorogoro Imai, commander of the escort at Erama-chi. He was captain of a company in rank. See appendix II, page 244.

hole about eighteen inches square scuttled in the roof. The houses are of one story and low. My host then took me to a stanchion in the middle of the room, supporting the ridge pole of the roof, and showed me thereon written, apparently with lead pencil, the following names—Robert McCoy, John Brady, and John————. The rest of this name and the other names I could not decipher.

Pointing to the hole above boarded up, "His Excellency" gave me to understand, by ingenious signs, and by uttering the word, "America," that fifteen Americans had made their escape by that hole; had been caught, hand-cuffed, dragged back, and "had their throats cut"—so said the sign language and manual of the narrator, who drew one of his two swords (the larger one) and made the sign of cutting the throat. He also pointed to the iron bludgeon hanging in the guard room; mentioned McCoy; and made the sign of striking.

All this made me reflect. The reported murder, or at least death of the Captain of the "Lawrence" [215] recurred to me, and I believed that my "fifteen" predecessors had shared the same fate.

However, I afterwards learned that this was the same American crew that was delivered up at Nagasaki when I was. The story of them, as I got it on board the "Preble," [216] when with them, and as given in Hildreth's *History of Japan*, 499 to 503, is as follows:

---

[215] See notes 175 and 219. George Howe was the second mate of the "Lawrence" of Poughkeepsie.

[216] The American sloop-of-war "Preble," Commander Glynn. The ship came to Nagasaki in April, 1849, to receive the ship-wrecked Americans detained there. For full account of the voyage see the official report April 12, 1852, U. S. Senate Ex. Doc't 59, 32nd Congress, 1st Session.

They were the crew of the whaler "Lagoda," [217] who had deserted her near the Straits of Sangar[218] near Matsmai, and on landing with their boat were taken in charge by the authorities, and were really kindly treated, while waiting an opportunity of being sent to Nagasaki, where, according to law, all foreigners were to be disposed of. There were fifteen of them, viz., eight Americans of the United States and seven Sandwich Islanders. [219]

[217] The "Lagoda," John Finch, Master, sailed Aug. 5, 1846, for the Pacific Ocean and North West Coast and returned home June 13, 1849. The "Lagoda," a ship of 371.15 tons burden, principally owned by Jonathan Bourne, Jr., of New Bedford, Massachusetts—father of Ex-U. S. Senator Jonathan Bourne of Oregon—was one of the famous vessels of the New England whale fishery. She was what is known as of billet head, square stern, two decks and three masts; 107.5 feet in length, 26.8 feet beam and 18.3 feet deep, and was built by Seth and Samuel Foster at Scituate, Mass., in 1826. Mr. Bourne purchased the ship in Boston, August 3, 1841, and in 1860 changed her rig to that of a bark. Mr. Bourne sold her in 1886 and she was condemned as unseaworthy at Yokohama, Japan, August 7, 1890. A half-size replica of the ship stands in the Jonathan Bourne Whaling Museum at New Bedford, Mass. From October 9, 1841, to July 10, 1886, when she was sold, the vessel, in twelve whaling voyages, made net profits for her owners of $651,958.99. The bark "Lagoda," Stephen Swift, Captain, was one of the five ships "in clear water south of Icy Cape" selected to bring down the 1200 seamen from the thirty-three vessels, wrecked in the Arctic ice in the early days of September, 1871. See note 144, p. 135. The cost to the owners and crew of the "Lagoda," in bringing down these wrecked seamen was approximately $51,000. After 20 years a benevolent Congress in a bill approved by the President on February 21, 1891, awarded $23,611.30 to the vessel. Taken from a *"History of The Jonathan Bourne Whaling Office"* by Benjamin Baker.

[218] The Straits of Tsugaru.

[219] In the *New Bedford Whalingmen's Shipping List* of January 16, 1849, we find the following: "Capt. Malherbe of the French whaling ship, 'Eliza' of Havre, at Hong Kong, spoke on September 5th in the sea of Okhotsk the 'Lagoda,' Finch, New Bedford, who reported that 18 of her men had deserted in three boats and are supposed to have landed on the Japanese coast." The names of the Americans: John Bawl of New York, chief mate; John Waters of Salem, 2nd mate; John Bull of Kempville, N. Y.; Jacob Boyd of Springfield, N. Y.; John Martin of Rochester, N. Y.; Melcher Biffar of New York City, Robert McCoy of Philadelphia and Ezra Goldthwait of Salem, all seamen, and eight Sandwich Islanders, a total of fifteen men, are given in a letter of the British Consul at Canton, China, January 25, 1849; Senate Ex. Doc. 59, 32nd

They were all young, violent, habitually quarreled amongst themselves, and gave much trouble. They preceded me here by about a month. As to the attempt to escape from the very room in question there were only two of them in that, and they were speedily recaptured. There was no "throat cutting," nor even corporal punishment, they were simply caged, and more closely guarded than the others. McCoy was one of the two. In fact, McCoy made a second or even third escape. He was then tied, and put into a sort of stocks. They were taken to Nagasaki.

All this time, and throughout their whole detention —a period of twelve months—they were according to their own account, well and certainly not cruelly treated; as prisoners ever, however. No punishment was inflicted. One American died; a natural death, and notwithstanding all medical care and humane treatment; the only other death among them was that of a Sandwich Islander, who, in the manner of his people, without compunction, hung himself.

To proceed with my narrative.

This monitory exhibition being ended, the Tajo or principal man of the place, with others, entered and went through the ceremony which had taken place on board the Junk. One of them, by making signs, of eat-

---

Congress, 1st Session, p. 3. On account of alleged harsh treatment of the captain, they deserted the "Lagoda" about June 5th, 1848, in three boats at the Straits of Sangar. near Matsmai. Landing on the island of Yesso, in a couple of days they were taken into custody by Japanese soldiers and held prisoners until their release through the efforts of Commander Glenn of the United States ship "Preble." During their imprisonment several attempts to escape were made, and in consequence the prisoners were roughly treated by their jailors. Ezra Goldthwait died on January 24, 1849, and Marrii (or Maury), one of the Sandwich Islanders, becoming despondent, committed suicide. For full account see statements of these men: U. S. Senate Ex. 59, supra. pp. 9-25. See also Alexander Starbuck, *op. cit.*, 142, 434.

ing, and saying *"Coojeen"*[220] (Boiled rice) asked me
whether I wanted to eat something. I said Yes!—nod-
ding at the same time.   They, thereon, brought in a
tray with a shallow bowl of rice, and chop sticks, I did
not use the chop sticks, though I could, having learned
to do so before I got to Soya.   The two principal men
talked together.

The Governor (as I called him) gave an order, and,
immediately, a bamboo spoon[221] and a wooden fork
were brought in. I brought them away, from Japan,
with me, but in subsequent wanderings, left them on
board the "Sea-Witch,"[222] when wrecked on her; on

---

220 Gozen.

221 This rude wooden spoon was cut out and left behind by one of
the crew of the "Lagoda."

222 There were several contemporary vessels named "Sea-Witch" at
least two of which were lost at sea.   The "Sea-Witch" of London was
lost in 1848 or 1849.   The editors have been unable to learn the date or
exact place of this disaster.   The "Sea-Witch" of Melbourne, 273 tons,
formerly the "Samuel M. Fox," built in New York in 1840 and transferred to Melbourne Registry from Sidney, N. S. W., in May, 1858,
foundered off the east end of Timor at Torres Straits in Timor Sea in
August, 1859.   An account of the disaster is found in *The Age* (Melbourne) of Thursday, Nov. 17, 1859—TOTAL LOSS OF THE SCHOON-
ER "SEA-WITCH."   Intelligence has been received in Melbourne of
the total loss of the schooner "Sea-Witch" in Torres Straits.   This vessel, which was the property of Messrs. Young & Martin of this city,
left this port on the 11th day of July (1859) for Timor and Sourabaya
(on the N. E. Coast of Java), with a general cargo and 8,000 sovereigns.
On the 29th day of July she struck on a reef and was, after some difficulty, got off by throwing over some fifty tons of ballast, and after losing both anchors, the Captain then endeavored to obtain fresh ballast
at Booby Island, but could not succeed. The vessel was at this time taking
a considerable quantity of water.   On the night of August 5th, when
off the east end of Timor, the vessel was pumped dry, and the mate,
whose watch it was, gave the alarm that the vessel was sinking.   All
hands were immediately called, and the crew had just time to throw
some provisions into the boat and get clear when the vessel went down."
The names of the crew and passengers (if any) are unascertainable.
Another vessel, the "Sea-Witch" of New London, Conn., a schooner of
109 tons, W. A. Reed, owner; Reed, captain, was added to the whale
fleet in 1856.   After a couple of short voyages the schooner was withdrawn in 1857. See A. Starbuck, *op. cit.*, 544-545.   At this late day it
is impossible to determine to which of the three vessels our author re-
fers, but he was probably aboard the "Sea-Witch" of London.

which occasion, I may observe, I lost all I had save the
clothes I had on and a little bundle, in a handkerchief,
containing, with other little precious things, only a few
of my notes in Japan.

That was in the Indian Ocean, near Madras, where,
for dear life, I had to swim ashore amongst the sharks,
knife in belt for them, with my little bundle on my head.
When in Soya, they made a spoon and fork for me of
brass. I left them there.

My supper consisted of nice fish, pickles and boiled
kelp. There were several (four or five) waiters on me.
Before partaking of it a person tasted of all the dishes.
These tasters—for there were more of them—wore
mantles of a peculiar color, like orange, the distinguish-
ing color, I believe, of the Tajo (Prince) of Matsmai.
I said grace before supper, in their presence, to be
Christian like before heathens.

Whilst I devoured the viands they devoured me with
their eyes, just in simple curiosity, and with a kindly
look of approval, rather than otherwise.

After supper, the Governor gave me a present of
clothing, Japanese, consisting of four garments, like
gowns, with large wide sleeves, viz., one, the widest of
silk; one of light grayish cotton, of native manufacture
evidently; one of some material—I don't know what
to call it—lined with white cotton; and another of blue
cotton, stuffed with cotton wadding; also a pair of Japanese trousers of cotton; two knives, a large and a small
one, and a box of confectionery, with a presentation
card [223] consisting of a piece about the size of half a

---

[223] This card is called "noshi"; even at present all presents have
"noshi" with them.

"Presents are presented with ceremony and covered with a paper
folded in a particular way." *Thunberg*, iii, 72. "On top of the present
was laid a folded paper, tied over with red and gilded paper thread at the

sheet of note paper, folded up in a peculiar form, the
ends tied with bows of paper—paper very thin, fine and
glossy. I was also presented with a bed and covering,
a large gown thickly padded, and a pillow, varnished,
of wood, about eight or ten inches long, bottom three
inches wide, upper part two inches, and on that, a small
pillow about the size of a man's wrist, apparently of
rice husk; it had a drawer also. The Governor kindly
made a sign to me to sleep, and said *"Noo"*—the Japanese, probably, for snooze. It was now about three
o'clock in the morning, and I gladly did so. I slept
well, in perfect confidence in my kind host.

Next day, I asked for my chest, to get at my books.
It was refused at first. I then made a sign of adoration
and said *"Kameni"* [224] their word, as I understood, for
worship, at the same time saying "God!" Thereupon,
they gave me my Bible. I had kept my Bible apart and
told them it was the book of my worship.

At my request, they made a shelf (tokiwari) [225] for
it. They seemed to respect it; in taking it up paying
it their usual compliment to books of a good character
by putting it up to the forehead.

I remained here about twenty days; with every comfort under the circumstances, but always a strict prisoner.

On the eve of my departure I wrote my name on the
wall where my Bible had been. They asked me to erase
it; which I refused, inducing them at the same time to
suppose that there was something sacred in it. They

end of which was pasted a strip of sea-weed. Around it were also several square pieces of the same sea-weed. All this is according to
etiquette; and is a demonstration of the highest respect. *Idem,* iii, 130-
131. See Capt. V. M. Golownin, *op cit.,* iii, 112. See A. H. von Langsdorff, *op. cit.,* i, 259.

224 Kami-ni; Kami, "God" or "Superior" and ni, "to," i. e. to God.

225 tokowaki.

allowed it to remain—at least while I was there. Throughout, in all matters, they treated me with very great kindness and gentle delicate consideration. I asked them for the name of the place, but they declined giving it. I think it was Erametz or Eremetz.[226]

Before leaving, they brought me a portion of my sail wherewith, myself, to make a bag for my clothing: which I did with twine and needle which I had among my things.

I ought to have mentioned that they sealed my chest by putting on seals[227] on the top and sides, connected with strips of paper, so that it could not be opened without discovery; when opened—as it had to be, when I got anything out of it—it was always in the presence of a large number of persons, and was resealed, when closed, before the same.

The official order for my departure was formally received and handed about in the company in my presence. On my asking what it was, they unrolled the scroll containing the order, and showed the representation of a long procession, each man's place being written where he was to take part in the procession accompanying me.

They shook hands with me at parting, and expressed regret.

We all walked down to the beach, about a quarter of a mile. The place was a village of about fifty houses. I saw a large village[228] not very far off.

---

226 Eramachi.

227 Everything was officially sealed lest trading or pilfering of the foreigner's goods might transgress the rules of the Government. The personal effects of the "Lagoda" crew were likewise inventoried carefully according to the statement of Robert McCoy. See also Golownin, *op. cit.*, ii, 207.

228 None of the villages near Eramachi had as many houses and inhabitants. Our author perhaps saw Matsumae, 7½ miles distant.

All—and there were many—who turned out to take part in the demonstration at our departure, were dressed in gay or honour attire: some of the Officers wearing chain armour on the body and legs: soldiers arrayed in different colours, principally red and blue: their coats reaching down a little below the knees; with one sleeve of one color and another of another. Their head coverings were caps apparantly of paper or japanned leather, perfectly flat except a small space in the middle for the queue ("ori") on the top of the head; they were padded, and fastened by a string passing round the chin and ears. It not being etiquette, generally, to wear them on the head, even out of doors at times, they, on this occasion, bore them suspended behind their backs, like shields. The only weapons I there saw in the hands of the soldiers were swords and lances. Each soldier had his own Chief's coat of arms ("*mondogro*") worked on each breast and on the back. Very many of these bearings were representations of the sun and moon, and a good many of diamonds (diamond shape) and flowers.

The flag or *mondogro* of the Prince of Matsmai was a square with diamond quartered.

The soldiers seemed to be ranked in different companies, under their respective feudal chiefs, and under distinctive standards: the companies also varying in numbers.

We embarked in an open boat, somewhat similar to the one I started in from Tootoomari, with this difference, that there were no oars other than that of the steersman. It was towed by several lines of boats, of which there must have been two and three hundred Our barge was full of officers and soldiers. Thus we made for a large Junk about three miles off.

The junk "Tenjinmaru"
From a picture illustrating the "Tour of Yezo by Muragaki, Awajinokami, in 1854."

The Junk[229] was adorned like the one I before described: it was larger however. Arrived at her side, we found her surrounded by upwards of a thousand boats. The curtains with painted port holes, the big swab, the glittering lances, and the flaunting flags of varied colors and designs, the whole floating on the heaving, changing sea was, to my gaze, more a phantasmorgia than an actual scene of human life.

We went on board by the port hole "man-gangway". On the lower deck, I remarked a pile of matchlocks, as long as our muskets, but lighter.

The vessel seemed to have been newly repaired. Having entered the cabin we all—that is to say, officers and myself—squatted ourselves on the mats which covered its floor. I found the position to be awkward. It consists in kneeling, crossing the feet, and sitting on the heels.

I would mention as a trait, not uncommon, of the character of my "barbarian hosts"—not that I consider them so—that on our leaving the place, I received from the Officer in whose charge I had been since my arrival at Matsmai, a present of some small apples, sweet and slightly acid, like our own.

When the parties from the shore had left, I was put into a small cabin, grated: was, in fact, caged. There I remained all the rest of the voyage, with a pile of arms at my door, unable to see anything outside except on two or three occasions.

I remonstrated against such close confinement, and on the following day the Captain ordered the removal of the grating, but I was told not to go on deck.

My cage—as I may call it—opened into the main

---

[229] This vessel was called "Tenjimmaru" and sailed from Eramachi on the first of October.

cabin, where the inferior officers and soldiers messed. At meals they squatted; eating, and supping with chop sticks, from delf dishes, wooden bowls (varnished), and drank out of a cup and saucer. Even for soup, the chop sticks alone were used.

The dishes were generally placed in trays about fifteen inches by twelve. In the centre bowl—generally the largest—was fish, boiled or broiled; in a smaller one, rice; in another of the same size, soup; in another vegetables; and in a smaller one, pickles.

The vegetables used on the voyage were principally pumpkins, squash, cucumbers, and cabbage. Further to the South, I saw, and myself ate onions, carrots, and potatoes like those called Irish, but smaller. Tea was taken by them regularly; sometimes mixed with rice. They used no sugar at their meals, though they have it, as I found by the sweetmeats given me. The average quantity eaten by each man, at a meal, I consider to be about three pounds in weight, soup included. They had four meals a day.

Before eating, they—as all classes of the Japanese do—so far at least as I saw—put the chop sticks to the forehead, as if saying grace. They were talkative at meals, ate fast; and seemed to enjoy themselves, especially at supper, when they had a greater variety of dishes, and about a pint of their grog (saki) each.

They were communicative to me, so far as they dared, and were able. I had picked up a smattering of Japanese, sufficient for some conversation: there was no interpreter between us then.

All said prayers, morning and evening, and some at noon also.

They had books, covered somewhat like ours, with boards of paper.

Some contained wood cuts, fairly well executed. The leaves were thin, doubled, and printed only on one side. Every person had a portfolio covered with cloth, with pockets containing paper for writing, and also for blowing the nose or use generally as we do a pocket handkerchief.

Their finer paper—more like gossamer than anything else I know of—is much thinner and more transparent than any of European manufacture that I ever saw. I speak of the finer kind used for writing, and fine art purposes. There are coarser kinds, for waste and windows, partitions and such ruder uses. It is manufactured, generally, out of the inner bark of the mulberry tree[230]—which is extensively cultivated also for their silk worms: silk with them—as it is generally known—is a staple of production, and its manufacture is one of the principal industries of the country.

All persons in Japan—men, women, and children of all classes from highest to lowest carry—or have at hand borne for them—paper, pen (brush), and ink. All are educated to read and write: and the people, even the lower classes, habitually write—their communications by letter being more general than amongst ourselves.

Their pen is, in fact, a hair pencil or attenuated brush of fine hair, of rabbit, hare, fox or other small fur animal. Their ink is like our India ink or that of the cuttle fish. Their writing is generally made up in rolls—beginning at the right hand or outer end of the roll, (or sheet), in vertical lines, from above to below,

---

[230] It is not from the mulberry, but from the "kodsu" tree the Japanese paper is made. See Dr. Englebreckt Kaempfer's *History of Japan,* Appendix III, thereof on the manufacture of Japanese paper.

arranged from right to left. In the books the "*foot
notes*"—as we call them are at the top of the page;
and the title page—as before stated is at what we would
call the *end* of the book.

CHAPTER XI

Voyage—Doctor—View of Country—Fruit—Arrive
at Nagasaki—Officials, Magistrates, and Interpreters—Examination on Board—Murayama—Questions and Answers—Disembark—Description of Bay
and Harbour—Enter City—Procession, Streets,
Houses, Etc.

On board the Junk, numbers were sea sick. A doctor,[231] with an attendant waited on them every morning, feeling the pulse, and immediately dipping his hand
into a basin of water. I had no need of them, being
neither sea sick, nor sick in any way.

I was, on the whole, well, and even kindly attended.
The military commander[232] visited me twice. I asked
him for leave to go on deck, but he refused.

The voyage from Eramets (or Eramatz) lasted about
ten days: the first three days were very stormy; the vessel pitching and *creaking* a great deal. She was rigged
like the other Junk, the big one, from Soya to Matsmai.

These Japanese Junks though strongly put together
are not taut like our vessels.

We stopped twice or thrice on the voyage. On
these occasions only, while on board, did I get a sight
of the outside world, and that was only through the

---

[231] The Doctor's name was Hosai Tani.

[232] The Commander of the escort was Tanemon Ujiie, Captain of a
company.

port hole of the entrance which, of course, had to be opened, and when in port, had merely a curtain; at sea, it was closed with boards. In my peeps, I saw junks, fields, and cultivated hill sides, and, of course, the cluster of houses about the port. In port we always got fruit, principally a kind like mangoes with large stones.[233] Its taste, to me, was nauseously sweet.

In the voyage from Soya to Matsmai we stopped as before stated, at only one place, for wood and water. We sailed along the West side of the Island of Yesso. We had frequent calms and headwinds on that voyage, which accounts for its comparative length in time to that from Eramatz to Nagasaki.

What of the West coast of Yesso I saw was high and even mountainous; wild; the sides of the hills and mountains covered with a dense forest of pine and other northern woods, with level parts only here and there. Of habitations, I saw only a few small villages, fishing stations, along the shore.

On the East coast of the main Islands of Japan—along which we sailed from Eramatz—the aspect was altogether of a better and more habitable country.

NAGASAKI

At length we anchored in the outer harbour of Nagasaki. A great number of the inhabitants—officials, I presume—came on board; among them *"Sherrei Tachachien*[234] *Sama"*, one of the five men who assisted

---

[233] The fruit seems to be the kaki (persimmon).

[234] Given as Serai Tasnosen (Shivai Tatsunosin) in Commodore Glynn's report and described with Matsmora Schall and Hagewara Matasak (Hagiwara Matasaku) as "a Japanese high military Chief of Nagasaki."

the Governor, ("*Obigue Sama*")[235] in the government
of the District of Nagasaki.

He, and another of note, sat, in Japanese fashion, in
the middle of the cabin, with two pale faced secretaries
by them, with writing materials, books of apparently
English or European binding, and a large book like an
atlas. *Saxtuero*,[236] interpreter, a very old gentleman,
with a benignant expression of countenance, rising a
little asked me, in a very kind tone, what my name
was. I told him and he repeated it to Sherrei.

The latter then asked me through *Murayama*,[237] another interpreter, where I was born.

I answered that I was born in Oregon: lived in Canada: and last sailed from New York.

Murayama—whose full name, I may state, was Murayama Yeanoske—interpreted all this.

---

235 Obugyo-Sama, governor.

236 Sakushichiro Uemura, see page 226.

237 Moriyama Einosuke (Mr. Mountain Grove) was a Japanese Samurai or two-sword retainer of a damio; he is frequently mentioned in the
following pages of our author's narrative. Moriyama Einosuke was
frequently with Robert McCoy and the imprisoned crew of the "Lagoda"
from September 2, 1848, on, and in April, 1859, with seven assistants
acted as chief Japanese interpreter during Commodore Glynn's negotiations for their release when he was officially described as "one who
spoke tolerably good English, but understood only as much as he wanted
to." U. S., Senate, *Executive Doc't* 59, 32nd Congress, 1st Session, pp.
11, 46. He officiated as the principal interpreter during the negotiations
of the Japanese Commissioners with Commodore Perry on his second visit
to Japan. His name first appears on page 396, i, of Frances L. Hawks
Narrative of the Expedition of the American Squadron as "Moryama
Genoske, who spoke a little English, which he is said to have acquired
from an American sailor who had been a captive in Japan, and who was
one of those taken away by the "Preble." It is evident that Moryama
did not feel free to disclose his intimate knowledge regarding the names
and experiences of the various shipwrecked American sailors who had
been held in Japan. See Francis Hawkes, *op. cit.* He was a frequent
visitor to Townsend Harris, the 1st American Envoy to Japan, who
seems to have grown peevish at Moryama's temporizing and evasions.
See Wm. Elliott Griffis, *Life of M. C. Perry* and *Life of Townsend Harris,* the latter pp. 59, 89, 91-2, 95. From the Japanese record it appears
that he saved our author some embarrassment by failing to render literal
translations of his statements regarding his Christian faith. See appendix IIB, p. 280.

Murayama and Tokojiro
Pupils of Ranald MacDonald, Chief Interpreters in negotiations
with Commodore Perry
From Hawks' *Narrative*, i, 348.

MURAYAMA

Of this young man a few special words are called for.

He was, by far, the most intelligent person I met in Japan.

He had a pale cast of thought, piercing black eyes which seemed to search into the very soul, and read its every emotion. He spoke English pretty fluently, and even gramatically. His pronunciation was peculiar, but it was surprisingly in command of combinations of letters and syllables foreign to the Japanese tongue.

He was my daily companion—a lovable one—ever afterwards, during my sojourn in Japan. When with me he always had books in Dutch,[238] and a Dutch and English dictionary. The Dutch factor at Nagasaki John Livessohn,[239] told me that Murayama spoke

---

[238] During the period of exclusion Occidental knowledge of Japan was derived through the Dutch. Three physicians attached to the Dutch factory at Nagasaki contributed principally to this knowledge of Japan: Englebrecht Kaempfer (Japan 1690-1692), author of a *"History of Japan and Siam,"* London, 1727; Charles Peter Thunberg (Japan, 1775-1776), author of *Travels in Europe, Africa and Asia;* and Philip Franz von Siebold (Japan 1822-1830), author of *Nippon, an Archive towards the description of Japan.* In addition to these, three directors of the Nagasaki factory, Isaac Titsingh, J. F. van Overmeer Fisscher and G. F. Meijan, furnished further information. Additional information was received through Russian sources from the published account of Georg Heinrich von Langsdorff, a German physician attached to the Reasanoff expedition (1804), and from Captain Vasili M. Golownin's *Memoirs of His Captivity in Japan, 1811-1813.*

In like manner whatever Japan received of the material civilization of the Occident during these years was obtained principally through the Dutch. After the Shogun Yoshimune (1716-1745) did away with the proscription of European books, so far as they had nothing to do with Christianity, the Japanese doctors, scholars and interpreters secured a number of European books, charts, etc. European books obtained through the Dutch leavened the mind of the Japanese and prepared it for the transformation of today.

[239] Joseph Henry Levyssohn, director of the Dutch factory at Nagasaki, 1846-1850. He later wrote and published a little book on Japan in the Dutch language entitled *"Blader Over Japan."*

Dutch better than himself. The books were on different subjects, but principally on the commerce and customs of European nations.

I asked him whether he, Murayama, had ever been out of the country, to which he replied in the negative. He told me that he had a large library; and also, that he was studying Latin and French.

But to return to my examination before the grandees:

In answer to their questions, I gave them to understand that I was, by birth, a British subject, but that I belonged to the Commercial marine and a citizen of the United States. I was desirous that they should regard me as belonging to both nations (British and American) in order that in the event of a vessel of either of them visiting Japan my case might attract their special attention. I mentioned Oregon. in as much as it was then in dispute (so then I thought) between the United States and Great Britain, and I thought it possible that a war might arise therefrom, and that some of the vessels of either side might approach the Japanese coast.

I was next asked whether I had a father, mother, brother, or sister then living. I told them I had.

They then asked me where my ship was. I told them I left her and went ashore; and that she went out to sea.

They then asked me my object in leaving the vessel in an open boat.

I told them I had some difficulty with the Captain. This I said, apprehending that if I told them that I had done so from curiosity and adventure, that they would treat me badly and perhaps kill me. When I said "difficulty", Murayama—who was then interpreting—seemed to be a little at loss, and handed me the Dutch and English dictionary to show him the word. Turning to the English-Dutch part I did so. They seemed to believe me. They said I must have had a great heart—so it was interpreted to me.

Then they asked me whether I believed in a God in heaven. They seemed to be satisfied with my answer in the simple affirmative.

They then told me that I would be taken to the Town Hall, before the Governor, on the morrow.

On the following day it rained and we did not go. The weather was mild, though then October: no fire in the cabin.

On the day following innumerable boats arrived. Sherrei, with a large company entered by the main gangway at the porthole. When they touched the deck (floor of the cabin) they knelt, salaamed to the Company, and, without rising, slid to a position at the sides on mats. Sherrei *walked* dignifiedly to his position, and as he sat down the rest salaamed to him, and he, in response, slightly bowed and uttered a low grunt in polite acknowledgment.

I was then taken out of the Junk; walked along a bridge of boats; and with two interpreters and four soldiers entered a boat. The people here (more accustomed to strangers) did not appear to be so curious about me as those further north. When we reached the inner harbour, all the boats except three dispersed. We stood off a little from the beach, and there waited about half an hour for somebody. In the meantime, tea was served out to all but me.

On the left of the harbour, looking towards the shore, was a bold steep bank, about a thousand feet in height. On the other side where in a valley, lay the Town, the shore slopes more.

Nagasaki is a Town, or City rather, of, I should say, about ten thousand houses. The houses, though small compared to ours of our cities, seemed, on the whole, to be of a better class than any I had seen elsewhere in the country.

The streets were about fifty to sixty feet in width, and were paved, in the middle, with stone.

In the inner harbour—which is about four miles in length and about a mile and a half in average width, with an Island (Papanberg)[240] at its entrance, was a Dutch ship anchored about two hundred fathoms from the small Island *Dessima*[241] with its Dutch Factory. There were also in port three large Chinese Junks, armed with cannon. Of the Junks of the country there was a large fleet.

While waiting, a large boat load of officers and soldiers approached us from the outer bay and passed on to the beach. We followed, and landed on a jetty with stone steps. Within about fifty yards from these steps we entered the City by one of its gateways. I saw no *gates*. The *gateway*, which was similar to those I saw at Tootoomari and Soya, was about fifteen feet in width and about thirty feet in height, with large cross beam or entablature, of wood, on the top. From it, along the street, soldiers, with side arms, were standing in a row on each side. Close to the gateway was a palaquin, into which I stepped. It being kept open, I had a good view as I was borne along between the files of soldiers. They and the citizens fell in behind and formed a procession. We passed through several streets, which were all of small wooden houses, nearly

---

[240] Takaboko, called Papenberg by the Dutch.

[241] De-shima, Outside or Jutting Island; shima meaning island in the Japanese language.

all of only one story, with peaked and projecting roofs, like ours, windows of oiled paper, on a sliding frame, and roofs, some of wooden covering like American shingles (but larger), some of reddish tiles. The houses were neither painted nor whitewashed.

There were, however, houses larger and of a better class; and I remember seeing two of brick or stone, two stories in height. These had gardens in front, sheltered by a stone wall, surmounted with broken glass or what looked like it. Vines and creeping plants were in great profusion.

There were not temples or pagodas, so far as I saw, although there were, I was told, many in the city; but on the rise of a hill a little out of the city, I saw white objects like monuments to the dead. The shops were merely open windows, with goods exposed. There were no shop signs that I remarked.

CHAPTER XII

Governor's Residence—Court—Reception—Plan of Court—"Devil of Japan"—Refuse to Bow to the Ground (Kotow) Before the Governor—Compliment by the Governor—Description of Things and Procedure—Examination—Answers Satisfactory—Treatment—Cage—Prisoner.

Arrived at the foot of a hill, where the palanquin rested, I stepped out. We ascended by large stone steps to the Governor's residence, three or four hundred yards off. Entered by a gateway. There were thousands of spectators. There was a porter's lodge. The porters at the entrance, in salute, bowed so as to touch the ground with their fingers. In front of the lodge was a stand of arms, with a guard of soldiers, seated. We turned to the right and entered a narrow alley between houses. A sliding low gate was shoved aside, by which I was conducted to a place railed in. Entered, by a small wicket gate, into a sort of a shed; where the flooring—elevated about two feet—was covered with dirty matting.

I was desired, by the Dutch interpreter to sit down. The soldiers retired and were replaced by men in long black dresses, looking grim, with inferior swords and daggers—looked like jailers.

The walls of the shed were plastered, covered with caricature and writing—it was altogether a filthy place.

After remaining there some time I was asked whether I wished to eat. I refused. However, they brought in and spread out some dishes for me. Not from hunger—for I had no appetite under the circumstances—but to show that I was not afraid, I ate. There was rice, pickled onions, fish, etc.

In half an hour after this repast Murayama came in and told me that in half an hour I would appear before the Governor to answer questions that would be put to me. He told me not to be afraid, "to take courage"; that he would interpret for me, and that he would be sworn. He instructed me also, that before seeing the Governor I should see an "image, on a metal plate;[242] at the foredoor"—these were his words—and further, that this image was the Devil of Japan and "that I must put my foot on it". I told him I would

---

[242] This was the efumi-e or image of the Christ-child and the virgin. Since 1669, after the expulsion of the Portuguese and the suppression of Christianity, bronze plates with the image of the Virgin and Child, Christ on the Cross, etc., were used to detect Christians by making them put their feet on the plates. In Nagasaki all the citizens in single file

do so, because I did not believe in images. "Very good ! Very good !" said he, and then retired.

While waiting, I saw several persons enter by the gateway. I had entered but instead of going into the shed where I was, they passed through a small opening with a panel—D in plan—of which, as best I can from memory, I now give a sketch of the whole place, with description references.

PLAN OF PLACE AND COURT OF
EXAMINATION

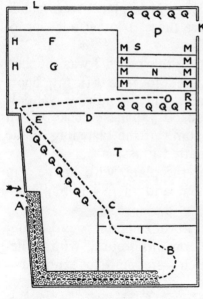

A. Gateway
B. Shed
C. Wicket
D. Small opening in panel
E. Panel slid aside, by which I entered the court
F. Magistrate trying criminal
G. Criminal
H. Goods on shelves
I. Metallic plate, Virgin and Child (bronze)
K. D o o r w a y—Governor's entrance
L. Windows of paper
M. Steps, broad, occupied by men in silks, sitting Japanese fashion
N. Murayama—Interpreter
O. My position, when examined
P. Governor
QQ. Soldiers on guard
RR. Gentry, sitting on heels
S. Secretary
T. Court yard
oooo. Pebbled pavement

had to put their feet on such plates once a year in the first month to show that they were not Christians. These images were made of cast copper and the ceremony was performed on the 4th day after the Japanese New Year (February 22) and following days. Everyone but the governor and his train participated and overseers were present to see that everything was duly performed, even the feet of infants and the infirm being pressed against the metal plates. See hereon Charles Peter

Through this opening at D they passed into a large building with walls painted black. Several were brought out of that opening, handcuffed. The walls of the court yard were also painted black.

About an hour after Murayama had left me, soldiers entered and formed a double line to the small opening E in the plan, to which I was directed to go. On approaching it, a large part of the partition was slid aside. Beyond it, was a pavement of large gravel, perfectly clean and dry, being under a roof.

Before me was a platform, F in plan, on which one of the officers whom I had seen, and one Tashnasheen [243] were, as magistrates, trying a prisoner standing before them. On the left—H in plan—were goods on shelves. Why they were there, I know not—probably they were stolen goods.

When in the act of entering this court, I was touched on the shoulder, and ordered to take off my boots (gaiter boots)—at the same time a pair of sandals being handed to me. I had on Japanese socks which are open at the big toe to admit of the fastening of the sandals. These were of matted grass.

In entering I looked for the plate, with image, "in the foredoor" of Murayama, and there—I in plan—saw it.

It appeared, to me, to be a bronze plate, round, about six inches in diameter, flat on the ground, with something delineated on it which—stooping to examine—

Thunberg, *op. cit.*, iii, pp. 89-93, see Mrs. W. Buck, *op. cit.*, 41. MacDonald did not know at first what it was, nor the purpose in requiring him to step on it. George Howe and party were forced to tread and spit on a similar figure in 1847; and the "Lagoda" crew in 1848. See U. S., Senate, *Executive* Doc't No. 59, 32nd Congress, 1st Session, pp. 20, 72. This custom of figure-treading has been referred to by Mr. Griffis and other writers on Japan; Richard Hildreth, *op. cit.*, i, 352.

[243] Tatsnosen of Commodore Glynn's report, U. S. Senate Ex. Doc't 59, supra, p. 35.

I took to be the virgin and child. Told to put my foot on it, being a Protestant, I unhesitatingly did so.

Looking around, I saw, towards the right hand, in front of me, broad steps serving as platforms—M M in plan—on which a number of Japanese, apparently of the highest class, dressed richly and principally in ample stiff silk gowns, with projecting shoulder pieces were kneeling (or sitting) on each side of the Governor's place—P in plan.

My place, on the floor or ground, paved, was at O in plan, in front of, and at a considerable distance from the Governor. The Secretary of the Governor was close beside him, while Murayama, about midway, but to aside, knelt on one of the platforms. All these were on fine clean mats. For me there was only a shabby dirty old mat. It aroused my ire; but I said nothing, till, when directed by Murayama to sit down on it, I refused, at the same time kicking away, or at, the dirty mat, saying I saw no chair nor seat for me. He then desired me to sit as they did. Being at the time dressed in my European sailor clothing, I answered I could not well do so. Seeing that he persisted in his request, with a friendly expression, I, after a little, made the attempt on one knee; but that did not seem to satisfy them. I was told by Murayama that I *must* sit as they did before I could see the Governor. He appeared to be annoyed at my hesitation. I finally complied; he showing me how.

Pointing to the door, K in plan, he said—"You will see the Governor enter by that door, but you must not look at him but bow low". I then heard a low rustling sound approaching toward us, as if by a given signal every one fell flat on his face. Behind me, close, and all about were soldiers, at arms—letters Q Q in plan.

The Governor[244] entered: Murayama repeated his injunction to bow low. Still angry, *I didn't*. I *"Kitu"*[245] (or *Kotow*) to no man! It required no effort to refrain, I just *would not* do it. Curious to read my fate at the hands of His Excellency, I looked him fearlessly but respectfully, full in the face. So did he me. I had just quickly, before that, looked around, and saw every one, even the soldiers, flat on their faces, the hands being placed on the ground, and the forehead resting on them. They all remained in this position for quite a time, say ten or fifteen seconds during which, in dead silence, the Governor and I stared at each other.

At length, rising from his sitting position, slowly, on his knees, and stretching forth his arms, resting on his hands on his knees, leaning towards me, the Governor addressed me a few words, deep toned and low, which though I did not understand them, I took, from his manner and look, not to be unfriendly. Afterwards —for I could not at the time—I asked Murayama what he said. He answered: "He said you must have a big heart". Had I known it at the time, I certainly would have acknowledged the compliment with a special bow, in true freeman's style, with a wave of the hands—"hats off!".

The ceremony of his entrance was impressive. In entering he was preceded by three or four soldiers, the foremost carrying a naked sword, hilt up, holding it by the point. The sword was like the ordinary Jap-

---

244 Ido, Tsushima-no-kami, who was one of the Governors of Nagasaki when MacDonald was there, was one of the Japanese commissoners who signed the first treaty with the United States. Hawke says [*op. cit.*, 404] "Ido, Prince Tsushima, was probably fifty or thereabout, and was corpulent and tall in person. He has a rather more vivacious expression than the elder Hayashi."

245 "Koto" means making an obeisance.

anese sword, about two feet of blade, with a circular bronze guard; blade about two inches broad, slightly curved.

The Governor was distinguishable by his portly bearing and bold look: Age, apparantly, about thirty-five years: Head shaved like other Japanese, except the top knot as before described. He was dressed in a pair of wide trousers of figured silk, greenish ground with flowery pattern; white lines socks; no sandals; a silk open gown to the ankles, and a belt: a blue overgarment of fine cotton, like two pieces sewed together behind, open in front, stiffened with starch or some such stuff, projected at the shoulders like enormous epaulettes.[246]

Features: — Nose, short, straight; mouth, well formed, indicating good nature; eyes, large, black, open to the utmost, not oblique: round full face, very florid —healthy looking; bearing, upright, majestic; hands, small delicate and white; nails not long.

He had a large plain fan of palm leaf like those in common use among us. In figure he was rather short —"chunky".

He knelt without crossing his feet. He stared very hard at me. I made my salaam to him without, however, touching the ground. After the lapse of a few seconds, when people had raised their heads he talked to Murayama: seemed to be swearing him.

There were writing materials before the Governor, and paper with writing, probably the questions to be put. My answers were written down by the Secretary as interpreted. His Excellency asked me, through Murayama as follows:—

My name ?—Where born ? etc.

---

[246] The usual ceremonial dress, Kami-shimo, for all officials, or on festal occasions.

In fact, the former questions already reported.

Murayama, always interpreted to him—addressing him in a full distinct tone, respectfully—bowing at the end of each sentence, resting on his hands on the ground, leaning over them, his eyes cast down, and at the conclusion of every sentence inhaling audibly through his teeth, as if afraid of offending.[247]

The Governor uttered not a syllable, except in putting the questions. Acted with great dignity.

One of the questions—as on a former occasion—was whether I believed in a God in Heaven. I said Yes!—Then I was asked what was my belief as to a God in Heaven.

I answered, first, that I believed in One God, and that He was constantly and everywhere present.

Then Murayama—as if not satisfied with the answer—asked what I believed in respect to God in Heaven. I answered by beginning to recite the "Apostles' Creed" —in my English prayer book—having been brought up an Episcopalean—my father's creed and my own; but when I had said "And in Jesus Christ, his only Son," born of the Virgin Mary";[248] Murayama suddenly stopped me, saying, quickly, in whisper "that will do! that will do!" He then proceeded to translate my answer, to the Governor, or, at least, so much of it as he thought necessary—refraining—I believe—from any mention of the "Virgin Mary," or "Christ." In that, he was my friend, indeed! After some conversation among

---

247 This inbreathing or drawing in of the breath is an ancient custom of politeness, that one should not offend in any way neither by one's breath nor what might possibly fly out of the mouth of the person. Gradually the custom became a mark of respect.

248 The account concerning MacDonald's views on religion given in the Appendix shows that the interpreters did not fully translate the prisoner's words.

themselves, viz: between the Governor, Murayama, and others, the grandees about, the Governor told me by Murayama, that a house would be prepared for me, and that—as it was expressed—"If I was good, I should live better and better"—so my friend Murayama put it, probably in his own kindly way.

I thereupon, in thanks, salaamed to the Governor, on my knees, and when on my feet, also bowed. His Excellency, however, did not return the compliment.

I was then conducted outside: went down the steps, entered a palanquin, and was carried through the streets to a place surrounded with a stone wall about six feet high, topped with broken glass.

There was a cluster of houses within the wall, and in the spaces between them and the wall were bamboo railings. There was a little garden in front. The house I was put in appeared to be an old building newly repaired: everything appeared neat and clean; flooring covered with mats. Entered by a lobby which communicated with my prison.

This, my prison, was partitioned off with bars about four inches thick and the same distance apart.[249]

EXTENT, SEVEN FEET BY NINE

The wall of the house had been removed and these high bars substituted, and a wooden screen about twenty-five feet high made in front of the bars about twelve

---

[249] The usual prison compartment all over Japan. This "roya" or cage was reasonably light and airy, with provision for cleanliness and warmth; and all prisoners confined therein were reasonably well fed according to the dietary of the country. Overmeer Fisher in his *Bydrage tot Kentis van het Japansche Ryk (Contributions toward the Knowledge of the Japanese Realm,* quarto, 1833) describes another form of prison —the "gokuya" for heinous offenders. These are dungeons within the walls of the government house, lighted and ventilated only by a small, grated window in the roof, and fully on a par with similar chambers of horror familiar in Europe prior to the middle of the nineteenth century.

or fifteen feet off.   Off this, to one side, was another room, for washing, and other conveniences, including bath, hot or cold.   All these were at my service.

There was nothing in the room (den, 9 feet by 7) but mats, a brazier, tea pot, and cup.   The mats—ordinary ones—were six feet by three—with a selvage of gauze-like stuff: mats of rice straw, three inches thick.

The Japanese bed and clothes, and a looking glass which I had got from the Governor of Matsmai were returned to me.   I had the use, also, of a mosquito bar (curtain) which was necessary even then—October— the weather being fine and mild, even warm, with the South West monsoon just set in.

In the evening, a tray with bowls of soup and rice, and a kettle of tea were brought in.   The tray—an ordinary one—was of light wood, varnished—japanned.

I supped alone.

On the following day I got a small table, about a foot and a half high, without having asked for it.   They don't use tables.

I asked Murayama, the first time he visited me after my examination, for my books.   He said I could not get them.   I then asked for my Bible. He answered: "Don't mention name of Bible in Japan, it is a bad book".   I replied I was lonsome.   To which he rejoined—"If you be good, the Governor will give you everything you want".

There was a guard over me, night and day; and my room was always locked.   I was treated coolly: Even Murayama being distant.

There were, at first, nine interpreters—Dutch—besides Murayama and Saxtuere—with me, by turns, one a day.   They were there then, merely to attend to my wants.   There was no conversation between us.   They looked: I looked. When I expressed my wants, they referred to their dictionary,[250]—Dutch-English—and I had the thing.

CHAPTER XIII

Second Examination in Court—Complimented—Third Examination in Our House—Information; Suggestions for Trade, Etc.—Sympathy—More Friendly—School for English, Fourteen Pupils, Interpreters—Language—Intelligence of Pupils—Religions—Morals—Eagerness for Information—Curiosity—Women, Dress, Etc.—Guards, Friendly—Interpreters, Reticence, Etc.—Fate of the Captain of My Guard.

About twenty days after my first trial—for indeed it was that—I was again taken to the Court. This time I was examined before Sherrei and another person.

They questioned me particularly as to the cause, means, and object of my leaving my vessel. I answered as I had before. They had asked me whether I did not, with the quadrant, intend to survey the coast. I said No!

They asked me again what relatives I had: Whether the Captain would be punished: what was the business of my father; what, my own business: and whether on arrival of my vessel in port there would be an enquiry instituted about me.

On all these points I gave them answers which seemed to be satisfactory.

---

[250] The third English edition of Charles Peter Thunberg's *Travels* (London, 1796) contains an English-Japanese vocabulary of approximately 1500 words; this was probably the first English-Japanese vocabulary published. It seems to have been unknown to our author and his scholars.

Again, they observed. "You must have a great heart to leave in a little boat, etc. I could only smile at the compliment, given, I believe, in all the sincerity of their good nature.

About a fortnight after that, I underwent another examination; but this time in my own "house", as the Governor called my cage.

They then produced before me, a Japanese copy of an English Atlas. They asked me to point out the course we had taken; what points we stopped at; and all about the people, products, etc., at these places. I told all I knew.

They seemed to be pleased.

When I pointed out Battan in the China Sea, as the last port at which the vessel I left had touched they observed that it was a "bad place". They conversed a long time about it, using often the word *"padre"*.[251]

They enquired particularly about whaling: the number of vessels engaged in it. I gave them to understand, as delicately as possible in the way of suggestion, that for such business particularly, Japan would be a good place for supplies; and that if Japan were to furnish them there would be no necessity for going to the Sandwich Islands or Hong Kong. I asked them whether in the event of the English, Americans, French, or Russians seeking to open trade with them they would consent. They said No! Murayama, with some emphasis, stating—"No ship can approach the Coast: No ship can enter our harbours: It is against the law". I often, after that, spoke to him on the subject. His answer was invariably the same. He assigned, as the cause of the law, the revolutionary conduct of the Por-

---

[251] "Padre" or more commonly "bateren" the common native term for a Roman Catholic priest.

tugese Christians early in the seventeenth century, for which they were expelled, and those remaining utterly annihilated in the land.

The matter is one of general history.

At every examination of me the Secretary (Governor's) was present with papers containing my former answers; and on each answer to a question, reference was made to my answer as taken down on a previous occasion.

They appeared to be satisfied.

A few days afterwards I was again questioned in the Town Hall: this time before Mr. Livessohn, the Dutch Factor. His questions were a mere repetition of former ones at my previous examinations. He was seated on a chair, on one of the broad steps, and had a small round table before him.

He told me that the Dutch ship[252] had gone, and that I would have to wait another year before I could be liberated.

I said nothing.

He expressed disapprobation at the conduct of the Captain for allowing me to leave the vessel under such circumstances. I told him that it was my wish.

After this examination they were more friendly. Murayama and Saxtuero almost daily with me. They would not consciously give me any information, but were very inquisitive[253] on several subjects; on which I told them all I knew.

In fact, during nearly all my confinement, and nearly daily, Murayama and others were my pupils. There

---

[252] This was the "Josephine Catherine" which arrived at Batavia in the fall of 1848. U. S. Senate Ex. Doc't 59, 32nd Congress 1st sec., p. 4.

[253] "They were continually asking questions for information upon every subject." Charles Peter Thunberg, op. cit., iii, 256. Hereon see Frances L. Hawks, op. cit., i, 464-465.

were fourteen of them. I give their names, phonetically, as pronounced to me by themselves:—

Names of pupils—interpreters[254] (*Tsoose-Gada*)[255] —Nagasaki 1848-1849 of Ranald MacDonald.

1. Nish Youtchero, (Nishi Yoichirō).
2. Wirriamra Saxtuero, (Uyemura Sakuschichirō).
3. Murayama Yeanoske, (Moriyama E-inoske).
4. Nish Kataro, (Nishi Keitarō).
5. Akawa Ki Ejuro, (Ogawa Keijurō).
6. Shoya Tanasabero, (Shioya Tanesaburō).
7. Nakiama Shoma, (Nakayama Hyōma).
8. Enomade Dinoske, (Inomata Dennosuke).
9 Sujake Tatsuetsero, (Shizuki Tatsuichirō).
10. Hewashe Yasaro, (Iwase Yashirō).
11. Inderego Horn, (Hori Ichirō).
12. Shegie Taganotske, (Shige Takanoske).
13. Namra Tsenoske, (Namura Tsunenoske).
14. Motoke Sayemon, (Motoki Shosayemon).

Their habit was to read English to me: One at a time. My duty was to correct their pronunciation, and as best as I could in Japanese explain meaning, construction, etc. It was difficult to make them catch some of our sounds especially the consonants, and some of the combinations, particularly were impracticable to them.

---

[254] In Thunberg's time (1770-1779) there were 40 or 50 interpreters attached to the Dutch Factory, who spoke Dutch with more or less accuracy and were extremely fond of European books, among which he noted an ancient dictionary in the Latin, Portuguese and Japanese languages. Charles Peter Thunberg, *op. cit.*, iii, pp. 32-37. The Japanese kept Golownin and his companions constantly busy translating with the view of familiarizing themselves with the Russian language, and Golownin mentions their having charts and maps showing Russia, Europe, England, etc., and many European books in their possession, including some *English* books. See Capt. V. M. Golownin, *op. cit.*, i, 259-262.

[255] Tsuji-kata.

Tatsnoski
Pupil of Ranald MacDonald, Second Interpreter in the negotiations
with Commodore Perry
From Hawks' *Narrative*, i, 485.

For instance: They cannot pronounce, except very imperfectly, the letter *l.*[256] They pronounce it *r.* So that they rendered my name Rana*r*do Macdona*r*do, with a strong burr of the *r.* They also had a habit of adding an *i* (short i) or *o* at the end after a consonant. As to the vowels there was no difficulty: They have all the full *ore rotundo* sound, and are all pronounced, even the final e (oe).

They were all well up in grammar, etc., especially Murayama; that is to say, they learned it readily from me. They were all very quick, and receptive. It was a pleasure to teach them.

The discussions as to signification and different applications of words were, at times, a little laborious, but, on the whole, satisfactory, by aid of the dictionaries, and my own natural aptitude in that way—of which I had no idea till developed by the effort. Without boast, I may say, that I picked up their language easily, many of their words sounding familiar to me—possibly through my maternal ancestry.[257]

However, having no grammar, nor any book of instruction about *their* language; and they all (except one or two of my guards) being studiedly reticent on all subjects pertaining to the country, it was only a smattering that I managed to pick up. Still, in the nature and unavoidable effect of our converse, it was a good deal; and on a variety of subjects; many of public moment.

---

256 The Japanese have no l, and every consonant is followed by a vowel or the liquid u.

257 On the question of the Japanese origin of the North American Indians, correspondence in language, vocabulary, etc., see the appendix to the 1st ed. of Wm. Elliott Griffis *The Mikado's Empire.* A close examination under the miscroscope shows the hair and muscular arrangement of the eyes is different and denotes the North American Indian a distinct race from the Japanese and other Asiatic people.

Amongst my visitors were some priests, some dressed in black, some in dark olive green and some in reddish or Spanish brown. Their garments differed from the ordinary Japanese dress only in the sleeves being wider, and the dress (robe) being longer.

They were perfectly bald—without the ordinary tuft (ori). They appeared to be intelligent. Though fat, they had no signs of high living. They are nearly strict vegetarians; not eating even fish. I believe they do not marry;[258] so I was told.

All I could learn regarding their religion—I speak of the Japanese people proper, and their original native religion was that they worship Deity (Sin[259] as their term is, but which strictly, means Way—*The Way*—to God, creator and father of all) in the abstract, as represented by material nature, chiefly the Sun—a pure Natural Religion; and they believe, that when they die good, they go to Heaven. What that Heaven may be, according to their conceptions, I cannot say. I never heard them speak of hell or purgatory. They have a Devil ("Onie"),[260] whom they fear; and when they imagine he comes across their course, they kneel, rubbing, at the same time, the palms of their hands together in sign of supplication to be spared from misfortune or evil. They are superstitious in signs; while having much faith in prayer for material blessings and purity of heart.

As to what is good (moral), and what the contrary, I know of no standard among them, acknowledged as such; no dogma, in our sense, no code, like that of Con-

---

[258] Priests do not marry except in the Shinshiu Sect. See hereon Wm. Elliot Griffis *The Religions of Japan.*

[259] Shin or Sin, as Shintoism; i. e. "Shin" or Kami, Superior or "God," and "to," the way or path. See hereon Wm. Elliott Griffis *Religions of Japan.*
[260] Oni.

fucius, or system of "Golden Rules" as amongst the
Chinese; but, so far as my observation and experience
went, it is as high, as pure, as humane, as loving of all
Nature, guileless and innocent as any out of Eden; more
Christian, in its beatitudes, in many aspects, than
Christianity itself (so called) in the world since its
primal purity.[261]

Where they got such religion; and how they so kept
it since they left the cradle of our (and their) race, it is
not for me to say; nor, so far as I know from my little
discursive reading, had anyone—historian, or chron-
icler, or savant—assumed to say, with any authority.
Themselves don't say; don't pretend to know.

The expression, given in a preceding page, of Murayama as to our Bible shows that they do not acknowledge a record of revelation from Deity. But on the
other hand, the approval, by the Governor and Court of
my emphatic belief in God, Omniscient, Omnipresent,
Omnipotent, Maker of all things, etc., shows clearly
their pure Theism—Monotheism—the Highest avowed
by man. Its avowal by me was my Shibboleth, in my
straits. It saved me!

We—of the so-called Christian Church, may regard
such Theism as an imperfect religion, and, in effect,
essentially heathenism, like that—said—of the Chinese, *Quaere!* Are we right? By what rule—law—
should we so condemn our brother? As God made
him; and has ever in his wanderings through the desert
of life, from generation to generation been his Preserver
and "Way of life," so he is today! Is it for us to condemn our fellowman?

---

[261] The Japanese told us that these principles (Christian) were not

I am no controversialist in religion. What I have in this way, I cherish, and try in my own weak humble way to live up to, in faith in Christ—as a Christian in profession and heart—and I thus speak because this have I learned my duty to Man as to God.

My place of residence, though really a prison—for I had no liberty beyond the bars of my cage—was the resort of quite a variety of people. Men of all sorts—students, officers, priests and people in general of the respectable classes, except women, came to stare at me, as a natural curiosity. The only exception as to women, was in the case of one of my guards, the Captain of them. He asked me for my consent to bring his wife and daughter and three of their females to see me.

Of course, I gave it, for I was anxious also to see how their women looked. They came; entering the guard room, and squatting there like men. I invited them, if they wished to see me, to enter my apartment—the "Lion's den." They all did so; giggling.

I cannot say that they were beautiful; nor, on the other hand, that they were ugly. Their general expression of countenance was that of smiling good nature and artlessness calculated to make a favorable impression.

Their dress, especially the head gear, was strange to me. After they left me, I made an attempt to sketch it, but found I was not equal to the artistic effort. In lieu, I attempt a description.

They were dressed alike, or nearly so. Wore a gown similar to that of the men, but longer, of cotton, striped, with wide sleeves, wider than those of the men; dress bound round the waist, loosely, by a very broad belt, of stuff like raw coarse silk. As to their under and foot dressing I cannot say. They shuffled in and out, and squatted in such a manner that they looked more like moving bundles of loose clothes than any thing else.

I had, however, a good view of their heads. Their complexion was a light brown; eyes black and slightly oblique; nose short, and almost straight, nor prominent but well developed. Face more round than oval, with well-proportioned mouth, cheek bones protrusive but not prominently; broad and intellectual forehead, fully exposed. Their hair black—intensely black—long, rolled up and tied on the top of the head, fastened with bodkins or hair pins (or arrows) about fifteen inches in length, apparently of wood inlaid with silver. The married woman (the Captain's wife) had blackened teeth;[262] the unmarried women, apparently young, had very red lips, and teeth slightly tinged with red; lips flattish, not large; the girl had white teeth and natural color in all her features.

So far as I could judge of their figures, they were short and not unshapely; bearing themselves with a graceful modest dignity. To judge of their general disposition, I should say it was a prevailing amiability.

Being nothing of a "lady's man"—poor at small talk —I had no conversation with them—merely, in "Lion roar," addressing them, on their entry and departure, with a few words—Japanese—in compliment. There

---

[262] "Among the women, the married were easily to be distinguished from the unmarried by the black front teeth, which from their delight and laughing so frequently, were often shown." von Langdorff, 248. See also Francis L. Hawks, *op. cit.*, i, 395, and Richard Hildreth, *op. cit.*, ii, 121-122.

Japanese ladies wore no jewelry or trinkets or ornaments other than their hair-combs and long hair-pins. They, however, painted their faces red and white, and the unmarried ones also painted their lips red and violet with a golden glow. Married women in addition to painting their teeth black, as noted above, sometimes extirpated the eyebrows. See Charles Peter Thunberg, *op. cit.*, iii, 77-78; Capt. V. M. Golownin, *op. cit.*, iii, 101-102; Mrs. W. Buck, *op. cit.*, 22.

was no tell-tale interpreter bye at the time—at least none that I saw—yet, the result proved that some "Peeping Tom," must have seen and told.

As to this incident I would state. That missing the Captain shortly afterwards—for we were close friends —I inquired about him, and was informed that his head had been chopped off—that was how they expressed it —for breaking the law, forbidding what he had done in bringing women to my prison. If so—which I could scarcely believe—the law seemed to me to be a very harsh one. I was sincerely sorry to lose, thus, the kind-hearted companion of many of my lonely hours. I used to talk to him as I could not to any one else; and he responded with marked intelligence and sympathy.

During the seven months and more of my close confinement in my cage in Nagasaki, I drew more comfort and sustaining companionship from my pupils the Official Interpreters. I picked up more of the colloquial language of the country, or of the place from them than from scholars.

In the higher matter of intellectual study and discussion I could draw only from the latter; but as before observed, they were ever studiedly on their guard against saying too much in exposition of their affairs and general public or even private life. Of this, more anon, perhaps, before I close. To proceed with my narrative.

CHAPTER XIV

Kindness, Effusive—Place of Honor for My Bible—
Food—Sundays, Specialties—Foreigners in the City
—Acquire Language—Change of Governor—Sys-
tem of Government—Harra-Karri—Sense of Honor
—Sacrifices to It—Personal Reflections on Ethics of
Such Course, and Japanese Life—Empire: How
Ruled—Character of People—Feudal System—
Laws—Aspirations—Kindness—Arrival of "Pre-
ble"—Military Display—Arms, Etc.—Liberation—
Departure in "Preble"

The above was the last examination I underwent in
Japan. After that, I was more kindly treated. I literally had—as the Governor had promised—everything
I wanted—except liberty outside. They even gave me
up my Bible; and seeing—as they expressed it—that "I
made a God of it," they made a neat shelf ("tokiwari")
at a corner of my room, to put it on, as a place of honor.

And further, they even at my request, did violence to
their religious prejudice against meat as food, so far as
to give me pork every seventh day. I was, by nature
and habit a meat eater. There was no beef, though they
had bullocks for work; no mutton; but I knew that, for
the Dutch, they raised pigs, and had pork. At the same
time I wanted to keep the run of our weeks—which are
different from theirs—and called pork day my Sunday.
According to my count of time I made it so.

The only thing I complained of was the smallness of
my cage, but in this I got no satisfaction; not even a reason for the refusal. It was, according to their ideas of
a "House to live in," good enough for a single man, who
had to be watched as an intruder; and, as I afterwards

learned, I was better off in this respect than other foreign prisoners then, in the same city, in confinement.

This fact of other foreign prisoners being in the city
was, I may explain, not voluntarily told me by any one,
but in course of conversation with my guards and visitors, I caught at certain sailor terms used by them
which I suspected they must have picked up from British or American sailors[263] about the place.   They used

---

263 From the days of Will Adams (1600-1620); Richard Cocks, the
English factor (1614-1623) and James Turner down to the time of our
author's visit there was more or less opportunity for the Japanese to
pick up some knowledge of England and America and of the English
language; especially after the withdrawal of the ban against foreign
books in 1720, which permitted a limited introduction of books of general knowledge through the Dutch.   For 60 years prior to MacDonald's
visit British and American sailors had been somewhat familiar with
Japan and the inhabitants along its coasts.   In addition to the official
attempts by vessels of Great Britain and the United States to open intercourse with Japan (mentioned in note 140, ante, p. 130,) it may be
stated that in 1796 Captain Broughton landed and buried Olason, one
of his sailors, on an island at Enderino Bay.

The war with England having deprived the Dutch from trading directly with Japan, they freighted ships in the United States with cargoes
for Japan, and these ships entered Nagasaki under the Dutch flag. The
first of these was the "Eliza" of New York, Stewart, captain, which
took the place of the regular Dutch ship in 1797 and again in 1798.   In
1803 Captain Stewart again appeared in the Bay of Nagasaki on a private venture under the American flag with a cargo from Bengal and
Canton, but he was compelled to depart without trading.   Mrs. W. Buck,
op. cit., 268; Capt. V. M. Golownin, op. cit., i, 289.

Other American ships visited the Dutch factory at Nagasaki in the
years 1799, 1800, 1801, 1802, 1803, 1806, 1807 and 1809, when the "Re-
becca" entered.   Archibald Campbell, a Scotchman, a common sailor on
board the ship "Eclipse" of Boston, Captain Joseph O'Kean, in his "Voyage Around the World," page 28, gives an account of the ship which,
chartered at Canton by the Russian American Company, entering the
bay of Nagasaki under the Russian flag in 1807.

Dr. Ainslie reached Nagasaki on one of the two ships dispatched to
the Dutch factory by Raffles in 1813, and the Japanese interpreters then
possessed some knowledge of the English and Russian languages. Mrs.
W. Buck, op. cit., 288, 294, 295.   The interpreters interviewing Capt.
Gordon in June, 1818, already knew a little English.

Dr. Phillip Franz von Siebold speaks of the frequent squabbles, in his
time, between the Japanese and the English and American whalers who
necessarily or unnecessarily violated the Japanese harbors, and adds that
since 1830 interpreters who had some understanding of English and
Russian were stationed at different points all around the exterior coast

—without telling me whence they got them—to ask the meaning of these terms, for by this time, I could speak a sort of "pidgin"—Japanese, or, at least, had the reputation for it.

Many of the terms I could not literally translate, as they were simply sailor objurgations, meaningless and innocent generally—such as "shiver my timbers!" etc. The Japanese don't swear; have no oaths—so far as I know. In such case, I paraphrased the expression, as best I could, for in common politeness, I had to answer them.

In all these communications to or with me each one seemed afraid of another informing on him. I was,

---

of Japan in preparation for the possible approach of any strange ship. Mrs. W. Buck, *op. cit.*, 294, 295.

In 1826 English convicts on the way to Australia in the brig "Cyprus" landed on the coast of Japan, and, according to an account in the Sidney (Australia) *Gazette*, February, 1842, the crew of the "Lady Rowena" destroyed a Japanese village in latitude 43.

During the period of exclusion much actual intercourse of necessity occurred between the Japanese of the Coasts and the British and American seamen, especially those in the whale fishery. *The Seaman's Friend,* Honolulu, Oahu, S. I., December 1, 1848, after commenting on the number of whaling vessels cruising within full view of the Japanese coast, says: "Several whale ships have fallen in with junks, exchanged civilities with them, and in some instances relieved those in distress."

Numerous British and American boats were wrecked on or touched the coast of Japan in the years preceeding MacDonald's visit. The ship "Tobey," Capt. Charles, which sailed for the Northwest Coast on March 11, 1822, was supposed to have been wrecked on the Coast of Japan and all on board lost or imprisoned. Starbuck, 242. The "Lady Adams" was wrecked off the Japanese coast in 1823—*Idem.*, 141; the "Lawrence" of Poughkeepsie, N. Y., Baker, captain, which sailed on July 10, 1845, was also wrecked, see note 175, p. 161; the English brig "Catherine" in 1847 was wrecked and the captain and crew imprisoned; the "Pocohantas" of New York, S. Carter, captain, and crew who re-shipped on the "Trident," were left on the island of Otatoe, North of Yezo, in July, 1850; Capt. H. H. Lovitt of Hobarttown and the crew of the English ship "Edmond" were wrecked on the coast near Yezo in 1850; the "David Paddock," which accompanied MacDonald's ship, was also wrecked on the Japanese coast. See note 148, pages 138-139, Reuben Andrews, first officer of the "David Paddock," states that the Japanese governor and the natives on the southwest cape of Saghalen, where the crew landed and remained there three days, knew several English words, such as "Jack," "Joe," "Grog Oh," "America," etc., and were friendly and supplied them with a hundred weight of rice when they left.

therefore, always careful never to tell tales against anyone; and they seemed to remark this, evincing perfect confidence in me. The people proper are, I would say, naturally trustful. Their spy system seemed to me more artificial than otherwise—an incident of governance in a country where, from the habit of intrigue in the *governing* classes, watch and ward have become the "order of the day." [264]

Towards the close of my confinement I was informed, one day, by one of my guards, that there was a change of Governor.

Governors, I understood, are (or were then) appointed by the secular Emperor *(Siogoun)* [265] and hold office for one year—the family of each Governor being retained, at Yeddo, as hostages for good conduct, during office.

In case of misconduct in office, and conviction for it, it is left to the guilty one, to kill himself, or allow himself to be killed, for die he must. The act of suicide is deemed the more honorable alternative, and is generally resorted to.

It is done with a short sword, always worn (for the purpose) in front, in a belt, with another, a longer sword, the two together as a sign of rank. [267] This smaller sword, is a blade about eighteen inches in

---

264 "We made our remarks to each other upon the nation with whom we were endeavoring to form new connections, upon their excessive closeness, upon the circumspection with which each step was taken; it seemed as if the least error would cost the life even of the person highest in rank. Every thought, every question, every word, was weighed in the nicest manner, and appeared to have some particular aim in view." G. H. von Langsdorff, *op. cit.,* 239. See also hereon Wm. Elliott Griffis, *op. cit.,* 295. See hereon Hawks, *op. cit.,* i, 15, 16.

265 Shogun.

length, covered with paper to within two inches of its point. This bared part is drawn across the belly (ripping the bowels) and across the wind pipe—cutting the throat. The act is called *"Harra Karri"* [268]—sounded as two words, which may be translated "Happy dispatch."

It is quite frequent: an ancient social habit. Most honorable in their regard, it is considered a perfect expiation for misconduct or guilt, and saves from confiscation of property, and imputation of disgrace to the family of the self-executioner.

Further than that: Sometimes, at the requisition of the Emperor, a number of them—high officers chiefly —have been known to thus execute Harri Karri to avert or check a public calamity; thus appeasing—as they imagine—by sacrifice of life blood—atonement—offended Deity.

These are things hard to believe of such a people, so far as I could judge of them from my own observation. Thus to find—or rather to hear—amongst themselves, of such superstition and "heathen darkness," is repugnant to our sense of the moral relations of God and man. I could not believe, and I don't believe, that such was, *then*, (when I was with them) still their code or creed in such matters. The tone and line of thought expressed by them—I mean particularly my pupils—forbade such belief. They were not Christians; but in their sense of Deity—regard and acknowledgment, at heart, of One Father of All, and of His infinite goodness and providential care to and *over* all men and all

---

[268] Hara-kiri, literally "belly-cut"; the polite word is seppuku, "abdomen incision." MacDonald's expression "Happy dispatch" is purely factitious. The term, however, appears in Mrs. W. Buck, *op. cit.*, (1841), 241; in Francis Hawks, *op. cit.*, and is used by Dr. Wm. Elliot Griffis in his *Life of Townsend Harris*, 82.

life they, certainly are not below any Christian people of any time or place, that I ever knew or read of. I may have said as much before, but as the occasion, now, here, presents itself, I repeat it. In my heart I cannot say enough on this score.

Living as I then was—a stranger amongst strangers —with no familiar converse on such themes save with my Bible—the Word (in it) ever speaking to me in aversion to such gross error and sin, while at the same time inculcating love to man, in his every aspect and relation, it strained my heart that I could not preach, then, and there, unto them, that Word as given unto me. My own proper sense of my situation as to them forbade any effort in the way of teaching a new or other faith to them. Moreover, I had no special aptitude, nor training for the purpose; and it did not enter into my personal aims to incur any martyrdom for any Church's sake. I went of the broad "platform" of a common humanity—thoroughly imbued with the idea that, truly, "The things of Christ are not of this world," or to put it briefly—Church and State *are not one*, whatever their accidental relations may be. Pulpits, polls and parliaments have each, in the order of things, their appropriate functions. I belonged to none of them. I was simply a wanderer, for knowledge—an adventurer in the broad field of adventure, for adventure's sake.

FEUDAL SYSTEM A. D. 1849

From what I saw and learned, the basis, then, of their government, was the feudal system; abolished since. I should say *a* feudal system, for, so far as I know it was not to be identified, precisely, with our general idea of the feudal system, as we read of it in Europe in the old-en time. I am not sufficiently familiar with the subject to offer any definition of it, or discuss it.

The Country, I understand, was then (in my time there) divided into twenty-eight feudal Lordships or Principalities *(Daimios)*, acknowledging, as a canon of faith (political) the *Mikado* (as he is called) as their Supreme, and *Divine* Head in government.

In theory, and really, he was—and is still—the Emperor in the sense of Civic and national governance; for there cannot, in the nature of things, be *two* "Emperors" *(Imperium in imperio)* of the same country, and people. From the theocratic character of this *Imperium* the Executive—functional—was placed in a Chief Minister of State—"Premier or Grand-Vizier"—with an Assistant Council, of highest Nobles, about a dozen, with separate Departments. In the course of time, accidentally and abnormally, this Chief Minister—originally also Generalissimo—while, ostensibly even admitting the theocratic supremacy of the Mikado, assumed the secular attributes of soverignty under the name of *Koboe,* or *Siogoun*—practically, Emperor.

This began in the twelfth century of our era, and eighteenth of the Mikado Dynasty, and has continued ever since till A. D. 1868—twenty years after my time in Japan.

The consequence of the Koboe[269] system was a chronic state of internecine strife amongst the Daimios —some claiming, in internal government, to be utterly independent. Now the Mikado, as sole Emperor, with a Parliament of his people, on essentially of British model, reigns, supreme, by divine right of kingship. To what their march in the progress of nationhood will ultimately attain no man can tell. In this they may yet lead

---

[269] Kubo; a 16th century appellation of the Shogun.

the world; their autonomy being of the strongest among men; and, now, the most active in national progress.

LAWS

As to their Laws I don't know much; and cannot enter into details. I know that in general character, they are very severe, and are rigorously enforced in defense of life and property.

The principle of compensation *(Lex talionis)* obtains amongst them. In case of murder the family of the deceased is allowed to kill the murderer if he runs away or attempts to do so. If he does not run away, nor attempts it, he has to be duly tried.

In case of theft and other crimes, trial is had before a Magistrate or Governor. The latter has the power of life and death. Government—in my time there—was essentially despotic; though practically not cruel according to general standards civilized or uncivilized.

NOTE IN CONCLUSION

In the above cursory statements, I have given only a mere skeleton sketch of what—in spite of difficulties— I managed to pick up in the way of information.

My imprisonment, though close, allowed me daily communication with people—many sorts—who, from curiosity, came to see me; in this regard I did not remark any special restraint on the part of the authorities. Naturally sociable, I always made friends; and at the same time managed not to excite any suspicion of the extractive ("pumping") process which, as occasion offered, I applied to my visitors, and attendants, and even pupils.

The Japanese, I would observe, are naturally chatty;

always in a vein of good humor.[270]   In this respect I
was *en rapport* with them. In look, facial features, etc.,
I was not unlike them; my sea life and rather dark complexion, moreover, giving me their general color—a
healthy bronze. I never had a cross word with any of
them; and I think I passed rather as a favorite amongst
them—eliciting, ever and anon, the compliment of the
Governor, as to my "heart."

Naturally, they are brave—I should say—utterly
fearless of death; their instincts markedly military. I
believe they would suffer annihilation rather than surrender in defense of their country. Unconquered; unconquerable:[271] that is their proud position.

Enjoying a well-guarded liberty[272] in their social life,
and a perfect toleration of creed, except as to that form

---

[270] "Of their friendly disposition and good nature towards foreigners
I have frequently with astonishment seen manifest proofs." Charles
Peter Thunberg, *op. cit.*, iii, 258. Capt. V. M. Golownin, [*op. cit.*, 89, et
seq.,] records many expressions of sympathy and benevolent acts by the
Japanese. See also Hawks, *op. cit.*, i, 267, 327, 512.

National characteristics change slowly, and for a proper understanding of the Japanese people observations made by Charles Peter Thunberg 125 years ago might bear repeating: "This nation is lofty, it is true,
but good-natured and friendly with all; with gentleness and kindness it
may be soothed and brought to hear reason, but it is not to be moved in
the least by threats or anything like defiance. . . . Pride is the principal defect of the Japanese. Whatever injury a Japanese might be inclined to put up with, he can never bear to have his pride touched."
Charles Peter Thunberg, *op. cit.*, iii, 258, 260. "The point of honor is
extremely lively in all ranks." Capt. V. M. Golownin, *op. cit.*, iii, 36.
Hawks, [*Op. cit.*, i, 17] states: "Among a people so sensitive . . . . . .
it is obvious that a great deal now depends on the fairness, good sense,
and good temper of our consular representative . . . . . . almost every
writer describes them as naturally frank in manner, communicative and
open in speech on ordinary topics, and possessed of a very high sense of
honor."

[271] Charles Peter Thunberg, *op. cit.*, iii, 261, likewise comments upon
the unconquered nation and the valor and unconquerable spirit of the
Japanese people.

[272] "The rights of the highest and lowest class of people alike are
protected by its laws. No nation in the whole expansive tract of the
Indes is more vigilantly attentive to their liberties." Charles Peter
Thunberg, *op. cit.*, iii, 254.

of Christian Faith known as Roman Catholic, banned, for reasons of State, over two hundred years ago—(I speak of the time I was then there)—they had nothing to complain of.

Yet, under that mask of placidity which they presented, I could see the inner working of aspirations for a higher life amongst the nations of the earth. I perceived this more particularly in Murayama and some of the younger of my pupils (all grown men), with minds of keenest search; acute enough to pierce the veil of their old traditional life, which, to them, was as the rotting shroud of a dead past.

During the full seven months and more I was thus immured, I never once stepped outside my prison. Yet I never suffered in bodily health. Of active habit, full blooded; great vitality; it was hard for me to be thus cooped up.

In the earlier part of the restraint, when, from my ignorance of their vernacular, I could not freely converse with my guards and visitors, and only with some difficulty with my pupils, time hung heavily on me. Yet I was content, as all being in the line of my venture. I had, moreover, some distractions, pleasant rather than otherwise.

In the first place, I was served with almost lordly state: with five or six waiters to attend on me at every meal—four a day—with special extra ceremony at my *Sunday* feast, on the pork ("good-so"[273] as they called it with its accompaniment *bread* ("*pan*"[274]—as they

---

[273] Gochiso, often pronounced "got-so."

[274] From the Portuguese pao—one of the indelible traces of the influence of Portuguese commerce with Japan prior to their exclusion in 639. In the Japanese language there are numerous other words of Portuguese origin, some of which, are so perfectly naturalized that their foreign origin is not at once apparent.

called it). They don't use bread, and very little flour, which they make up, only as a rarity, into sweet cakes. I had also butter, which they call *boutre*[275]—from the Dutch. They don't use butter, nor milk in any way from animals. All these (to them) rarities they seemed to take a pleasure in procuring for me, and were effusively demonstrative in, *most regularly,* laying before me, with the appropriate table service of knife, fork, etc. I forgot to mention that they made me a "comfortable" according to order and directions from myself. They are singularly expert in such work.

In the course of time came our New Year's day (January 1st, 1849) [276] and with it, a present from the kind Dutch Factor (John Livessohn) of a bottle of exquisite coffee, some small loaves of wheaten bread—also, more precious still to me—sixty-eight numbers of the *London Atlas* newspaper, and *Weekly Dispatch,* the whole with his polite card of compliments.[277]

---

[275] Botoru, from the Dutch boter. The Japanese do not use butter. Charles Peter Thunberg, (1779), *op. cit.,* iii, 73.

[276] The Japanese New Year begins, generally, in our February.— [Original.]

[277] Levyssohn, in his *Bladen over Japan,* 55, mentions MacDonald on this occasion:

"Ter gelegenheid van het nieuw ingetreden jaar werd op den 1 January, door my aan den avonturier Ranald Macdonald eene hoeveelheid levensmiddelen en andere benoodigdheden, na alvorens dienaangaande van den gouverneur van Nagasaki verlof gevraaged en verkregen te hebben, ten geschenke gezonden, hebbende gezegde Macdonald voor wyn of sterken drank bedankt."

Levyssohn also says that Macdonald was suspected of being a missionary or spy, and attributes his kind treatment to his affability and his having taught English to some interpreters: "Dit verhaal (account of his arrival at Notsuka) veroorzaakte veel wantrouwen of argwaan by het Japansch bestuur, dowyl men hem voor een zendeling of spion beschouwde, en het was alleen aan zyn goed gedrag, aan zyne fatsoenlyke manieren en doordien hij aan eenige der tolken voor het Hollandsch onderwys in de Engelsche taal gaf, toe te schryven, dat hem wederkeerig eene beleefde en goede behandeling te beurt viel."—*Idem.,* 53.

The Dutch superintendent also extended his generosity to the "Lagoda" crew, sending them sugar, coffee, Holland gin, some flasks of wine and also some white cotton for John Bull, who was destitute of clothing. See U. S., Senate, *Executive Doc't,* No. 59, 32nd Congress, 1st Sesson, 1.

In fact, every one was kind to me; and I must say, that whether or not I was "good," the Governor—good, kind soul!—kept his word to me to the letter and to the spirit in this respect.

Much—if not all—of this must, no doubt, have been due to the kind report of me by my pupils. In this, I feel ample reward for all the service—such as it was— I rendered them.

They improved in English wonderfully, for their heart was evidently in the work, and their receptiveness quick and comprehensive aptitude in learning was, to me, extraordinary; in some of them, phenomenal. Their minds are exceptionally acute—far more so than mine, though, in my conceit, I did once lay some pretension to "seeing as well through a mill stone (with its hole) as most people."

They, I would say, are naturally, the cleverest people I know of: I say "cleverest" not in the sense of deceit, but in its highest and purest meaning. All they require is light from without; the (to them) mystery of their now fast rising East, with its cumulative wisdom of Western life. On this head I could say much as the result of my experience and reflections, but refrain, and confine myself to my narrative.

To proceed—At last, about the end (26th) of April,[278] I heard, for the first time in the country, cannon shots. I asked whether the new Governor had arrived. With a leer, they said Yes—at the same time looking at each other. At this time, I had several or all of the interpreters with me. I did not know, at the time, what made them crowd in then.

They, and all my guards except one, then suddenly

---

[278] The ship arrived at Nagasaki on the 26th of the third month or on April 18th.

went out. This one, when they had gone, came up to the bars of my cage and told me that a foreign ship had arrived, and that the guns were fired as a signal for troops from the interior.

On the following morning there was a pile of papers displayed beside my then single guard. On asking him what the papers meant, he said that they were lists of soldiers that had arrived that night; he mentioned the precise number; it was about three thousand five hundred. I thought it singular that the lists should be left at my door. Was it for effect? Of course it must have been! viz., for me, afterwards to tell others, and like a singed rat, to warn them of the "danger" of getting into such a trap.

On my inquiring, he (my guard) told me that the ordinary garrison of Nagasaki was from three to four hundred. He also told me, spontaneously, that on such occasions as this they always called troops from the interior.

They have a few real forts, and always put up sham ones[279] in the shape of canvas curtains with embrasures painted on them, when demonstration is called for. They have the idea also that a duplication of these curtains would keep off cannon balls; as no doubt they would, with *enough* of them. The cannon and mortars which I saw represented in their books, and which they told me they used, were very inferior to ours. I saw none of their real forts, except possibly, at Soya, Matsmai and Nagasaki, where, however, I did not notice

---

[279] For a similar account of sham forts see statement of George Howe, U. S. Senate Ex. Doc. 59, 32nd Congress, 1st Session, 1; Richard Hildreth, *op. cit.*, ii, 217. This idea of canvas sham forts, undoubtedly true of old China, was incorrect as to the Japanese, and arose in part from that confusion of ideas as to China and Japan and misconception of the character and purpose of these military curtains—a very old custom in Japan. See notes 188 and 189, page 173.

them. Their powder is black, dusty and bad; they prefer our's.

Their matchlocks are of steel barrels, well finished; with a smaller bore than our old muskets. They showed me a target they had been firing at, from which it would appear they were good shots.

The foreign ship which had just arrived was the American Corvette, "The Preble," of eighteen guns, in command of Captain (technically commander) Glynn.

About three days after her arrival, the Official Serrei, Murayama, and others told me that a ship had arrived from my country, and that the Captain had asked for my liberation. (Here let me say, this was not strictly true, for the Captain knew nothing about *me;* nor, I presume, had heard of me as a prisoner; it was the crew of the "Ladoga" that he was after.)

That—Serrei and Murayama went on to say—on the following day, I would have to go to the Town Hall to pay my respects to the Governor.[280] Went next morning, accordingly; carried thither in palanquin.

The new Governor had arrived since the arrival of the "Preble," and in the interval since, had immediately visited me, in my cage, *incognito.* I did not know that he was the Governor until I saw him in the Town Hall, seated afterwards, beside the old Governor. While I was in the shed—BB in the plan—thirteen American seamen were brought in. They had on their ordinary sailor dress. I had on my best Japanese dress, plain and respectable. They appeared very pale and thin. We all appeared, at the same time, before the Governors. They made me kneel apart from the rest.

The Governor, through interpreter, then told us of the arrival of the ship; and that they had, after consul-

---

[280] Oya, Totomi-no-kami.

tation, decided on allowing us to depart by her; but that it would be necessary for us to go to the Dutch Factory first.

We returned our thanks through the interpreter.

On leaving, each was borne in a palanquin. The streets were crowded. The other seamen singing "Cheery men, Oh!" [281]

We crossed, by a covered bridge about sixty yards in length, to the Factory, which is on the little Island of Dessima. [282]   At the further end of the bridge, at the Factory, we were searched.

Taken, before the Chief Factor (John Livessohn) he told us not to kneel, observing—"This is a Christian house!"

We, were entertained with a good dinner, with knives, silver table service, chairs, pork, bread, etc.— all which we duly relished, with a parting cup of best Dutch Java coffee, and then, with a true "Cheery Men Oh!" embarked in the good ship "Preble"; warmly welcomed; and with her noble Captain and right good crew, sailed for freer and more genial shores.

CHAPTER XV

Sequel—Official Record: Historical—Treaties—New Constitution

On board the "Preble," a statement, at considerable

---

[281] —
>   "O o-ly-i-o cheerly man
>   Walk him up O cheerly man,
>   O-ly-i-o
>   O-ly-i-o cheerly man."

Found in *"English Folk-Chanteys"* by Cecil Sharp (London), 50; also in Capt. W. B. Whall's *Ships, Sea-Songs and Shanties,* 111, and Miss Smith *"The Music of the Water,"* 22.

[282] This was on April 26th.

length, of my experiences in Japan was made by me to
an officer named Wilson. It was taken down by him
in writing and signed by me, and possibly sworn to, for
official record. It is, I understand to be found, printed
or alluded to in blue book, in Senate Documents of
1851-1852, ix. *"Executive Document 59,"* of the
United States.

Historical reference to it is to be found in Hildreth's
History (American) of Japan, 503, where, alluding to
the rescue, by the "Preble," of a shipwrecked American
crew detained, at the same time, in Nagasaki, he says:

"At the same time with these men, another seaman, from an
American whaler, was delivered up, who had landed a month or
two later, on some still more northerly Japanese Island. As this
man, named MacDonald, and who described himself as twenty-
four years old, and born at Astoria in Oregon, had made no attempt at escaping, he had no occasion to complain of severity.
In fact he lived in clover, the *Japanese having put him to use as a
teacher of English.* The very interpreter who boarded the "Preble"
had been one of his scholars.

Hildreth—as he states in his book—got this information from the official report above referred to.

As he truly says in his work, there was no demand
made for *me* on the occasion—for there was no knowledge or report of me, or of my position; but the Japanese authorities at Nagasaki were afraid to keep me: a
fear arising not so much from any apprehension from
the American Government, as from their own Imperial
Government, in its policy in such case. This is hereinafter explained in comment by a very intelligent Japanese gentleman on the subject. The default of such
surrender might have been fatal to the governor of Nagasaki, and even to his predecessor who, in the first instance, had so put me "in clover."

Here I may state, that on the arrival of the "Preble"

in Chinese waters, I—a penniless waif on the ocean of life—took ship again before the mast. Thence, after many adventures, the world over, including Australia during the first "gold diggings," [283] I returned, after several years, to my native land, or rather to that portion of it (British Columbia) which had been left to the Old Flag by the Oregon Treaty. Of this portion of my life —matter for a book, and of some public moment as pioneer work, in close connection with my old and ever good friend, Sir James Douglas, first Governor of that Colony—I shall not here speak: confining myself, strictly as possible, to my story of Japan, briefly, merely stating what followed in the way of immediate sequence.

SEQUENCE

On April 26th, 1849, after ten months of sojourn in Japan, including about seven months of teaching of English to a class of fourteen government interpreters, I was, as stated, delivered over to the American (U. S.) authorities.

Evidently there was no relaxation, then, of the Japanese rule of exclusion of foreigners.

On March 31st, 1854, the *first* "Convention"—first in all history, I believe—was made by Japan with a foreign power.

That was with the United States of America.

It was followed with a similar one with Great Britain on October 14th, 1854—the same year.

---

[283] While gold was first discovered in Australia in 1823, it was not until 1851 and 1852 that the important discoveries were made in New South Wales, Victoria, South Australia and Tasmania, attracting the great rush of gold miners. Shortly afterwards important gold discoveries were made in Queensland.

These conventions—so called—were not Treaties in the ordinary sense; were not for a commerce; but were merely to provide ports of refuge and means of relief to vessels and crews in distress in the navigation of Japanese waters. Certain of their seaports were, under these conventions, opened for the purpose; and a restricted trade for necessary commodities—such as water, coal, wood and food—was allowed.

Four years after that, on August 26th, 1858, a solemn "Treaty of Peace, Friendship and Commerce"— such is its heading—was made between Great Britain and Japan. It is, I believe without alteration, in force still; and, if I be not mistaken, is the basis, still, of communication between these two Powers.

This Treaty, with its incidental trade and postal regulations was—so far as I know—the first Act of State of the kind which Japan had ever entered into.

It was soon followed by others, in like tenor, with other foreign powers, including the United States of America.

Now, not only in commerce, but in general international comity, qualified only by general consular relations, Japan is open to the world.

By a social revolution since; unexplained, in the history of the world, in its depth, force and effect, it now stands practically abreast of the most advanced nationalities of Europe in political status.

With a Constitution framed upon the best exemplers in Europe,[284] but *au fond* essentially Prussian with the

---

[284] The Occidental constitutions of Europe and America were the outgrowths of popular uprisings against despotic rulers and a declaration of popular rights, while the Japanese constitution emanated from the Emperor as the fountain of power. The Japanese constitution was therefore to some extent framed on the Prussian model in making the Ministers responsible not to the Diet, but to the Emperor.

English language as a subject, amongst leading classes, largely of private, and even, to some extent, of public education, it promises, fairly, to soon become—and is now fast becoming—the New England of that further India which Columbus sought and led to. In this acceptiveness by furthest Eastern of furthest Western civilization is the resurrection of Aryan Asian death to the *Lux Mundi* of a "Better Day"; the completion of that globe chain of humanity in the bonds of peace, when, sooner or later, all Waterlooes, and Armageddon itself shall have dropped their trail of sword, forever!

CHAPTER XVI

Suggestion for Change in International Policy. Agency of Author in It—Japanese Appreciation of His Service.

Here, in reference to this incident of my having been the first, during their hermit seclusion, to be teacher of English to the Japanese, and in that was the first instructor—apostle in a sense—of English thought, influence, and power for good, to this people—then in darkness in such matter—the following questions suggest themselves. I give them as they present themselves to me; though with diffidence, from their seeming egotism:

1. What moved the Japanese to thus, exceptionally, make me a teacher of English to them?

2. Was there any pressure brought to bear upon them by Great Britain, or by the United States of America, or any other foreign power, for such action?

3. Was there any special inducement, external, or internal, held out to them for it?

4. If it was their own spontaneous act—as seems to have been the case—what enlightened or prompted them to it?[285]

In answer, from my knowledge of them, I would say:

1. That their own self-enlightened appreciation of their position, in the family of nations so moved them.

2. That there was no external pressure brought to bear on them in that direction; and that in receiving my teaching and its incidental advocacy of international relations on the general principles of comity of nations, they but followed their own spontaneous desire for that.[286]

This covers questions 2 and 3.

3. To question 4, I would say, in all sincerity, but with all proper diffidence:

That that enlightenment with its own inherent suggestions, probably prompted them to the course taken by the Conventions and Treaties referred to.

The Chinese and Dutch, with whom alone they held communication, were naturally, and in actual public polity, opposed to such opening of their ports.[287] It took time—a little—for my humble teaching to ma-

---

285 See hereon Dr. Tuazo Ota Nitobe's *The Japanese Nation,* on intercourse between Japan and the United States; also Wm. Elliott Griffis, *The Japanese Nation in Evolution.*

286 "From their insatiate curiosity respecting European affairs nothing but the absurd jealousy of the government prevents them from rising high in the scale of science, and should a revolution in manners once take place and the ports of Japan be opened, we may anticipate changes, both moral and political of the most extraordinary nature through all the oriental region." Note Capt. V. M. Golownin, *op. cit.,* (1824 ed.), iii, 34-35.

287 The Dutch King, William II., in 1844 sent a letter to the Emperor of Japan advising the opening of the country, and later recommended that the American Expedition be well received. See Wm. Elliott Griffis, *Townsend Harris, First American Envoy to Japan,"* for further light on this question.

ture: its inculcations had to reach the Imperial Executive itself, far off, high, on its Throne of State. Under Providence, in time, it did so. So at last, I flatter myself: and so, in generous concession, have intelligent Japanese themselves declared.

In this connection, in evidence of the appreciation of these facts by them, I take it upon me to give the following communications and incidents.

The first I shall give (with permission) is a letter, in form of a critical report, in English, from a very intelligent Japanese gentleman, the Reverend Mr. K. T. Takahashi (a Presbyterian Clergyman) a resident of Montreal, Canada, to whom had been submitted by my friend Judge McLeod, of Ottawa, Canada, with the story of my adventure there. After a prolonged and critical reading of the M. S. Mr. Takahashi wrote of it thus:

"This story of Mr. MacDonald's adventure in Japan is of immense interest to me, and the Japanese generally as it is a story hitherto unknown in our Country." (After narrating, briefly, the leading facts, he proceeded to say.)

"The special reason for which the narrative is interesting to us Japanese is the light which it throws upon the inner current of thought which was gradually changing its course then, in Japan. It will be seen from his narrative, that though a prisoner, he was a teacher, much beloved and respected, over fourteen scholars, quick and intelligent, ever zealous of gathering information of Western nations. Such information the Country needed at the time very badly; although the Government was jealous that it should be shared by the people, and even made it the subject of very severe punishment if they dared to do so. In all probability it was these fourteen scholars in turn who made themselves invaluable, when, later on, Japan had become involved in foreign intercourse.

"Moreover, it was no doubt through these fourteen that the foremost intellects of the country had gathered better knowledge of foreign countries, and better prepared themselves to formulate the future plan of their national course. Yet it is remarkable that today, in Japan, there is hardly any one who can recount the names of those fourteen, and possibly none who know of this seven months' study under MacDonald. Such was the secrecy of the Government of the day kept in regard to all foreign affairs. Severe comment is apt to be passed on such secrecy, but it has done good to the country in one sense; for, under the circumstances, none but sincere patriots, of far sight and high intellect, cared to seek access to such secret; and, indeed, it was through them only, that Japan has been safely steered through its crisis—beginning with the ports opening, and ending with the revolution and reformation of twenty years ago [288] and landed on to the present state of progress.

"It is not in vain that Mr. MacDonald should flatter himself the fact that he has been the first instructor and propagator of the English language in Japan, and much that was needed to enhance their notion of Western nations to the Japanese of the time. We, of today, would gladly acknowledge his immense service, so long cast into cruel oblivion; and if he should happen to revisit the Country now, our people will not be slow to show him their sincerity in this respect."

Such is the comment and intelligent criticism of one who is an utter stranger to the writer. It shows a keen and far searching appreciation of the circumstances in question. In this, he, from his particular stand point as a Japanese, is not alone.

In the incident of Mr. Oda's visit to my friend Judge McLeod in Ottawa, in this connection, as the bearer of a special present from the son of my dearly beloved pupil Murayama Yeanoske, as hereinafter related, I flatter myself with the same generous appreciation of the service in question. That was done when I was supposed to be dead: a fact which but enhances the merit of the act. The whole—in its "In Memoriam"—presents a phase of Japanese character which touches the finest feelings of the human heart. The communication through Mr. Oda came in this way, and I have it from his host at the time Mr. McLeod.

In 1869, the story of my adventure in Japan had,

---

[288] This was written in 1888.—[Original.]

briefly, been given in one of a series of articles in the public press of Canada by Mr. McLeod, under the pen-name of Britannicus, advocating, from personal know-ledge and special authentic data, a feasible line of transcontinental railway through British North America—the whole as already stated in introduction.

Many years afterwards, in November 1896 or about then, on the establishment of postal communication di-rect with Japan by the Canadian Pacific Railway, hap-pening to see in the newspapers the name of Murayama (pronounced Moor-ei-ama, with accent on second syl-lable) as that of one of the proprietors of a leading newspaper bearing the name "*Assa Hi-shim*"[289] (mean-ing literally, "Rising Sun News"—Morning Chroni-cle) published in Osaka, Japan, Mr. McLeod, thinking that he might be the Murayama of my story, sent him, by the C. P. R. a copy of one of his Railway pamphlets containing the account, in brief, of my adventure in Japan, in which special laudatory notice was made of my said favorite pupil.

At the same time he wrote Mr. Murayama a letter explaining the circumstances, and stating that he be-lieved that I had been dead several years. He also en-closed a list—taken from my original one in his hands —of my fourteen pupils in Nagasaki. The packet was duly received; but Mr. Murayama being unfamiliar with English, it was handed to his partner and co-editor, Mr. Oda, who, as an English barrister of thirteen years standing, and collegiate (during three years) of Edin-burgh University, Scotland, and the translator of sev-eral standard English books into Japanese, was perfect-ly competent to translate the communication.

---

[289] The *Asa Hi Shimbum—Rising Sun Newspaper*—is one of the great newspapers of Japan.

It turned out that my Murayama had died, and that this was his son.[290]

None of the other pupils named in the list were known to them, but in a searching enquiry they traced them. All had died: but they found out their heirs; who, however, knew nothing of *me*—had never heard of me or my teaching. However, Messrs. Murayama (the son) and Mr. Oda were convinced of the truth of my story, and they published it in their paper just as it was given in Mr. McLeod's railway pamphlet.

Some months after that—the occasion arising—Mr. Oda received a request from his friend His Excellency Minemitsu Mutsu[291] (a nobleman of princely standing; closely related to the Emperor; and a leader of the party of progress) to accompany him to Washington, as newly appointed Ambassador, there, for Japan. He did so; not in any official quality, but simply as a friend.

Mr. Murayama availed himself of the opportunity of learning more, if possible, about me and my story.

Mr. McLeod and myself had ceased in our correspondence for twenty-five years or more, and—as he wrote to me afterwards—had supposed me to be dead, and so informed Mr. Murayama.

Mr. Oda kindly offered to go to Mr. McLeod to make further enquiry on the subject; and at the same time to be the bearer to him of a testimonial from Mr. Murayama (the son) for such mention of his father. In

---

290 Moriyama and Murayama are two different family names. Mr. Murayama, proprietor of the *Asa-hi-Shimbun,* is not related to the interpreter.

291 Munemitsu Mutsu, afterwards Count Mutsu, was appointed Japanese Minister at Washington in February, 1888. It is not true that he was related to the Emperor. He was a great friend of the United States. He was afterwards Japanese Minister of Foreign Affairs. A bronze statue in memory of him stands before the Department of Foreign Affairs buildings in Tokio. His son, Count Mutsu, is still living.

due time, in the summer of 1888, Mr. Oda—making a digression for the purpose on his way to Berlin—arrived at Ottawa, and for three or four days was the welcomed guest of my friend Judge McLeod.

The testimonial—carefully packed in two boxes, one within the other—was an ancient despatch or letter (in roll) box; in form, peculiarly double, in that one open box fitted in, or over another; dimensions, about twelve inches in length, five in depth, and four in width; of *papier-mache*, with a mixture of gold dust—composition technically called, in Japanese, *Kahamashee*.

The sides, inside and out inlaid with plates of gold, in different arabesque forms; the top having a specially deep rich moulding, all in gold, in different and appropriate hues, of a perfectly natural scene, of lake (or sea), river, land, trees, herbage, flowers, and foliage in most minute and exquisite detail. Mr. Oda said it was the work of a Lost Art—lost for two hundred and fifty years back. Yet it looked, in its bright sheen, as fresh from the artist's hands, save, (a little) in its time shaded silk cords with tassels. A princely testimonial truly!—Princely! not only in its intrinsic value; but, more still, in the motive of its giving.

To Mr. Oda, in evidence of my story, were handed all my papers which, now forty years ago, I had left in the hands of Mr. McLeod when his guest in Canada. Amongst these were little scraps of Japanese paper— quite different from our own—on which, with a crow quill, I had written, while in the country, a glossary of Japanese words and colloquial terms, with English. This alone was very strong evidence, and was accepted as such. Mr. McLeod also as already stated, showed my original list of pupils. As to my Journal proper, there were only a very few pages, scarcly a dozen.

MR. ODA

A word as to this gentleman: it is due to him. As my friend (M) wrote me of him, he seems to have been a personage of highest culture and finest feeling; and deeply interested in my story. According to his own account, he had received a thorough English education; and, as before stated, had then been an English barrister of thirteen years' standing. My friend being himself an old lawyer—a Queen's Counsel—a retired Judge in fact—and, in his earlier days, an active and influential politician, had much to say to his brother in the law, about law and politics, and remarked to me afterwards, when we had resumed correspondence, that while thus conversing with this stranger from strange Japan, and unaware of his position, in these matters in his own country, he was surprised to find in him such a grasp of intellect—grasp beyond far, what my friend (himself of much advanced views in our higher law and politics in national life) had found in Canada: but with all, there was such a modesty in the bearing of the gentleman with his abnormally large head (on a small body, and large eyes (scarcely Monghol) glowing in their intelligence, there was no gauging the intellect thus touched.

Aryan, or not, I regard the Japanese intellect the most subtle—finest and keenest—in the world.[293] My friend says he considers it *pre* and *supra* Aryan, with a literature pre—or *ante* Aryan, and has a theory of their genesis which—he contends with much learning and

---

[293] "The inquisitiveness, the readiness at learning and the memory of these people surprised us exceedingly." G. H. von Langsdorff, *op. cit.*, 238.

force—naturally and logically explains it. On that question I cannot here enter.

It was only on leaving, when, in return for certain books (chiefly on law and political constitutions) which my friend had presented to him, he offered, and insisted on my friend's acceptance of a present from himself, viz: of three thick volumes (duod) gleaming in gold; all in Japanese "black letter"—which he called "The Codes of Japan"—Codes Civil, Criminal, and—as he expressed it "Administration of Government", that my friend accidentally learnt who and what he was. Accepting with all thanks, my friend turned at once to the title page, which, in Japanese is at the end (as we would call it) of the work. There, he saw, and knew well enough to recognize, the full name, viz: Oda-Ian-Icki-Ro [294] printed in Japanese characters, which some of the ladies of the house had, before that got him, in pleasantry, to write down for them, to keep as a curiosity. Asked whether that was his name and whether it meant himself, he answered "Yes". As what? asked Mr. McLeod. "As editor", was the answer. "Editor for revisal, or for Composition?" asked M. Answer—"Composition".

There being two names at the same place—his first —my friend asked him what that was. "Name of the other editor" was his answer.

It is to be explained—that in Japan all public or official function by twos, or generally so; one as a check on the other, an old custom.[295] Mr. M. then got him to write his "presentation" on the title page, "J. Oda, chief Editor of Code of Japan."

---

[294] The name correctly spelled is Oda Jun-ichi-ro.

[295] This was pursuant to an old Japanese custom.

Thus, in grateful recognition of my humble service to Japan, had I, after my supposed death, "In Memoriam", the grateful homage of its Gamaliel[296] and possibly, of its ambassador to Washington.

Mr. Oda, I understand, went direct from Canada to London, by the St. Lawrence, promising my friend to return by the Canadian Pacific Railway. Delicate, and taking ill in London, his physician advised him not to risk, at that season (October-November) the rigours of such a northern route, but to hasten home by the warmer one by the Suez Canal. Starting, on it, from Marseilles, in Steamer named "Le Caledonien" of the French Line ("Messagerie") to the East, he seems to have died on the way.[297] We have learnt nothing of him, since: Enquiry has totally failed on the subject. Probably his body was "buried at sea". dropt into Ocean!—unhonoured; unknown!

CHAPTER XVII

RETROSPECT: CONCLUSION — DUTCH FRIENDS — A LAST WORD.

It is long, nearly half a century—since my adventure here sketched: Yet even now, after the vicissitudes, varied and wearing, of my life, I have never ceased to feel most kindly and ever grateful to my fellow men of Japan for their really generous treatment of me. In that

---

296 The Elder Gamaliel was a descendant of the family of David and a grandson of Hillel, the celebrated president of the Sanhedrin and patriarch of the Jewish community in Palestine. Gamaliel was a teacher of the apostle Paul and dissuaded the Jews from taking strict measures against the apostles. (Acts. v, 34.) Our author's allusion is due to the well-known characterization of Gamaliel as *"a doctor of the law,* had in honor of all the people."

297 He returned to Japan, and died shortly after at Kyoto.

long journey and voyage from the extreme North to the extreme South—fully a thousand miles—of their country; throughout my whole sojourn of ten months in the strange land, never did I receive a harsh word, or even an unfriendly look.   Among all classes, a gentle kindness to the fancied cast-away—the stranger most strange—pervaded their general regard and treatment of me.   From the time I landed on the beach of Tomassey in the Straits of *La Perouse,* when Inoes took me gently by the wrist, one on each side, to assist me to the dwelling of their employer, while others put sandals to my feet, to the time of my joining the United States Sloop of War "Preble," it was ever the same uniform kindness.   Truly I liked them in that congenial sympathy which, left to itself—unmarred by antagonism of race, creed, or worldly selfishness—makes us all, of Adam's race "wondrous kin".

Among them were individualities which particularly attracted my regard.   First I would mention the Governor (Obigue) in Nagasaki, before whom I was brought and tried, surrounded by his officials in the Town Hall or Court, he assumed all the dignity of a Chief Justice.   When presiding he assumed as much gravity and austerity as his good sound heart would allow—for I know that it was through his clemency and favor that I was well provided with all the comforts and accommodations I enjoyed. It was not treason, according to their laws, I suspect that he, at least, exceeded his prescribed duty in such leniency towards me: for by the then existing laws of the Empire—laws then unalterable in such matter as those of the Medes and Persians of old—my landing in Japan soil was—I repeat—an offense that might; in course, have consigned me to a dark dungeon for life, or to the more speedy

fate of summary execution.   So I was told, at parting,
by the Obigue himself: and that, not in reminder of
favor shown, but in warning, friendly and kindly,
against running such risk again.   At the close of my
first interview with him, in full court, as already described, he encouraged me by saying that I had a "big"
heart, without adding a sound heart.   At the close of
my last interview with him, his advice was—and that
in tone and manner more tenderly, warmly friendly—
"Never to put my foot on Japan soil again, or it would
be worse for me".

Really, I don't believe that he meant it in reproof for
my having done so, but in pure friendly warning.

Whether or not he had the secret approval of the
Emperor in his course towards me; or that the Emperor
or the Ministers of State had any knowledge of my position, I cannot say.   As there was no time then, by
any means at their comand, to communicate with the
Emperor[298] at Yeddo,[299] about 500 miles distant
from Nagasaki—between the time of my first trial
and the Governor's order for employment of me as a
teacher of English, I infer that the thing was done on
the responsibility of the Governor himself.   It was a
bold, brave deed, involving deep peril to his own life,
for public law—I mean law of administration of government—was then—as it had ever been in Japan—essentially draconic.   The considerations in public policy—
for there could have been no other—that so weighed
with His Excellency of Nagasaki must have been
weighty indeed.   In this vicarious heroism, for purely
national weal, the deed is worthy of historical record.

---

[298] The only Emperor (Mikado) was at Kyoto; the Shogun-chief *de-
facto* ruler—was in Yedo.

[299] Since called Tokio.—[Original.]

There were other individualities who, although sub-ordinates, specially attracted my attention, and won my regards.

Among them was a gentleman, evidently a high of-ficial, at Nagasaki. I forgot his name. He was the tallest person I saw in Japan. He frequently visited my quarters with books, maps, etc., accompanied always by my friend Murayama. He showed great interest in me; and appeared to be anxious to learn something of the outer world. Soft and gentle in his conversation, this fine old dignitary showed all the refinement of a gent-leman. It was to him, I suspected, that I owed the completeness, regularity, and perfect comfort of my quarters. I owe him many thanks for lightening many hours of my prison life.

The next person still impressed on my mind was the distinguished venerable Mr. Sjerrei, one of the Chief, if not the chief interpreter. He was aged: sev-enty-four years, if I remember right, as he then told me. His face was dark; features good; aquiline or rather so; nose long and chin long: with the habit of mumbling his words before speaking. He was fre-quently the medium of conversation between officials and myself.

The next—the dearest to me in every regard, and most esteemed, and ever loved—was the brilliant Mur-ayama Yeanoske, of medium height among his people, say five feet six inches; of delicate and finely cut fea-tures; with signs of great intelligence; eyes intensely black, brilliant, and penetrating, yet with an expression mild and loving—truly magnetic: of very light com-plexion—like the white of the Southern States of Am-erica, lighter much than the average Japanese. His countenance, when in repose, had the air of mild dignity, such as is observable in our clergy, as a class. When speaking to me before officials it was always with a smile, as if to give me encouragement and confidence. He showed a great desire to learn English, and displayed much aptitude in doing so. He was fluent in Dutch, for he was one of the official interpreters of that language: and I take it for granted that he was well grounded in the history and musty traditions of his country: of which, however, he never spoke to me; nor did I ever ask him. His general appearance was that of a studious and earnest scholar; and a refined gentleman.

He was my favorite.

MY DUTCH FRIENDS

Whatever influence a European resident might have had with the Government I don't know. It was evident to me in my case, that that influence was given in my favor, for I have the assurance of Mr. John Livessohn, the Dutch Chief Factor resident at the time at the Port (Nagasaki), that they would give me a passage in the next annual ship, subject of course to permission from the authorities of Japan. He, as stated in my narrative, was ever most kindly attentive to me in the way of relieving the monotony and wants of my foreign confinement. I can say the same of the good Doctor (Dutch also) of the Establishment. They were all good and clever: and we all esteemed each other.

A LAST WORD

In my old age; while living out, still in sweat of brow, the fast falling evening shades of life, in my na-

tive homeland of the Columbia, after having, in my
wanderings, girded—I may say—the Globe itself, and
come across peoples many, civilized and uncivilized,
there are none to whom I feel more kindly—more
grateful—than my old hosts of Japan; none whom I
esteem more highly.

As to their wonderful progress in civil life and government within the last few years, I am not surprised.

From what I saw of them, their aspirations—scarce
concealed though studiedly covered—were, to my view,
even then, in that direction. I felt at the time, that some
such change, possibly soon, would come—come, not
over them, as from some external force, but from within themselves—in process of that inherent principle
of progressive national life, in evolution, which from
the very *origin* of their nationhood has—uniquely, as
a sort of "chosen people", but not "Jew"—preserved
them throughout our ages of human life, in their singular integrity. Whence their origin, we know not.
Themselves don't know. History, even legend, on that
point, is a myth. From my own limited observation
and study I can advance no satisfactory theory on that
point. Suffice it for the present to say, that they are
truly a wonder among the nations; commanding, in
their present position, the respect and admiration of
the world.

Often in conversation with my pupils—pupils themselves infinitely superior to me in intellectual power
and learning—I was struck with the readiness with
which they grasped what I told them of the principles
of Constitutional Government of Great Britain and of
the United States respectively.

As to the former, there was no difficulty; being somewhat like their own, save in its electoral franchise and larger individual liberty. They seemed to understand it perfectly, and approvingly.

As to the latter, however, with its repudiation of the doctrine of the "Divine right of kings," it was evidently mystery to them—mystery in that they could not accept the principles of government *from* and *by* the people: govern*or* and govern*ee* in one and the same. Still, since my time among them, I note that their relations with Republican Powers, such as the United States, France, Mexico, and other American Republics have been most amicable. The spirit of popular sympathy —though scarcely *demos* itself—is there; in the Nobles as in the Masses. This silver cord is the very bond of their New Constitution. In that Constitution is the "Golden Bowl" of—if not a new—certainly a better life in national existence: in consonance, more, with our later times; in dawn—let us hope—of a better day —for Peace on earth! Good will to all men!

APPENDIX I

Identification of Manuscript.

Malcolm MacLeod, Q. C., 172 Wellington Street,
Ottawa, March 24, 1894.

Ranald MacDonald Esquire, Old Fort Colvile, Columbia River,

Very Dear Friend: Your's of the 13th inst. with required sketch came duly to hand; for which please accept thanks. I have, thereon, made up a nice, and, to me, interesting looking sketch. That of the Court, etc. of trial I have also filled up. The M. S. thoroughly revised, is now off to England by parcel post with accompanying letter to my good friend there, viz: Rev. H. M. Fletcher, Grasmere Co. of Westmoreland, England—a cousin (2nd) of Marquis of Lorn & intimate with many of the leading nobility of Engd. & Scotland. In my letter to him is the following for use with the publishers.

"Memo of Offer of Ranald MacDonald. M. S. (Japan) to publishers in Britain.

1. Copyright for British Empire only.
2. Copyright for British Empire and U. S. A.
3. Copyright if not to for *both* B. & U. S. author to be at liberty to sell to latter, as well as to former—each independently.

Address of author holding copyright
    Mr. Ranald MacDonald, Old Fort Colvile, Columbia River,
        Marcus P. O., Stevens County, State of Washington, U. S. A.
    Or, to his agent *ad hoc*:
    Malcolm McLeod Q. C., City of Ottawa, Ontario, Canada.
    Agent in England: Rev. H. M. Fletcher, Rectory, Grasmere Co.,
        Westmoreland, England.
    M. McLeod, Agt. for said MacDonald.

In my letter (private) to Mr. F.—as to price, I limit, to a *minimum* copyright to Br. Emp., to L100 Stg. say $500 and for *both* B: Emp. & U. S. to double that. I tell my friend we are both too poor to pay for publication. On this head I feel assured of my friend doing his best for you in the matter.

Much—if not most—will depend on his own impression from a reading of the work, but, I think, that in any case, he will try the publishers. I am aware that he is intimate—or acquainted with Mr. Murray at the head of the great publishing house of that name. On this score I leave all to him. What use he may make of the thing in the way of pushing it into notice in high quarters— the very highest—as he, spontaneously, used to do with my pamphlets and even private letter for C. P. R. & N. W. I cannot say. Possibly, even Roseberry & Co. may have their notice drawn to it, especially yr chap. V with the Quelpert Wand suggestion. I note your report as to Mrs. Haskin's failure to find a publisher. I am not surprised. You ask my advice as to Mr. Burnet's offer to look at the M. S., with a view (if advisable) of trying to find a publisher on the Pacific slope, who would take it up, on purchase, or even on his own risk. As to that—as financial matters are, there, as elsewhere in the U. S. and as such matters are conducted in the typo world of the U. S. I have, *now*, no faith. Cash on the nail—as you put it—and high at that is their motto.

At the same time, if convenient to you and Mr. Burnet, it would do no harm to show him the M. S. Candidly—with the present fast increasing antagonism between U. S. & B. I think he would consider it *too British* for American Press. In any case I would advise you to take no less than $500 ("Cash on nail") for copyright in the U. S. only. This won't interfere with present arrangements as proposed by me through Mr. Fletcher.

The British version is framed for Br. interests and sentiment.

I expect to be able to report progress in—say abt. 6 weeks. With all best wishes, in which my sisters join me. Yours ever sincerely,   Malcolm McLeod

Marcus P. O., Stev. Co., Wash., May 7, 1894.
A. D. Burnett Esqr., Spokann.
Dear Friend:

Dear Friend: Some time since Donald showed me a letter he had received from you wherein you stated with regard to my manuscript on Japan that you thought that after reading and judging of the matter it contained if of sufficient merit that there would be a chance to have it published in our immediate neighbourhood on the Pacific Slope. So I herewith forward you the M. S., also last letter from my friend Mr. Malcolm MacLeod, 172 Wellington St., Ottawa, Canada, from which you will learn what he has done, also the terms. You will please advise and what you think of it. Should there be an impossibility to do anything with it I will send stamps for the return of the M. S.

The amendments which I received at different times I stuck as you will observe for safe keeping. If I have done wrong it was with the best intentions.

The M. S. was in the hands of Mrs. Haskins of Kettle Falls with her best efforts had failed to get a publisher. Should you find anything of sufficient interest to publish you may do so. I would suggest the article about Doctor McLaughlin and my connection with Canadian Pacific Rail Road should that, or anything in the M. S. be published you would favor me much were you to send a

copy or two to Mr. MacLeod. I know he can make good use of
them to forward the interest in the Book.

I would have gone to Spokann and had a personal interview
with you long before this but I have been very unwell during the
winter and getting over it slowly, now the weather is milder.

I will expect to hear from you at your earliest convenience. I
am, yours sincerely,   Ranald MacDonald

Marcus P. O., Stev. Co., Wash., May 20, 1894.
Alex'r. D. Burnett Esquire, Review Office, Spokann.

Some time since say about the 7th May I wrote advising you
that I had sent you my M. S. on Japan.

I am not a little anxious to know whether you got it. The letter and parcel were addressed as above to the Review office. I
sincerely hope that you got it all right. I would not like to lose
it, a loss to me. Yours sincerely,   Ranald MacDonald

Marcus P. O., Stev. Co., Wash., June 15, 1894.
A. D. Burnett Esquire, Review Office, Spokann.

Dear Friend Your letter found me sixty or seventy miles up the
Kettle River on the Colville Reservation, being on a visit to a
Niece, who was left a widow and desired my immediate presence,
ever since I may say I am shut out of the world, our nearest Post
office is at Boundary Creek, British Columbia 4 miles from my
niece's Ranch which is a fine one and well stocked. Your letter
relieved me of great anxiety when I learned that you received the
precious document all right, for I had neglected to tell the person
who posted it also to register it.

Knowing the hard times, I hardly expect you will succeed in
finding a publisher. To date I have not received a line from my
friend Mr. MacLeod altho; letters may await me at Marcus.

Communication with the rest of British Columbia is open with
Boundary Creek, but with Marcus it quite different all the Bridges
and Ferry boats are either carried away or damaged. I am dear
Friend.   Ranald MacDonald

Spokane Public Library, Spokane, Wash., Jan. 16, 1913.
George W. Fuller Librarian: This manuscript was left in my
care, by Mr. A. D. Burnett, of this city. It is the property of the
heirs of Ranald MacDonald, and it is their wish, as they want to
sell it, not to allow the public to read it, without their permission.
I consider this a very valuable document. Read the article in the
Quarterly of the Oregon Historical Society, XII, 220. (Sept.
1911).   Caroline Hathaway

APPENDIX II

Authentication of Manuscript

A. A SAILOR'S ATTEMPT TO PENETRATE JAPAN

SEAMAN'S FRIEND, (Honolulu, S. I.) December 1, 1848

"There is a growing conviction throughout the civilized world that the time is rapidly approaching when the exclusive policy of the Japanese will be done away with, and a commercial intercourse be opened between that and other nations of the earth besides the French and the Dutch. Occasionally the rumor reaches us that the British East India Squadron is hovering upon the coast of Japan, but no sooner have we begun to credit the report than we learn that it is a mere rumor. The report flies around the world that an American commodore, on board a 'line of battleship', is bound for Japan. Now something will be done. The stately vessel anchors near Jeddo. Communication is attempted with the Japanese authorities. The emperor sends word to supply the 'big junk' with what she wanted, up anchor, be off and never return. All this was done in the most genteel and civil style, and what could a gallant commodore do? He had fought the British, but he must not fight the Japanese.

"While the great commercial and naval nations of the world are meditating upon some great expedition, our numerous whale ships are really doing something in the way of opening intercourse with the Japanese. The 'Manhatton' made a far more satisfactory visit to Japan than the 'Columbus.' (See Friend, Feb. 2 and Sept. 2, 1846.) During the last season for ships to cruise in the Japan sea, not scores, but hundred of vessels spread their canvas within full view of the coast. Several whale-ships have fallen in with junks, exchanged civilities with them and in some instances relieved those in distress,

"As the reading world is not likely, for some time to come, to be favored with an account of the conquest or opening of Japan by the naval forces of England, France or the United States, our readers on ship and shore may not be uninterested in the following facts and documents relating to the adventure of a sailor belonging to the American whale-ship 'Plymouth'. of Sag Harbor, Captain Edwards. If his plans were not upon so gigantic a scale as those which might emanate from a board of admiralty or a naval bureau, yet to answer his purpose they certainly indicate some head-work. It appears that a man named Ranald MacDonald shipped on board the 'Plymouth' when she sailed from the United States. After remaining in the vessel two years, while in Lahaina in the fall of 1847 he requested his discharge, unless Captain Edwards would consent to leave him the next season somewhere upon the coat of Japan. Young MacDonald is a son of Archibald MacDonald, Esq., formerly in the employ of the Hudson's Bay Company, Fort Colvile, Columbia. On application to the agent of the company in Honolulu we learned that this young man received a good education, but instead of pursuing a mercantile life on shore, betook himself to the sea. Soon after the 'Plymouth' left Lahaina, he began to make arrangements for penetrating the hermetically sealed empire of Japan. Captain Edwards allowed him to make choice of the best boat belonging to the ship. The carpenter partially decked her over. Having gathered his all together, he embarked upon his perilous and adventurous enterprise. One of his ship-mates has furnished us an extract from his journal giving an account of MacDonald's embarkation:

"Thursday at 4 o'clock this morning all hands were called, the reefs shook out, the top gallant sails were set. We had a fine breeze on our starboard beam, steering for the Tee Shee Islands. It was a beautiful morning; a light mist hung around the island, but as we neared the island we could see plainly the green covered hills. We stood in until 9 o'clock, when all hands were called and the mainyards were hove aback. We launched a boat, put water and provisions of different kinds into her. She was a centre-board boat, partly decked over and very strong for one of her kind. One of our crew was to be her only navigator. After all these things were in the boat he was towed astern by a line; two men stayed to help him trim her. After the boat was trimmed they came on board. He let go the line and was clear from us forever. His little vessel dashed over the waves like an arrow. All hands had gathered aft to see the last of the bold adventurer. He took off his hat and waved it, but in silence. The same was returned from the ship's company. Soon the order was given to brace the main yard, and the gallant ship was going in an opposite direction. From our ship's mast he was viewed with a naked eye as long as he could be seen; then the spyglass was handed from one to another, that they might have a last look at the little vessel. He was watched from the masthead until he was gone from our sight forever.

Every man on board felt sad to see a shipmate leave the ship under such circumstances. He was a good sailor, well educated, a firm mind, well calculated for the expedition upon which he had embarked. His intentions were to stay at this island and learn some of the Japanese language and from there go down to Yeddo, the principal city of Nepon, and if the English or Americans ever open trade with the Japanese, he would find employment as an interpreter. He had other intentions which I never mention only in a secret manner. The last we saw of the little vessel she was standing in for a small bay on the north side of the island.

He was a man of about five feet seven inches, thick set, straight hair and dark complexion. It was his wish to be left here and he agreed for the same before we left port a year before. He had a good voyage in the ship which he forfeited for his boat and his little cargo, such as a quadrant, epitomy, two pistols, two small kegs of water, keg of meat, barrel of bread, anchor, thirty-five fathoms of tow line and oars. His own chest was nearly full of books of various kinds. No one can blame Capt. Edwards for leaving the man in such a manner, for he advised him until his boat was launched over the side not to go on such a hazardous voyage, but no, his mind was not to be changed."

E. P. F.

The following is a copy of a pass or certificate of a discharge furnished by Capt. Edwards:

"Ship 'Plymouth,' Japan Sea, June 20, 1848.

"To Whom It May Concern: This will certify that Ranald MacDonald has been duly discharged from the ship 'Plymouth,' for the adventure to the Japan Islands, and that the boat and apparatus fairly and honestly belong to him."

L. B. EDWARDS, Master of Ship "Plymouth."

"Captain Edwards allowed us to peruse two unsealed letters which MacDonald had written to his friends, one to his father and the other to a relative with whom he had resided. They were well written epistles and bespoke a young man of good information and education. We took the liberty to copy a few lines from the letter addressed to his father which reads as follows:

"I again shipped for another Cape Horn voyage with the intention of being discharged at some of the islands or on the Spanish Main. These intentions I have altered and as Capt. Edwards was going to China and from there to the Japan sea, I thought it a good opportunity to crown my intentions, that if I went with him I would be discharged before he left the sea. He has kindly undertaken to teach me navigation—he allowed me the choice of a boat out of seven—he has also furnished me with a sail and anchor, quadrant and compass, bread, meat and water—in fact, everything to insure my reaching the shore. He tried to persuade me to give up the adventure, but I am going."

Everyone who reads the account of MacDonald's adventure will no doubt be anxious to learn the fate which attends him. The letter to his father closes with an emphatic . . . We can furnish only a single item of intelligence to fill up that blank. Some days after his embarkation, while the ship 'Uncas' was cruising in that region, she picked up the rudder of his tiny craft which we will venture to name the 'Young Plymouth'. Whether she reached the shore or was swamped in the surf remains a profound mystery. We shall not fail to make all necessary inquiries, when ships return after the next Japan season; and hence, should any cruisers on that coast gather the least intelligence of the young MacDonald's weal or woe, they will do us a favor and perhaps relieve the minds of anxious parents and friends. Oh that the same unseen hand which conducted the 'Mayflower to the rock of Plymouth might now conduct the 'Young Plymouth' and preserve the life of her adventurous commander! Who does not fervently hope that a successful issue may crown the bold, daring and hazardous enterprise of Ranald MacDonald, an adventurer in the Japan Sea.

In *The Seamen's Friend* of October 1, 1849, we find the following related to Ranald MacDonald:

"We will now furnish some facts relating to that American who was none other than Ranald MacDonald. It may be recollected by some of our readers that this young man left the American whaleship 'Plymouth' and was furnished with boat, sextant, compass, etc., by Capt. Edwards. On landing he intentionally capsized his boat and was kindly received by the Japanese. After being on shore eight days he was taken under the charge of four Matsmai officers. At Matsmai he was imprisoned from the 6th day of September until about the first day of October. Subsequently he was removed to Nagasaki and brought before the governor in the town hall. On entering he saw upon the pavement a crucifix and an image of the Virgin Mary, and the Savior when an infant. He was compelled to tread on these when he entered with the crowd into the town hall. Then he was questioned in regard to his coming to Japan and whether he believed in the God of Heaven. To which he replied that he did. He was given to understand that the images he had trampel upon was the devil of Japan. During his imprisonment he had several scholars among the Japanese interpreters which doubtless contributed to the kind treatment which he generally received. MacDonald for the first time met the other captives on the 26th day of March at the town hall, although they had been prisoners for months in the same city.

"Knowledge that these young men were imprisoned in Japan led Commodore Geisenger, Commander of the East India U. S. Squadron, to dispatch the 'Preble,' Commander Glynn, for their rescue. This vessel arrived in the Japanese waters about the first of April. On her approach, Japanese officers warned her commander off, but he pushed forward and came to anchor near the city of Nagasaki, where the prisoners were in confinement. The report of the 'Preble's' guns inspired hope in their bosoms, although the Japanese evidently designed to keep from them all knowledge that an American man-of-war was in port. McCoy reports that he had threatened the Japanese with the visit of such a vessel if he was not treated better, but they only laughed at his threats. They hold foreigners in supreme contempt.

"Several interviews were held between Commander Glynn and the authorities. The Japanese evidently intended to evade any direct communication between the commander of the 'Preble' and the Emperor. He was put off from day to day and given to understand that 'by and by he might expect to have the business attended to.' The prompt and decisive action of Commander Glynn seemed to infuse some new ideas into the minds of the Japanese. He distinctively told them the object of his visit and if the Japanese authorities were determined not to surrender the prisoners, that he should leave immediately and report to his superior officer. A time was appointed for their delivery, but if they were not forthcoming the 'Preble' would sail. Before the time had elapsed they were delivered over to the Dutch merchants and transferred to the 'Preble.'

"During their captivity these young men gathered much interesting information respecting the country and Japanese government. MacDonald, but more especially McCoy, succeeded in acquiring a tolerable knowledge of the colloquial Japanese language. We hope that ere long a more full report of these young men will be spread before the world, together with the visit of the 'Preble.' It opens a new chapter in the intercourse of foreigners with the exclusive Japanese.

"The 'Preble' returned to China where the Americans were left to be sent to the United States, but the Sandwich Islanders were brought to Honoluly.

"In our next we intend giving some account of the Loo Chooans and the visit of the 'Preble.' "

A further article in *The Seaman's Friend* of December 20, 1849, mentions MacDonald.

B. EXTRACTS FROM OFFICIAL JAPANESE RECORDS.

Entries in the *"Memoranda of the foreigners forwarded to Nagasaki and their escorts"*.

On the second day of the sixth month of the same year (the first year of Kaei, i.e. July 2, 1848) a foreigner landed at Notsuka in Rishiri Island; on the twenty-fifth day of the seventh month (August 23) he was forwarded in a *fune* (Japanese junk) from Soya (to Esashi).

The name and the age of the foreigner and the escort are as follows:

Makiton, about 23 years of age, 5 *shaku* 7 *sun* 5 *bu* (about 5 feet 8½ inches) high.

The escort in the *fune*:

(*Samurai*)	Togoro Shinagawa
(Superintendent of foot-*samurai*)	Kujuzo Oba
(Foot-*samurai*)	Kumanojo Taketa
(Physician)	Yoseki Kakizaki
(Soldier)	Tokusaburo Kawasaki
(Soldier)	Zenji Shibayama
(Soldier)	Teikichi Shimizu

As the *fune* arrived at this town (Matsumae) the foreigner was forwarded in a *kago* (Japanese Palanquin) to the village of Eramchi. The escort were:

(Captain of a company)—Katoda Araida with five foot samurai, ten soldiers and Kujuzo Oba (superintendent).

The escort in the village of Eramachi were:

(Captain of a company)—Gorogoro Imai.
(*Samurai*)—Shunzo Nakashima, Zenji Shimura, Matsugoro Kubota.

In place of Zenji during his illness.

Superintendent of foot-*samurai*—Eijiro Yokoi.

Foot-*samurai*—Kozo Tahara.   Asaichiro Kamada.   In place of Kozo during his illness.   Mineji Okumura.

Foremen—Matasaburo Mikami, Bangoro Ono.

Soldiers—Nesaburo Sasamori, Yokichi Kakemura, Tettaro Takahashi, Kotaro Amamoto.

Purveyor's assistant—Renzo Ito, with one soldier.

Two secretaries who asked to serve in turn—Tokusaburo Yoneda, Tokubei Yamada.

The foreigner was forwarded to Nagasaki in the "Tenjinmaru" and the escort were:

Captain of a Company—Tan-emon Ujiye.
Superintendent—Bansaku Murata.
Superintendents of foot-*samurai*—Nazaemon Saito, Katsugoro Nagae.
Samurai—Kyogoro Tamura.
Physician—Hosai Tani.
Foremen—Koji Yamamoto, Hyotaro Miyamoto.
Soldiers—Tatsuyemon Tamura, Wajiro Mori, Kyusaku Sato, Zengoro Honda, Kintrao Ikeda, Rokusaburo Yoshida.

The escort on the shore on the foreigner sailing from the port were:

Tatsunoshin Wada, Eitaro Murakami, Teita Etagaki, Tsunetaro Murayama, Renjiro Makita, Gonzaburo Tsuji, with six soldiers.[301]

Report to the Shogun's government from Shima-no-kami, *Daimyo* of Matsumae and Yezo.   Matsumae, July 22, 1848.

On the 2nd inst. about the hour of ape (4 p. m.) a foreigner was driven in a boat to the shore of Notsuka in Rishiri Island in my domain of Western Yezo.   As he had wet clothes on and seemed very tired, he was immediately taken to the guard-house at Notsuka and given food, etc.   On being informed of the event some of my retainers at the Guards station of Soya went to Notsuka and tried to get information (from the foreigner).   As, however, they could not understand each other the questions were put by signs and the foreigner also answered by signs, so that the precise facts could not be ascertained, but he was understood to say that he left the mothership alone in the boat and after some time the wind and the sea getting high his boat capsized twice; that his compass dropped into the sea and he was drifting aimlessly when he saw a high mountain and rowing towards it

---

300 The *"Memoranda"* from which the above entries are taken is a manuscript from the archives of the *Daimyo* of Matsumae and Yezo.

landed on the shore. As the boat had suffered[301] no damage he was told by signs to sail home, but he seemed to hesitate to go out into the wide sea in that small boat. He was therefore told by signs that he would be allowed to stay and as he nodded assent he was taken to the guards station of Soya and was well treated and escorted. The preceding is the report of my retainers at the station:

According to the report the boat in which the foreigner came is about 4½ *ken* (26 feet 9½ inches) long and about 6 *shaku* (5 feet 11½ inches) broad. The boat and all the gear are kept in the station. They have also sent the appended list of articles in his possession. I inform you of the above and wish to know what is to be done with this foreigner.

On the 22nd day of the 6th month, Matsumae, Shima-no-kami.

Draft of instructions affixed (to the above report.)

The foreigner whose landing is here reported ought to be examined at Nagasaki. He should, therefore, be forwarded to that place as you did with the foreigners who arrived some time ago. All the books in the foreigner's possession should be put under seals in presence of your officials and care taken that no one should see them without leave.

The articles in the foreigner's possesson are as follows:

One small firearm, about 4 *sun* 5 *bu* (5 1-3 inches) long and the diameter of the muzzle about 3 *bu* (one-third inch).

One boat, about 4½ *ken* (26 feet 9½ inches) long, about 6 *shaku* (5 feet 11½ inches) broad at the widest part and about 3 *shaku* (3 feet) deep.

One mast, about 2½ *ken* (14 feet 11 inches).

One sail, of white cotton cloth.

One oar.

One article like the handle of a rudder, about 5 *shaku* (4 feet 11½ inches) long.

Two ropes, of which one is about 50 fathoms long and the other 6 fathoms long.

One article like an anchor.

One article like a buoy for an anchor.

Two water casks.

One bag with all sorts of clothings.

One cask containing animal flesh.

Twenty-three large and small books with covers.

Fifteen books without covers.

One bundle of different kinds of books.

One map of the world.

One box containing an article like a telescope.

---

[301] The materials contained in the following pages, are taken from the *"Tsuko-ichiran"* (collection of documents relating to foreign relations), 2nd series.

One leather hat.
A kind of dagger.
A kind of knife.
A kind of flint.
Two articles like round chisels, one large, one small.
A kind of pincers.
A kind of spear.
One article like the cover of a kettle.
A kind of pot with a silver chased cover.
A kind of copper ladle.
A kind of borer.
A kind of comb-brush.
A kind of comb.
Two balls of white cotton thread.
One article like tusk.
One packet of sulphur.
Two balls of pine resin, large and small.
One ball of pitch.
A little tobacco.
A kind of spectacles.
A kind of candle-stick, silver colored.
One small box with lock.
One varnished board.
A kind of mat.
A kind of broom.
A pair of boots.
The articles are as given above.

A letter from the officials of the *Daiymo* of Matsumae and Yezo at Yedo to the Shogun's government requesting instructions.

August 9, 1848.

Concerning the foreigner detained at the guards station of Soya, about whom our master Shima-no-kami has sent a report. As it is a little more than 190 *ri* (1 Japanese mile equals 2½ miles) from Matsumae to that place and as every year the sea becomes gradually rough after the 210th day (from the 1st of the 1st month; on this day frequently occurs typhoons) and the voyage is stopped and as also the place is very cold two of the soldiers (stationed there) go to winter at Mashike and the remaining officers of the station return to Matsumae every year in the end of autumn. If the foreigner is taken to Ishikari, a little more than 113 *ri* distant there will be no difficulty even in autumn and winter. It might seem too presumptuous on our part, but if he is likely to be forwarded to Nagasaki it will be possible to make a voyage early next spring if he is taken to Esashi. We should prefer to take him to Esashi if that is permissible. As it concerns a place which is very distant and whence the sea must be crossed we take liberty to request your instructions in order to notify our master at his residential town.

On the 11th day of the 7th month.

Orders given on the 19th day of the same month. (August 17.)

The drifted foreigner mentioned in your letter should be first taken to Esashi and forwarded to Nagasaki at the earliest convenience.

(Extract from the "*Nagasaki Kiji*," (Record of Nagasaki.)

On the 2nd day of the 6th month of the 1st year of Kaei a foreigner drifted in a boat to the shore of Notsuka in Rishiri Island in Western Yezo governed by Shima-no-kami of Matsumae,

The news reached the residential town of the *Daimyo* on the 22nd of the same month and on the same day a report was sent to Yedo. On the 11th day of the 7th month of the same year they requested instructions of Abe, Ise-no-kami, (member of the Shogun's cabinet) and Shima-no-kami was told to send the foreigner to Nagasaki, treating him as the foreigners of some time ago. Ise-no-kami informed Inaba Dewa-no-kami, (governor of Nagasaki) resident at Yedo of this order. The latter accordingly sent a notice to Ido, Tsushima-no-kami, (governor of Nagasaki) resident at Nagasaki.

Report to the Shogun's government from Shima-no-kami, Daimyo of Matsumae and Yezo. Matsumae, October 2, 1848.

The foreigner who landed at Notsuka in Rishiri Island and concerning whom you instructed me on the 19th day of the 7th month sailed from Eramchi for Nagasaki yesterday the 5th inst. (Oct. 1), the wind being favorable. As my retainers sent there informed me of the fact, I hasten to report the same.

On the 6th day of the 9th month. Matsumae, Shima-no-kami.

As you instructed me to take the foreigner mentioned in the other report first to Esashi and at the earliest opportunity to forward him to Nagasaki, I sent an express messenger to the guards station at Soya with the necessary orders. The foreigner accordingly sailed from that place on the 26th day of the 7th month (August 24), but as the wind was not good the *fune* came to the road of this town on the 10th of last month (September 7). The *fune* ought to have gone to Esashi, but the wind not being favorable it had to put into the port of Eramachi. While waiting for a favorable wind at that port preparations for the voyage (to Nagasaki) were finished and he sailed yesterday. I mention this fact as it was not the place in your instructions.

On the 6th day of the 9th month. Matsumae, Shima-no-kami.

Report from the resident officials of the Daimyo of Matsumae and Yezo to the Shogun's government. Yedo, November 7, 1848.

The foreigner, who landed at Notsuka in Rishiri Island and concerning whom you gave instructions on the 19th day of the 7th month, was forwarded to Nagasaki. The officers who accompanied him there have notified us by an express messenger that without any accident during the voyage he arrived in safety (at Nagasaki) on the 15th of last month (September 12) and that on the 17th of the same month (September 14) Ido, Tsushima-no-kami, received the foreigner in charge at his own office. Although Shima-no-kami, who is now in his residential town, will report on hearing the news we hasten to inform you of this.

On the 12th day of the 10th month.

Report, from Shima-no-kami, to the Shogun's government.

Matsumae, December 8, 1848.

As my officials have already reported to you the foreigner, who drifted to Notsuka in Rishiri Island and concerning whom you instructed me on the 19th day of the 7th month, was forwarded to Nagasaki. Without any accident during the voyage the foreigner arrived (at Nagasaki) on the 15th day of the 9th month and on the 17th of the same month Ido, Tsushima-no-kami, received him in charge. This is to report the said fact.

On the 13th day of the 11th month. Matsumae, Shima-no-kami.

Extract from the "*Nagasaki Tomegaki*", (Nagasaki notes).

Ranarudo Makudonaruto, fisherman of Canada, 24 years old, has been received in charge.

He said that there was no god nor Buddha. He cultivated his heart and will and worshipped heaven in order to get clear understanding and enjoy happiness. He has nothing else to repeat.

C. EXTRACTS FROM OFFICIAL AMERICAN RECORDS.

Contemporary deposition of Ranald MacDonald.[302]

Before me, James Glynn, commandinig the United States ship "Preble," personally appeared, this 30th day of April, 1849, Ranald MacDonald, who, being duly sworn, deposes as follows:

I was born at Astoria, in Oregon; I am twenty-four years of age. I shipped at Sag harbor in the whale ship "Plymouth," Captain Edwards, on a whaling voyage, on the second day of December, 1845. Being off the island of Japan, I left the ship at my own desire, agreeably to a previous understanding with the captain. He was to furnish me with a boat,

---

[302] U. S. Senate, *Executive Docket*, 32nd congress, 1st session, No. 59, pp 25-28.

etc., and drop me off the coast of Japan, under favorable circumstances for reaching the shore.

Ranald MacDonald further deposes that on the 28th day of June, 1848, after losing sight of the "Plymouth," I hauled on the wind, standing to the northward and eastward for the land. In entering a bay I observed some rocks ahead. I endeavored to tack, but failed. I then wore to the southward and westward, just clearing the rocks. I kept on the wind until I cleared them. I then ran free to the northward and westward, standing for the opposite side of the bay. I passed through a channel in the reef, and anchored under a shelter, where I tried my pistols by shooting a sea-lion. I then got under way, and stood for the bottom of the bay, where I landed, having understood from the captain that it was inhabited; but finding no inhabitants I made an experiment of a premeditated design, which was to see if I could capsize my boat and right her again. In this I succeeded to my satisfaction. I then ascended the heights to take another look at the ship. With a view to lengthening my absence from the ship, I remained two nights in this bay. In the meantime I made an excursion into the interior, but I saw nothing of interest.

That knowing there were inhabitants on the island of Timoshee (or Dessey of the Japanese) about ten miles distant, I put to sea on the third day to go there, with a view of representing myself as destitute.

That between the two islands, about ten o'clock in the morning, I turned out the reef in my sail, capsizing my boat intentionally, making no effort to save anything but my chest, which I wanted for ballast, and for trimming my boat. My rudder was let go also. Unstepped my mast, righted my boat, re-stepped my mast, set my sail, and stood towards the land. I saw a vessel that day about six p. m., to the northward. That night I spent in the boat, lying off and on. Next morning early I approached the land, and was becalmed. I first discovered smoke, and when day broke, saw some natives launching a boat. They came towards me, within a hundred yards. On my beckoning they approached me timidly, and I jumped into their boat, fastening the painter of my boat to theirs, and made signs to go ashore.

On my landing they took hold of my wrists, one on each side, in a gentle manner, put sandals on my feet, and led me to a house. Here a breakfast was provided for me in their best manner; and they also gave me dry clothes. I remained in this house eight days, when four Matsmai officers arrived from Soya. These officers took me to the capital of the island situated on the seashore, to the northward and westward. There I was imprisoned. At first my apartment was quite small; but on my remonstrating, they enlarged it by moving the partitions.

After remaining here thirty days, an officer arrived, and took me to a town called Soya, on the island of Yesso, distant about twenty-five miles. I was placed in prison in Soya, and remained there about fifteen days, waiting for a junk, which I was secretly told they expected from Matsmai. This vessel not arriving, I was placed in a small boat, and after a day's journey met a junk, and was taken back to Soya, where I was delayed four or five days longer; after which I was put on board this junk and sent to Matsmai. On the passage, stopped to get wood and water. On board this vessel I was permitted to go about abaft the mast. I arrived at Matsmai, after a passage of fifteen days, on the sixth of September. Here they put me in confinement, where I remained until the first of October. Whilst here I learned that I had been preceded by other fifteen Americans, who had made attempts to escape. Here they gave me sweetmeats, and in all other respects treated me kindly. I was given a rude spoon, which had been manufactured and left by one of the party of fifteen Americans who had been imprisoned here before me. On the first of October I left in another junk for Nangasacki; arrived at Nangasacki on the 15th; remained on board two days, and landed on the 17th. I was taken, in the first place, to a small enclosure adjoining the town hall. Here I was met by an interpreter, (Morreama Einaska), who told me that in front of the first door of the town-house I would see an image, and to put my foot on it, telling me that this image was the "devil of Japan." In passing the door I put my foot on it, but was not able to see it clearly, in consequence of the crowd, who pressed me forward. It appeared to be a metallic plate, of about a foot in diameter, on which I thought I could see a representation of the Virgin and Infant Saviour. In the town-house I was requested to kneel, after the Japanese fashion, upon a mat. I attempted one knee, but they insisted upon my getting down on both knees; which I finally assented to. Soon after this I heard a *hissing* noise, and was told by the interpreter that the governor was coming, and that I must make "compliments to him;" which was to bend low, and not look up. I made a low bow to the governor, though not before I had taken a look at him.

The Japanese inquired my name, my place of birth, and port from whence I sailed, and my place of residence. I answered them Oregon, New York and Canada, with the hope that in the event of an American or English vessel arriving here, either of them would taken an interest in me, and that I might be restored to my own liberty, and for the opportunity of giving information to the people of the United States that some of their countrymen were imprisoned in Japan, and in all probability would remain in prison for life. They then inquired the name of the ship I had left, the name of her captain, and my reasons or motives for leaving the ship. I told them I had some difficulty with the captain. They finally asked me "if I believed there was a God in Heaven." I answered, yes; that I believed in the "Father, Son and Holy Ghost, and in our Lord and Saviour Jesus Christ." I was then told that I had permission to leave the hall; and I was then taken in a *cago,* attended by a number of soldiers, to my prison, which I was told was a sort of temple or priest's house. I remained in this prison up to the present time. During this time I was taken to the town-hall twice, and also questioned on several occasions at my prison. The day after being put in this prison I asked for my books, particularly my Bible. The interpreter told me, with a good deal of fervor or interest, "not to speak of the Bible in Japan; it was not a good book." During these interviews the object of their questions appeared to be to ascertain if I had any influential friends at home who would seek for me. If I had, they would send me away; if I had none, then they would imprison me for life in Japan.

About the seventeenth day of April I heard signal guns. (About three months before, I was told that when the Dutch ship, or any ship appeared approaching the coast, the guns would be fired.) I was told by my guard, secretly, that these guns announced the approach of a yearly Dutch ship, and they were also fired to call in the troops from the neighboring towns and districts. On this occasion there were fired six guns; two were in close succession, being repeated at longer intervals. In the hands of the same soldiers, the next morning, I saw sheets of paper, with writing on, which did not appear to be a letter. On inquiry, he told me it was a list of soldiers who had arrived at Nangasacki from the neighboring cities. The number he gave me was "three thousand five hundred and four." I asked how many soldiers there were in Nangasacki on ordinary occasions. He said that the ordinary number was six hundred and fifty; but on this occasion he thought there were about six thousand, besides an unknown number of attendants or followers—an extraordinary force.

On the afternoon of the 24th, the chief "Serai Tatsnosen," accompanied by the interpreter, "Morreama Einaska," came to me in my prison, and told me that as a new governor and a number of gentlemen had arrived from Yedo, they had concluded to send me to the Dutch factory. After a while, they asked me if I knew the reason of this. I replied, "No." Then they told me that a vessel had arrived from my country. As I had hailed from three different countries, I asked if the ship was from Oregon; that having been assigned as the place of my birth. They said "No, from New York." I told them that was the place I sailed from. From thence I was taken to the Dutch factory at Decima, and delivered over to the Dutch superintendent of trade, where I was kindly treated. The superintendent sent me to the ship. I have heard other cannon fired before the arrival of the "Preble," which I suppose was a salute on the arrival of the winter fleet of Chinese junks. I was told there were five cannon in Soya, but I never saw any except those I saw on coming from Nangasacki. The troops that I have seen in Japan were clothed in a coat of mail, with hats of paper, japanned, broad-rimmed, low-crowned, and fitting close to the head. These hats did not appear to be worn for defense. They were armed with two swords, and, in addition to these, with bows and arrows, and also with match-locks, (the ignited match being carried at the waist.) I never saw any mounted cavalry, but heard of such being in the country. The match-locks were with very short breeches to the stock, which was brought against the cheek in firing, as shown to me by one of the soldiers. In firing, they kneel upon the right knee, throwing the left foot forward, keeping both eyes wide open.

The common people appeared to be amiable and friendly, but the government agents were the reverse.

During my imprisonment I had a number of scholars among the Japanese interpreters, which probably procured me more kindness than I would have otherwise met with. Morreama speaks better English than any of the Japanese I heard attempt it. Two or three of the other interpreters speak a little English. I was told that there was an abundance of mineral coal in Japan, and some not far from Nangasacki.

That I was fully under the impression that the fifteen men, whoever they might be, who had preceded me from Matsmai, were still in Japan, and doomed to perpetual imprisonment; and that I believed that their liberation depended entirely upon the success of my efforts to return to civilization, and send them relief.

Upon the arrival of the ship there appeared to be a general excitement among the government agents. On the morning of the 26th of April, the interpreter came to my prison, and exhibited a letter, translated into English, purporting to be a communication to the commanding officer of the "Preble," requiring him to leave the harbor of Nangasacki, on the reception of the fifteen men.

The interpreter wished me to give him the relative rank of the captain of the ship, by counting in the order of succession from the highest chief in the United States. First, I gave the people, which they could not comprehend, then the President of the United States, the Secretary of the Navy, commodore, post captain, and commander. This rank appeared to be sufficiently elevated to excite their surprise.

RANALD MACDONALD.

Sworn and subscribed before me, this 30th day of April, 1849.

JAMES GLYNN,
Commanding the U. S. ship "Preble."

Narrative of the shipwrecked seamen in Japan, as furnished by the Japanese authorities at Nagasaki. Presented to Commander James Glynn by Mr. Bassle, on the 25th day of April, 1849, and orally translated by him. (The original is written in Japanese Dutch.)[303]

Fifteen men from an American whale ship, said to be wrecked near Matsmai. As customary, the men were taken into the custody of Japanese officers, and the edict of the Emperor orders that all foreigners shall be taken to Nangasacki; and these men were accordingly placed on board a vessel and transported to that place. (This paragraph was supplied by me.)

At Matsmai they were placed in confinement. John Bawl and Robert McCoy escaped by breaking through a water-closet. They ran into the mountains, but, after a short time, were recaptured.

John Martin and Robert McCoy afterwards made a successful attempt to run, by breaking through the roof of the house. They were retaken.

These three men, John Martin, Robert McCoy and John Bawl, were then placed in a boat by themselves. They afterwards asked forgiveness. It was granted on their promise to behave better. They were then restored to their companions.

On the 27th day of August Robert McCoy again escaped by breaking through the side of the house. He was retaken and put in solitary confinement. He was questioned as to his reasons for running away, and his reply was well received by the governor. He was again cautioned as to his conduct, pardoned, and placed with his companions. At this time all the men were warned to keep still and to behave properly.

Their wants were supplied. The superintendent wrote a letter to the Americans, requesting that they would keep quiet, and show a proper behaviour towards those who had them in charge. The men replied in English, promising that they would behave themselves.

On the 18th day of October, John Bawl, Robert McCoy and Jacob Boyd escaped, by burning through the floor. They were retaken, being discovered in a farmer's house. They were questioned, but the reasons they gave proved unsatisfactory. They begged to be forgiven; it was again granted. But they were separated from their companions.

The men gave so much trouble that the Japanese authorities scarcely knew what course to pursue towards them.

Sick.—Makea was taken sick with a fever on the evening of the 6th

---

303 U. S. Senate, *Executive Docket*, 32nd Congress, 1st session, No. 59, pp. 38-39.

of August, 1848, and received medical advice.

Robert McCoy was seized with a pain in his stomach on the 19th of August, and received medical advice.

Makea, James Hall, Manna and Steam took cold on the 19th of August and received medical advice.

John Martin, on the 19th of August, was seized with a pain in his teeth, and by fever. He was given medicine.

Maury and Hiram, on the 20th of August, were attacked with cold, and received medical advice.

John Waters, on the 1st of October, was atacked by fever, and seized with cramps in the stomach. He got well by the use of medicines.

Steam, on the 4th of October, was attacked by cold and swelling of the face. He recovered of this, and was afterwards seized with a cough, and threw up much phlegm. He got well by using medicines.

Jacob Boyd, on the 25th of January, was taken sick with a pain in his stomach. He recovered.

John Bawl, on the 8th of January, was seized with a pain and swelling of the face. He recovered. He was afterwards taken with the same kind of disease, but used medicine and got well.

John Waters, on the 5th of January, was taken with a cold, but recovered.

Melcher Biffar was seized with a pain in the face on the 19th of March.

James Hall was seized with a similar pain on the 24th of March. These two men have been under medical treatment ever since, and are yet upon the sick list.

Henry Barker and Jack have not been sick.

Ranald MacDonald (the sixteenth man) has never complained of being ill.

Deaths.—Maury committed suicide by hanging himself on the night of the 12th of November, whilst his companions were asleep. This statement was made by the men to the officers, who instituted an inquiry into the cause of Maury's death. His associates begged and obtained permission to bury him.

Ezra Goldthwait and James Hall, on the 16th of December, were both seized with a swelling of the face. They recovered of this; but on the 21st of December Goldthwait was taken down with a fever. He had medical advice and attendance; but became worse and worse, and on the 1st of January died. His companions asked and were given permission to bury him.

The narrative concludes by stating that the wants of the above men have been at all times supplied them by the government of Nagasaki, as is well known to Mr. Levyssohn.

APPENDIX III

GLOSSARY OF ENGLISH AND JAPANESE WORDS, FROM
COPY IN THE PROVINCIAL LIBRARY, VICTORIA, B. C.,
ARRANGED BY MALCOLM McLEOD FROM ORIGINAL
NOTES OF RANALD MACDONALD.

The following glossary is inserted to permit the curious reader
an opportunity to judge our author's aptitude and success in learning something of the Japanese language. The glossary has neither
philological value or accuracy, as our author's hasty autograph
notes are hard to decipher, and neither the late Malcolm McLeod
who compiled the glossary from the notes, or the Amercan
editor who is responsible for their appearance here had any fitness for the tasks they assumed.

Prior to the restoration, the language of Kyoto, the ancient
capital of Japan, was considered the standard of language, and of
highest authority, but since the restoration and the removal of the
capital to Tokyo, the dialect of the latter place has taken pre-
cedence. Other dialetical differences are numerous and the language abounds in provincialisms and vulgarities: moreover in
many Japanese provinces the pronunciation is so varied that it was
a very difficult task for an uneducated person speaking only one
local dialect to make himself thoroughly understood by another
native speaking an entirely different dialect. It should also be
borne in mind that our author, even in his limited intercourse
with the Japanese people, doubtless heard and noted down a number of provincialisms, which in his phonetic rendering are now
well nigh unintelligible. Since MacDonald's time, through the introduction of a standard system of schools and Japanese text
books, the Japenese language has become standardized. Many
words in use at the time of MacDonald's visit are now obsolete.
Notwithstanding all this, a glance through the following pages
will disclose that a high percentage of the words, so imperfectly,
transcribed from Mr. MacDonald's notes are either identical with,
or closely approximate the present standard Japanese word.

A

English	MacDonald's Japanese	Standard or Recognized Japanese
Admiral	Fene Tajo	Suishi teitoku
Adultery	Metano	Kantsu
African	O'shaka	Afurikajin
Again	Mena	Mata
Anchor	Ekat	Ikari

English	MacDonald's Japanese	Standard or Recognized Japanese
Ankle	Asnoko	Ashi-kubi
Angry	Nakin (or) Negur	Ikaru
Apron	Hakama	Maekake
Arms	Oude	Ude
Arrive	Ketaru (or) Kista	Itaru
Arrow	Yaa	Ya
Ashes	Hie (or) hae	Hai
Aunt	Oba	Oba
Autumn (next)	Ake	Aki
Awake (or get up!)	Okaro	Okiru

B

English	MacDonald's Japanese	Standard or Recognized Japanese
Bad	Warka Waree placed after noun, Tremara, not good.	Warui
Back	Senaka and Tamasha	Senaka
Barley	Mogi	O-mugi
Bathe (to)	You or Me	Yuami, Yu
Bay	Ere	Irie
Beans (Dumpling of ground beans)	Tove	To-fu
Bear	Koma	Kuma
Bed	Feto or Ftone (quilt)	Futon
Beef	Cos	Gyu-niku
Beginning	Hagemii	Hajime
Belly	Harra	Hara
Belly, to cut the	Shepuk, and Harra Kari	Seppuku
Belt	Obea	Obi
Bite	Kweetsko and Fconouku	Kamu
Black	Kufraka	Kuroki
Blacksmith	Caggy	Kajiya
Blind	Momoka	Mo-moku
Blood	Tse	Chi
Boat	Funa	Fune
Boatswain	Soefo Kasera	
Body	Kanaa	Karada
Boil	Taquiru	Nie tatsu
Book	Hone	Hon
Bow (to)	Orae	Soru
Bow, a	Yomme	Yumi
Bow, string	Yomme tsure	Yumi-zuru
Breakfast	Assahan	Asahan
Breast	Mony	Mune
Breathe (to)	Ekee	Iki

Heru shiar	day(light)	Sno or Coneye	To day
Yousii	night	Kino	Yesterday
Ussa	morning	Usta or Munige	Tomorow
Yomobee	last night	Omoroka	Entertaining
Comban	this evening	Warro	laugh
Eets	When	Regur-hakion	Angry
Nande	What	Ootso	Strike & hit
Doconee	Why	Wagshash	dagger
Douka	Who	Catano	Sword & Sabe
Buich	Which	Uamaso	Sham or lie
doa	How	Sta	Tung
Aku	Sunshine	Sta	Under
Kerkomatink	Fine day	We i	High
Hanaso	to tell	Geesing	Earthquake
Kotoba	Speak	Come mare	Thunder
Warka	Bad	Noor	Sleep
Youka	Good	Okeeroo	Awake
Ftuska	large	Nakoo	weep
Oke	Great	Gosashse	Sorry
Comaka	Small	Watakuyshe	Me
Tsesa	little	Anata	You
Tucksan	Plenty	Mumoruf	Ignorent
Oka	a Great deal	Baka	fool
Epe Epe	Full	Oboye	Memory
Otoka	presently	Oboyewary	Bad memory
Otakra	by & by		

Photographic copy of a page of MacDonald's glossary of English-Japanese words

From his original notes made in Japan, 1848-1849, now in the Provincial Library, Victoria, B. C.

English	MacDonald's Japanese	Standard or Recognized Japanese
Bride	Hanayoume	Hana-yome
Bridegroom	Hanamko	Hana-muko
Bring (back)	Motoqua	Motte Kaeru
Bridge	Bas	Hashi
Broke	Otshewan	Kowareta
Brother	Qudae	Otoko Kyodai
Bugler	Yamabush	Yamabushi
Burn	Yokedo	Yaketo
By and By	O-tagkra	Imani
By and By warm	O-tagki atse	Sugu Atsukunaru

C

English	MacDonald's Japanese	Standard or Recognized Japanese
Cabbage (Pickled)	Tagana	Tamana
Calm	Nage	Nagu, Nagi
Candlestick	Shockudie	Shokudai
Capital, The Sacred of Japan	Meyako	Miyako
Capital, The Secular of Japan	Ieddo (Yeddo)	Edo
Captain (Chief)	Tajo	Taicho or Taii
Card-visiting	Nafda	Nafuda
Carpenter	Dicku	Daiku
Carry	Catsu, or	Hakobo
	fenow (on shoulder)	Katsugu
	(on back)	Seou
Cat	Nekoe	Neko
Catch	Tsecam	Tsukamu
Change	Kawaro	Kawaru
Charcoal	Some	Sumi
Cheap	Yaska	Yasni
Cheeks	Hoe	Ho or Hoho
Chin	Agi or Ake	Ago
Chopsticks	Hass	Hasui
Clean	Kerce or Kreen	Kirei na
Christ-Jesus	Kibac Kogin	Kirisuto, or Yaso Kurisuto
Colonel	T Kusho	Taisa
Come	Kivo	Kiyo
		Kuro
Come here	Kistamii	Kitamae
Compass	Holly, and	Rashinban
	Hare	Hobari
Compliments	Urosu	Okurimono
Cook	Yaking	Taku, Ryo-rinin
Cover (to)	Feta-suru	Feta-suru
Cover (to) un(cover)	Fta toru	Futatoru
Coverlet	Conotnak	Yagu
Cup	Wan	Wan
Cut (to)	Kure or Korri	Kiru

D

English	MacDonald's Japanese	Standard or Recognized Japanese
Dagger	Wagsash	Tanto
Dance	Odoo	Odoru, buto
Dark	Katraka	Kurai
Darkness	Yeen	Ankoru
Daughter	Musme and Gosokujo	Musume
Day	Shear, and Heru	Hiru
Day, to	Quo, or Conege	Kyo Kon-nichi
Day yester	Kino	Kino
Day fine	Koekonatink	Yokitenki
Deliver (to)	Sane	Watasu
Dear Me!	Narhodu!	Oyama
Devil	Oneye	Oni
Different affair	Fseaury	Betsuji
Dig	Hor	Horu
Dinner	Shearhan	Hiruhan
Dirty	Eswashy	Kitanai
Dog	Yeegan	Inu
Dragoon	Ma (horse)—Oyakoonu (soldier)	Ryu-kihei
Drink	Nonɩ	Nomu
Drummer	Kinwoche	Taiko-uchi
Duck-Tame	Aheer	Ahiru
Duck-Wild	Kamo	Kamo
Duke	Kakush	Koshaku

E

English	MacDonald's Japanese	Standard or Recognized Japanese
Ears	Memee	Mimi
Earthquake	Geesing	Jishin
Eat	Mesagaro	Taberu
Eight	Hatch and Yoka Yoka (days)	Hachi Yoka
Eighteen	Ju hatoinai and Ju Hatch	Juhachi-ban (18th) Juhachi
Elbow	Hege	Hiji
Eldest (born of woman)	Ane (daughter)	Ane
Eleven	Ju itch Ju estinge	Juichi
Emperor, before division	Quoto Mikado	Kotei Mikado
Emperor, Spiritual	Dairi	
Emperor, Temporal	Kobo. Ziogoun	Sho-gun
Empress	Neotae	Nyo-tei, Ko-go
Ensign	Hatakasra	Hata jirushi
Entertaining	Omosroka	Omoshiroki
Entertaining—days for	Mokash	Asubihi

English	MacDonald's Japanese	Standard or Recognized Japanese
Evening-this	Conban	Komban
Eyebrows	Unegie	Mayu-ge
Eyes	Mea	Me

F

English	MacDonald's Japanese	Standard or Recognized Japanese
Face	Cow	Kao
Farewell	Sinara	Sayonara
Fast-quick	Eiaka (Highaka)	Hayaku
Father	Weyage	Chichi, Teteoya
Fifteen	Ju-jwonge or Jugo	Jugo
Fight (to) with both hands	Netoe	Sumo
Fingers	Yonbe	Yubi
Fire place	Shevals	Irori
Fish	Sugana	Sakana
Fish—Dumplings of	Camabuco	Kamaboko
Fine day	Kakonatink	Yokitenki
Five	Goka, (elements) (virtues)	Gogyo Gojo
	Itska	Itsutsu
Fled	Heku	Heru
Flowery pattern	Iakinmoyo	Hanamoyo
Follow (to)	Orae	Shitago
Fool	Baka	Baka
Foot	Ash	Ashi
Forehead	Hetye	Hitai
Fork	Hoko	Hoko
Fort	Dieba	Daiba
Four	Yoka, or She-yoka (footed)	Yotsu Shi-soku
Fourteen	Ju-Yoka	Ju-shi
Friend	Hoyou	Hoyu
Full—to overflowing	Epae or Epe	Ippai
Fur	Kawaoso	Kawa, Kegawa

G

English	MacDonald's Japanese	Standard or Recognized Japanese
Garment	Kremono	Kimono
General	Diemn	Rikugun-Taisho
Gentleman	Kenshe	Kunshi, Shinshi
Ghost	Yourin	Yurei
Ghost, Holy	Magoe	Seire
Give	Yar	Yaru
Glass	Vetro (probably from French *vitre*, introduced by French Jesuits)	Biidoro, Gurasu
Go—To	Ego, or Youkfla (?)	Iku Yuku

English	MacDonald's Japanese	Standard or Recognized Japanese
Go—to—away	Kiro	Yuku
		Koeru (by)
Goat	Yagie	Yagi
God (of the Shinto)	Kamoui or Kami-Sama	Kami
Good	Youka	Yoi, Yoki
Good—not	Kemara	Yokunai, Aku naru
Goodnight	Weya Timi	Oyasumi
Goose	Ga	Gacho
		Gan (wild)
Governor	Bougio, or Bunyo	Chiji
Grandfather	Geesan	O-ju-san, Sofu
Grandmother	Babasan	Baba, or obaa-san, sobo
Granddaughter	Hoska Musme	Mago-musume
Grandson	Hoska Musko	Mago-musoko
Great	Oke (Same in Cree)	Okii
Great deal	Oka or Oke	Yohodo, Takusan

H

English	MacDonald's Japanese	Standard or Recognized Japanese
Hail	Arare	Arare
Hair	Kamee	Kami, kami-no-ke
Hall—Large	Zashjee	Zashiki, Yashiki
Hand	Tae	Te
Handkerchief	Tenewe	Tenugui, Hankachi
Hark	Tsur	Jitto-kiku
Haste	Ohio	Isogo, Hayai
Haul	Hekoe	Hiku, Hakobu
Have—got	Aro	Aru, Motsu
He	Konata (applied also to personal pronoun Thou)	Kono okato, Kare
	Onata	Ano-hito
Head	Adama	Atama
Hear	Keku	Kiku
Heaven	Sin	Ten
High	Wee	Takai
Hit—knock to	Tadakul	Tataku
Hold—to	Negor and Negeem	Sasaeru
Hold—to with finger and thumb	Tsema mu	Tsumamu
Hook (a fish)	Tsure	Tsuri
Horse	Ma	Uma
House	Eyae	Ie, Iye
House—Large—Mansion	Yashke	Yashiki
How	Doa	Do, Ikani
How do you do?	Sonomotoo merucotowi	Kon-nichi-wa

I

English	MacDonald's Japanese	Standard or Recognized Japanese
I	Watakshewa, also Wataksuwa	Watakushi
Ignorant	Iummo Kul	Ahona
Ink	Sim	Sumi
Island	Sona	Shima
Itch	Kasa	Hizen, Kayui

J

Jug—Oil	Kodash	Aburatsubo
Jump	Tob or Toeb	Tobu

K

Kelp	Coub	Kobu, Kombu
King	O'	O, Tenno
Kitchen	Dikokoro	Daidokoro
Knee	Heza	Hiza
Knuckle	Fush	Kushi

L

Lame	Chimba	Chimba
Lampwick	Toshin	Toshin, Toshimi
Lantern	Andon	Andon
Lantern Box	Backwandon	
Large	Ftukoi	Futoi, O-ki
Last Night	Yombee	Yube, Saku-ban
Laugh	Warro	Warau
Law	Okete	Okite, Horitsu
Left—side or direction	Hedier	Hidari no, Hidarigawa
Legs	Sene	Ashi
Lend me	Okash nasaramosh	Kashite Kudasai
Lend		Kasu
Lie—Falsehood or Sham	Damaso	Damasu
Lieutenant	Kasra	Chu-i
Lift	Omka	Ageru
Light	Hera	Akarui
Light day	Hera Shear	Akarui Hi
Lightening	Enabeky	Inabikari
Little—size or degree	Isesa	Chiisai
Little, a small quantity	Scose	Sukoshi
Little—too	Tcheto	Chitto, Chotto
Lobster	Abegama	Yebi
Long ago	Mokash	Mukashi
Loose	Toketa	Toku, Tokeru

English	MacDonald's Japanese	Standard or Recognized Japanese
Lord—Highest term of address to all of superior rank in society, corresponding to the term "Monsieur"	Sama	Sama, Kami
Love	Tsecatzicke	Itsukushimu, Ai

M

Maid	Sara	Gejo
Make	Cosherioni	Tsukuru, Koshi rae-ru Koshiraeru
Man	Fito	Hito
Man—old	Rogin	Rojin
Most	Hasra	Mottomo
Master	Shugen	Shujin
Mat	Tadiame	Tatami
Me	Watakushe	Watakushi
Meet	Mestaro	Au, Matsu
Memory	Oboye	Oboe, Kioku
Memory bad	Oboye waig	Oboye Warui
Merchant	Tschoja	Shonin
Mile—one of ours	Egere	Jushicho Amari
Mile—their mile about 2½ ours	Ri	Ri
Mistress	Weran	Mekake, Oyeran
Mistress pleasure for	Youjoe	Yujo, Jujo, Joro
Money	Gin	Jeni
	Kin (ready)	Genkin
Monkey	Sar	Saru
Month—a	Stotske	Tsuki, Hitotsuki
Moon	Tske	Tsuki
Morning	Assa	Asa
Mother	Kakosan	Okka-san, Haha
Mountain	Yamma	Yama
Mouse	Nezume	Nezumi
Mouth	Quich	Kuchi
Moyat—a kind of water vegetable	Moyat	
Muck	Oka	Koyashi

N

Nails	Takatakado	
Navel	Heso	Heso
Neck	Cubee and Nodo	Kubi Nodo
Neck—to stab thru the	Gegii	Jigai
Necessary (Water Closet)	Shetseyeen	Setsuin, Bengo

English	MacDonald's Japanese	Standard or Recognized Japanese
Nephew	On	Oi
Net	Amee	Ami
Niece	Mac	Mei
Night	Yousii or Usii	Yoru
Night—last	Yombee	Yu-be
Nine	Quoo a koo, or Kokonoka	Ku Kokonotsu
Nineteen	Juquinge, or Kooinge	Juku
No	Eya, and Na	Iiye, Iye Bai
Nose	Hana	Hana
Not	Nigh	Nai
Not any	Naka or Naran	Hitotsumonai
Now—at present	Fadima, or Atska	Ima

O

English	MacDonald's Japanese	Standard or Recognized Japanese
Oar	Kam Hatm Rama	Ro, Kai
Obliged, greatly	Okearin gado	O-kini Arigato
Obliged, greatly for attention	Osheva	Osewasama
Ocean	Diikii	Taiyo Kai
Of	Ga, and no (affix)	No
One	Sto, ege, itch	Ichi
Onions, pickled	Ranque	Rakkyo
Onions	Stomoge	Shitomogi, Hitomoji
Open	Awkur, mow kado	Akeru
Orange	Mecan	Mikan

P

English	MacDonald's Japanese	Standard or Recognized Japanese
Pain	Etaka	Itai, Itaka
Paper	Kame	Kami
Pease—blue	Yokone	Aoendo
Pen	Fede	Fude
People—Common	Heyo	Hito, He-min
Pickle—red	Cal-na	Hikabu
Pillow	Magraw	Makura
Plank	Ekooru	Ita, Ita wo haru
Play	Go otts, (checkers) Amaroo	Go wo uts Asobu, Tawamureru
Plenty	Tucksan	Takusan
Police	Tesak Tesak (detective)	Seiji, Junsa Teisakuri
Pork	Buda "good-so"	Buta no niku, Buta Niko
Post Captain	Sindo-sama	Sencho
Pot—kettle or saucepan	Nabee (T?)	Nabe

English	MacDonald's Japanese	Standard or Recognized Japanese
Potatoes	Emo	Imo
	Pantsiol	Baresho
Potatoes, a vegetable like	Quy	Kuwai
Pray	Ogama	Ogamu
Pregnant	Quitii	Ninshin
Presently	Otska	Ottsuke, sugu
	Fadima	
Pretty	Tsukuseka	Utsukushii
Prince	Wakagime	Wakagimi
Princess	Shemaegim	Wakahime, Himegini
Private	Takinmoyo	Kojinno
Pull or Haul	Hekoe	Hiku
Put—to put on	Kier, or	Kiru, Oku
	Kista	Kiseru

Q

Quarrel	Kinkwa	Kenkwa
Queen	Neo O'	Nyotei, kogo
Quiver—Arrows of	Yaat	Ya, Yugi
Queue—on top of head	Ore, bach	Chonmage
Quy—a vegetable like a potato	Quy	Kuwai

R

Radish—pickled	Digoon	Daikon
Rain	Ame	Ame
Read	Yom	Yomu
Red	Aka	Akai
Return	Atomodoru	Kaeru, Modoru
Rice	Come	Kome
Right—side or direction	Megie	Migi
Right—a little to the	Younoke	Sukoshi Migi
River	Kawa	Kawa
Road	Menato	Michi
Room—bed	Haeya	Heya, Shinshitsu
Rope	Tsena	Tsuna
Row—to	Row os	Kogu
Rudder	Kage	Kaji
Rump	Koshe	Koshi
Run	Hiaka,	Kakeru
	Hasure	Hashiru
Run away, to	Negaer	Nigeru

S

Saddle	Kura	Kura
Sail	Ho	Ho

English	MacDonald's Japanese	Standard or Recognized Japanese
Sailor	Fenagada (Sailor's Inn)	Funanori Fenayado
Salt	Sheo	Shio
Same, the	Onashoto	Onaji, Onajikoto
Sash—window	Shoge	Shoji
Sauce, of dark colored fish	Shon ("Son")	Shoyu
Scratch	Cakul	Karu, hikkaku
Sea	Oome or Owme	Umi, kai
Seal (mark or stamp)	Ingu	Ingyo, Han
See	Metae	Mitai, Miru
Seed	Zance, guo	Tane
Seen, not, you for	Otodo-shue	Omeni Kakaranai
Servant	Kerii	Kerai, Yatoinin
Service—at your	Kawdra Kotonika	Anatano Kotode, Katte ni otsukai nasare
Seven	Sitch Nanca	Hichi, Shichi Nanatsu
Seventeen	Ju stinge, Ju sitsh	Ju hichi
Sew	Noo	Nu
Shipwreck	Hashaen	Hasen
Shave	Sorktse	Soru or sogu
Sheep	Hetsuge	Hitsuji
Ship	Fenee	Fune
Shirt	Hadake	Hadagi, Juban
Shoulders	Kata	Kata
Shower	Fore ante	Yu-Dachi, Niwaka ame
Shut (a port)	Shaku	Sakoku
Sing	Fushets kateota, or futs kate	Utau
Sir—yes	Hea, hea, hea	Hei
Sister	On a Qudae	Onna-kyodai
Sister second	Qudii	Imoto
Sit	Suwar	Suwaru
Six	Rock, Muyouca	Roku, Mutsu
Sixteen	Ju Rockinge, Ju Roste	Juroku
Sleep—a	Noor	Nemuru
Sleepy	Neptaka	Nemui, Nemutai
Small	Comaka, Tsera	Komayaka na Chiisai, chi-sana
Small pox	Kemoore	Hoso
Snow	Youkee	Yuki
Snuffers	Shinkere	Shinkiri
So—Just	Siode, Sonotor	Sho-do
So—So	So so (probably from Dutch	Su So
Socks	Tabee	Tabi
Soldier (common, not impl.)	Oyokonu	He-tai
Soldier, Imperial	Oosieu	Konoe Hei
Sole	Asnohara	Ashi no ura

English	MacDonald's Japanese	Standard or Recognized Japanese
Sometime—ago	Hesabesa Oshasu	Kono Aida
Son	Muska	Musuko
Son, second	Ototo	Ototo
Sorry	Gosashe	Kanashi, Kuchi-oshii
Soul—mind	Koo, zkee	Re-kon
Speak	Kotoba, You	Kokoro, Hanasu
Spectacles	Megame	Megane
Spill	Cobose	Kobosu
Spit	Tsubake	Tusba, Tsubaki
Spit box	Hyvek	Tantsubo, Haifuki
Spring—next	Harr	Haru
Spy—a	Cacksomaetoke	Kanjya, Metsuke
Stab	Tsuku	Tsuku
Stab, through the neck	Gegii	Jigai
Stamp	Mgu	Inshi, Han
Stand—to	Tatsu	Tatsu
Star	Hose	Hoshi
Stink	Qusaka	Kusai
Stirrup—leather	Warazore	Warazori
Stop	Mate, Ocheru	Mate, Tomaru Osaeru
Strait	Masugu (space) (time)	Masugu Massuguna Jikini
Straight along	Gekene	Massugu
Stranger	Tabenosto	Tabi no hito, Tanin
Street	Meech? (Matz)	Machi, Michi
Strike	Dotso Tadokul	Butsu Tataku
String	Tsure	Tsuri-Hi-Himo
Summer—next	Natts	Natsu, Natsu or ka
Sun	She	Hi, Taiyo
Sunshine	Skii	Hinata, Taiyo Kagayaku
Supper	Yoohan	Yuhan, Yu-gohan
Swallow—to	Nameken Notodormoka	Nomu, Nomi-komu
Sweep	Hoke	Haku
Swim	Wyaegoo	Oyogu
Sword	Catana	Katana, ken
Sword, to draw the	Nuge	Nuku, Ken o nuku
Sword handle	Tska	Ken o Tsukau
Sword blade	Sia	Saya, Yaiba

T

Table	O'gen	Shokutaku, Zen
Take	Torr	Toru
Talk—tell	Hanasoo	Hanasu

English	MacDonald's Japanese	Standard or Recognized Japanese
Tea	Cha	Cha
Tea cup	Chawan	Cha-wan
Tea Tray	Chadi	Cha-bon
Teeth	Ha	Ha
Tell	Hanaso	Hanasu
Ten	Ju, Tokatoka	Ju, To
Thank (you)	Aringodo	Arigato
Then	Carera	Kara, Shikaraba, Shikarutoki
Thighs	Shere	Momo
Think	Wasreta Mo	Watakishi, Kangoern Omou
Thirteen	Ju Tange, Ju Tan	Ju-san
Thirty	Kenata san ju	San-ju
Thou	Eto (applied also to the third personal pronoun in eastern style of address	Anata
Thread	Waga	Ito
Three	San Meca	San Mi, Mitsu
Throw	Nagur	Nageru
Thumb	O'Yoube	Oya-yubi, Oyubi
Thunder	Camarare, Rye	Kaminari, Rai
Tie	Mosobo	Musubu
Tiger	Tora	Tora
Tired	Kiska	Tukareta
To	Ni, ye	Ni, ye
To—up or towards	Dokono	Uyeni
To—down	Darega	Shitani
Today	Quo, Conege	Kyo Konnichi
Toes	Asno yoube	Ashi no yubi
Tomorrow	Asta, Munege	Ashita, Myo-nichi
Tongs	Shebas	Hibashi
Tongue	Sta	Shita
Town	Enaka	Machi
Tray	Di or Dy	Dai, Bon
Trousers	Momoshegi	Momohiki
Tsua—a kind of water herb much used by natives	Tsua	
Turkey	Karacoon	Choseicho, Hichimencho
Turtle	Gamme	Kame
Twelve	Ju ne	Juni
Twenty	Hatska or (years) Ju Hatska	Hatachi
Twist, to	Naegera, Quahe	Nejiru, Nigu
Two	Ne, Fitoka	Ni Futatsu

U

English	MacDonald's Japanese	Standard or Recognized Japanese
Uncle	Oge	Oji
Under	Sta	Shita

V

Varnish	Rush	Urushi
Viceroy	Rotshew Grotsu Tajo	Sotoku Taishu

W

Wash	Sintaku	Sentaku, Arau
Wash, to, the face	Tchozu	Kao Arau
Walk	Sorosure Youk	Hoko suru Aruku
Wall	Kabee	Kabe
War	Takado	Senso
Warm	Atse	Tatakau Atsui, Atataka
Water	Meze	Mizu
Way—Short	Miskii	Michi, Michikai
Way—long	Toga	Nagai
We	Wara ware	Warera
Weather—Dark	Otoshe	Uttoshe
Weep	Nakoo	Naku
Whale	Quisra	Kujira
When	Eets	Itsu
Which	Quich	Izure, Dochira
Whip	Bugee	Butsu
White	Shruka	Shiroi
Who	Douka	Tare, Dochira
Who is it?	Dareyo	Tareka
Why?	Doconee	Doshite, Naze
Wife	Ogatson	Oku-sama, Tsuma
Wife, second	Sho Tetake	Sho Tekake
Will	Dozo	Daro, dozo
Will—I, not	Scan	Senai
Wind	Kagee	Kaze, Kaje
Wing (feather)	Hanee	Hane
Winter, next	Juyou	Fuyu
Wipe, to dry up	Nogow	Nugu
Wish	Dozo	Negau, dozo
Wish I, you joy	Oyaro cobee (much joy)	Oyoro Kobi Omedeto
Wood	Kee	Ki
Write	Cakut	Kaku

Y

English	MacDonald's Japanese	Standard or Recognized Japanese
Yawn	Akubet	Akubi
Year—this	Quotosh	Kotoshi
Year—next	Muning	Myo-nen, Rainen
Year—past	Zuning	Kyonen, Saku-nen
Year—one	Egening	Ichinen
Yes	Hea	Hei
	Yos	Sayo
Yesterday	Kono	Kino
You	Anata	Anata
	Sokamoto	Sokka

BIBLIOGRAPHY OF RANALD MacDONALD

(Including magazine and newspaper articles containing mention of MacDonald's Japan Adventure.)

Astorian (Astoria, Ore.), February 8, 1891. The oldest Native Astorian.

Britannicus Letter No. 7, Ottawa Times, Ottawa, Canada,1869. Contains Ranald MacDonald's Adventure in Japan.

Canadian Pacific Pamphlets; 1875-1880; some contain mention of Ranald MacDonald's story.

Century Magazine, New York, Aug. 1913, vol. 86, pp. 597-605. Wm. Elliot Griffis. American Makers of the New Japan.

China Mail, May 31, 1849. Vol. 5, No. 224, p. 86. Report of return of the Preble with men from the Lagoda, and MacDonald from the Plymouth.

Chinese Repository, S. Wells Willams, ed., June, 1849, vol. 18, pp. 315-323. Cruise of the United States Sloop of War, Preble, commander James Glynn, to Napa, and Nagasaki.

Corrector, (The) Sag Harbor, L. I., N. Y., H. D. Slight, editor, various dates, 1905; A History of Sag Harbor's Whaling Industry.
Same article, reprint, Brooklyn Times, (various dates) 1905.
————Sag Harbor's Whaling Fleet, various dates.

Dye, Eva Emery. MacDonald of Oregon; a tale of two shores. 395 p. Chicago, A. C. McClurg & Co., 1906.

Griffis, William Elliot. America in the East; a glance at our history, prospects, problems and duties in the Pacific Ocean. 236 p. New York, A. S. Barnes & Co., 1889. Ranald MacDonald p. 103, 167-168.

————The Japanese Nation in Evolution, New York, Crowell & Co., 1907. pp. 226, 308-309.

Harper's Weekly Magazine, New York. July 18, 1891. Vol. XXXV, No. 1804, pp. 534-535, Elizabeth B. Custer. An Out of the Way Outing.   ;
Same article, Kettle Falls Pioneer, Haskins ed., Kettle Falls, Wash., Aug. 6, 1891.

Hildreth, Richard. Japan As it Was and Is; a handbook of old Japan, 2 vols. Chicago, A. C. McClurg & Co., 1906. Ranald MacDonald; Vol. 2, p. 271-272.

Kettle Falls, (Wash.) Pioneer, Aug. 6, 1891, Mrs. Custer's article copied from Harper's Weekly of July 18, 1891

————Sept. 3, 1891. Was Uncalled For—A cutting rebuke to Mrs. General Custer's criticism. The Oldest of Pioneers. An interesting letter from our honored and respected Patriarch, Ranald MacDonald.

————Nov. 16, 1893; Nov. 23, 1893; Dec. 7, 1893; Dec. 21, 1893; Jan. 4, 1894; containing the first chapters of MacDonald's *Narrative.*

————Aug. 30, 1894. Notice of death of Ranald MacDonald.

Levyssohn, John H. Blader ubs Japan. 's Gravenhage: Belinfante, 1852. MacDonald, pp. 53, 55.

Littell's Living Age, Boston, E. Littell &. Co., Oct. 27, 1849, vol. 23, No. 284, pp. 145-152. Americans in Japan. Cruise of the U. S. Sloop of war Preble.

McLeod, Malcolm, Pacific Railway, Canada. Britannicus Letters, etc., Thereon, p. 36. Ottawa, Canada. A. S. Woodbury, 1875, Ranald MacDonald p. 18.

Morning Courier & New York Enquirer (N. Y. City) Thursday morning, Sept. 18, 1849.

Niles National Register, Philadelphia, May 30, 1849, vol. 75, p. 340. Intercourse with Japan. (Referring to the Seamen's Friend, Honolulu.)

Nitobe, Inazo Ota. The Japanese nation, its land, its people, and its life, with special consideration to its relations with the United States, 334 p. New York, G. P. Puttman's Sons, 1912. Ranald MacDonald, pp. 272-273.

Oregon Historical Society Quarterly, H. G. Yoring, ed., vol. VII, Dec., 1906, pp. 435-437. Review of Eva Emery Dye's MacDonald of Old Oregon.

————Sept., 1911, vol. XII, pp. 220-223. A Hero of Old Astoria, Eva Emery Dye.

Providence (R. I.) Journal, Thursday, Sept. 18, 1849.

Portland Oregonian, (Portland, Oregon) February 12, 1891, page 5. The Oldest Native Astorian. A brief sketch of the Life of the Grandson of King Kum Kumly, the old Indian Chief, copied from the Astorian.

————Nov. 27, 1893; Nov. 29, 1893, Chinooks' Lawful King.

Scott, Harvey W., History of Oregon. Leslie M. Scott, ed., 2 vols. MacDonald mentioned, vol. ii, pp. 140-141.

Spears, John R. The Story of the New England Whaler, New York, Macmillan Co., 1908. MacDonald mentioned pp. 146-148.

Spokane (Wash) Review, Nov. 24, 1890. Old Com-Comly's grandson, copied in the St. Thomas (Ontario) Journal.

————Nov. 27, 1893, vol. X, No. 191, p. 2, col. 1, Long Live King Com-Comley, copied from Kettle Falls Pioneer, and copied in the New York Sun and various other papers.

Spokesman Review, (Spokane, Wash.) Aug. 31, 1894, vol. ii, No. 116, p. 1, col. 1. Old MacDonald Dead. Link broken that Bound us to the Savage Post.

Starbuck, Alexander. History of the American Whale Fishery from its earliest inception to the year 1876. Waltham, Mass., the author, 1878. Ranald MacDonald mentioned p. 142, note.

(The) Seaman's Friend, Honolulu, Oahu, Sandwich Islands, Rev'd Samuel C. Damon, seamen's chaplain, editor, Dec. 1, 1848; A Salior's Attempt to Penetrate Japan. Appendix herein.

————October 1, 1849.
————December 20, 1849.

Tyrrell, J. B., ed.; David Thompson's Narrative of his Explorations in Western America. Toronto, Champlain Society, 1916. p. 505, note 2.

Victoria (B. C.) Times, Sept. 21, 1888. An interesting Visitor. (Visit of Mr. Ada to Ottawa contains brief mention of Ranald MacDonald's Japan adventure as told in Britannicus letter.)

Same Article: Ottawa Daily Citizen, Ottawa, Canada, Saturday, Sept. 1, 1888.

Same article: (copied) Colville (Washington) Miner.

United States Senate Executive Documents, 59, 32nd Congress 1st session. President Message . . . communicating . . . . certain official documents relative to the empire of Japan, and serving to illustrate the existing relations between the United States and Japan. April 12, 1852.

Story of Ranald MacDonald as told by himself; in 1849. pp. 25-28.

Story of Ranald MacDonald as told by James Glynn, commander United States Ship Preble, pp. 55-57.

OTHER WORKS AND AUTHORITIES CITED IN FOOTNOTES

Age, The, of Melbourne, Australia, Thursday, Nov. 17, 1859.

Baker, Benjamin, History of the Jonathan Bourne Whaling Office, and some of those connected with it. Quoted in extenso in Old Dartmouth Historical Sketches, No. 45. New Bedford, Mass., March 16, 1917.

Bancroft, Hurbert Howe. History of the Northwest Coast. 2 vols., illus., 1 map. San Francisco, A. L. Bancroft & Co., 1884.

Beechey, Capt. F. W. (R. N.) Narrative of a voyage to the Pacific . . . 1823-1824, 2 vols. London, Henry Colburn and Richard Bentley, 1834.

Belcher, Sir Edward. Narrative of a voyage around the world, performed in Her Majesty's ship Sulphur, during the years 1836-1842, including details of the naval operations in China from Dec. 1840 to Nov. 1841 . . . 2 vols, ills. pl. maps. London, Colburn, 1843.

Bible, The.

Blanchet, Francis Norbert. Historical sketches of the Catholic church in Oregon; during the past 40 years; 1838-1878, 186 p. Portland, Oregon, Catholic Sentinel Society, 1878.

Boas, Franz. Handbook of American Indian Languages, Bulletin 40, part 1, Bureau of American Ethnology, Wash. D. C. Government Printing Office, 1918.

Bryce, George. The remarkable history of the Hudson's Bay Company, including that of the French traders of northwestern Canada and of the Northwest, X Y, and Astor fur companies. 501 p. pl. maps. London, Low, 1900.

Buck, Mrs. W., editor. Manners and customs of the Japanese in the 19th century, (based partly on Dutch accounts and the German of Dr. D. H. Fr vonSiebold, London, 1841.

Campbell, Archibald. A voyage around the World from 1806 to 1812. Edinburgh, Constable & Co. 1816.

Corney, Peter. Voyages in the Northern Pacific, Narrative of several Trading voyages from 1813 to 1818, (Reprint from London Literary Gazette of 1821) Honolulu, H. I. Thos. G. Thrum, 1896.

Correcter, The. Sag Harbor, Long Island, N. Y. March 7, 1874.

Coues, Elliot, ed., New Light on the Early History of the Greater Northwest: The Manuscript Journals of Alexander Henry and of David Thompson. 3 vol. New York, F. P. Harper, 1897.

Cox, Ross. Adventures on the Columbia River, including the narrative of a residence of six years on the western side of the Rocky Mountains. 2 vols. London, Colburn, 1831.

Davidson, Gordon Charles. The North West Company. 349 p. front (fold map) 4 fold maps. Berkely, University of California Press, 1918.

Douglas, David. Journal kept by David Douglas during his travels in North America, 1823-1827. London, William Wesley & Son, 1914.

Dunn, John. History of the Oregon territory and British North-American fur trade; with an account of the habits and customs of the principal native tribes of the northern continent. 359 p. 1 map. London, Edwards, 1844.

Ermatinger, Edward. York Factory Express Journal, being a record of journeys made between Fort Vancouver and Hudson Bay in the years 1827-1828. Transactions Royal Society of Canada vol. VI, Royal Society of Canada, Ottawa, 1912.

Elliot, T. C. David Thompson, Pathfinder and the Columbia River. 9 p. The Scimitar Press, Kettle Falls, Wash. 1911.

Fairhaven (Mass.) Star, Friday, July 5, 1918.

Fissher, J. F. van Overmeer. Bijdrage tot de Kennis van het Japansche Rijk (Contributions towards the Knowledge of the Japanese Realm.) 320 p. plates. Amsterdam, 1833.

Franchere, Gabriel. Narrative of a voyage to the Northwest coast of America in the years 1811, 1812, 1813 and 1814; or, The First American settlement on the Pacific. Tr. and ed. by J. V. Huntington. 376 p. 3 pl. New York, Redfield, 1854.

Golownin, Captain Vasilu Mikhailovich. Memoirs of a captivity in Japan, 1811-1813. English ed., 3 vols. London, Colburn, 1824.

Gray, William Henry. History of Oregon, 1792-1849. 624 p. 1 pl. Portland, Oregon and New York, Harris, 1870.

Griffis, William Elliot. Life of Mathew Calbraith Perry, a typical American Naval Officer. Boston, Houghton, Mifflin & Co. Ditto. Boston, Cupples and Hurd, 1887.

————The Mikado's Empire, a handbook of Japan. New York, Harper & Brothers, 1876.

————Townsend Harris, First American Envoy in Japan, Boston and New York, Houghton, Mifflin & Co., 1895.

————Japanese Nation in Evolution. New York, Crowell, 1907.

Harper's Weekly Magazine, New York, Dec. 2, 1871.

Harris, Dr. J. Arthur. Graphics of the American Whaling Industry, Popular Science Monthly, July, 1914. Vol. 85, pp. 83-86.

Hawks, Francis L., D. D. Narrative of the Expedition of an American Squadron in the years 1852, 1853 and 1854 under command of Commodore M. C. Perry. Government Printing office, Wash. D. C., 1856. (Ex. Doc't No. 79, 33rd Congress, 2nd session.)

Holman, Frederick Van Voorhies. Dr. John McLoughlin the Father of Oregon. 301 p. Portraits. Cleveland, The Arthur H. Clarke Co., 1907.

Hudson's Bay Company Correspondence.

Irving, Washington. Astoria, or Anecdotes of an enterprise beyond the Rocky Mountains. 2 vols. 1 map. Philadelphia, Carey, 1836.

Jaggar, Charles A. Ph. D. Entering a Forbidden Port. The Manhattan's Log near Japan. The Southampton Magazine, vol. i, No. 1. Southampton, N. Y. The Southampton Press, 1912.

Kaempfer, Dr. Englebrecht. A history of Japan and Siam, containing an account of the voyage made by the English in 1673. London, 1727.

Kane, Paul. Wanderings of an Artist among the Indians of North America from Canada to Vancouver's Island and Oregon . . . . 455 p. illus. 8 pl. 1 map. tab. London, Longmans, 1859.

Langsdorff, George Heinrich von. Voyages and Travels in various parts of the World, 1803-1807. 2 parts, illus. London, Henry Colburn, 1813.

Lee, D. and Frost, J. H. Ten years in Oregon. 344 p. 1 map. New York, J. Collord, 1844.

Lewis, (Meriwether) and Clark (William) Original journals of the Lewis and Clark expedition, 1804-1806, printed from the original manuscripts . . . . ed. by Reuben Gold illus. New York, Dodd, 1904-1905.

Lyman, Horace S. History of Oregon, the growth of an American
    State. Associate board of editors; H. W. Scott, C. B. Bel-
    linger and F. G. Young. 4 vols, port pl. and maps. New
    York, North Pacific Pub. Soc., 1903.

Martin, R. M. Hudson's Bay Territories . . . . with an Ex-
    position of the Chartered Rights (etc.) of the Honorable
    Hudson's Bay Corporation, London, 1849.

Macfie, Mathew. Vancouver Island and British Columbia, 574 p.
    illus. 1 pl. 2 maps. London, Longmans, 1865.

Martin, Archer. The Hudson's Bay Company's land tenures, 238 p.
    1 port. 2 maps, 2 plans. London, Clowes, 1898.

Masson, D. R. (les) bourgeois de le compagnie, du Nord-Ouest,
    recits de voyages, lettres et rapports inedits relatifs au
    Nord-Ouest Canadien; publies avec une esquisse historique
    et des annotations. Ser. 1, 2 vols. maps. Quebec, Cote,
    1889-1890.

McLeod, Malcolm. Peace River. A canoe Voyage from Hudson's
    Bay to Pacific, by the late Sir George Simpson (Gov. Hon.
    Hudson's Bay Company.) in 1828. Paper xix 119 p. map.
    Ottawa, J. Jurie & Son, 1872.

————Oregon Indemnity, Claim of Chief Factors and Chief Trad-
    ers of the Hudson's Bay Company, 1892.

Nantucket Inquirer, (Nantucket, Mass.,) February 2, 1849.

Nantucket Journal (Nantucket, Mass.,) 1887.

National Intelligencer, January 22, 1821.

New Bedford, (Mass.,) Whalingmen's Shipping list, January 16,
    1849.

Niles National Register, Baltimore, March 10, 1821.

Oliver, E. H. ed. The Canadian Northwest, Its Early Develop-
    ment. Government Printing Bureau, Ottawa, 1914-1915.

Parker, Rev. Samuel. Journal of an Expedition from Singapore
    to Japan.

————Journal of an exploring tour beyond the Rocky Mountains
    . . . in the years 1835, 1836 and 1837 . . . 371 p.
    1 pl. 1 map. Ithaca, Author, 1838.

Palliser, Capt. John. The Journals, Detailed Reports and Obser-
    vations relative to the Exploration, by Captain Palliser . .
    325 p. London, 1863.

Portland Oregonian, Portland, Oregon. Nov. 29, 1893.

————Dec. 17, 1899 p. 28. Comcumly's Followers, Their Empire
    about the Mouth of the Columbia, etc.

————December 18, 1899 p. 9. Mr. Smith's Address. He tells of Early times in Oregon. Arrival of the First Ships—Wrecks on Clatsop Beach, etc.

Provincial Archives Department of Province of British Columbia, Report of, for the year 1913, Victoria, B. C., 1914.

Ross, Alexander. Adventures of the first settlers on the Oregon or Columbia River; being a narrative of the expedition fitted out by John Jacob Astor to establish the "Pacific Fur Company" . . . . 352 p. 1 map. London, Smith, 1849.

————The Fur Hunters of the far west; a narrative of adventures in the Oregon and Rocky Mountains. 2 vol. 1 port. 2 pl. London, Smith, 1855.

————Red River Settlement; its rise, process and present state. 416 p. London, Smith, Elder & Co. 1856.

Scouler, Dr. John. Journal of a Voyage to Northwest America. Oregon Historical Quarterly, vol vi. pp. 54-76, 159-205, 274-289. Jan., June, Sept., 1905.

Siebold, Dr. Phillip Franz von. Nippon, Archiv zur Bescreibung von Japan (Nippon, an archive towards the description of Japan) 6 vols. folio, Leiden, 1832-1852.

Singapore Free Press (Straits Settlement) January 6, 1848.

Sharp, Cecil. English Folk-Chantey's, London.

Seamen's Friend, The, Honolulu, S. I. October, 1884.

Smet, Pierre Jean de. Missions de l'Oregon et voyages aux montganes Rocheusses aux sources de la Colombie, de l'Athabasca et du Sascatshawin en 1845-1846. 423 p. 15 pl. 3 maps. tab. Schelden, Ghent, n. d.
Ditto . . . . 406 p. Paris, 1848.

————Life, letters and travels of Father Pierre-Jean de Smet, S. J. 1801-1873; missionary labors and adventures among the wild tribes of the North American Indians. ed. by Hiram Martin Chittenden, and Alfred Talbot Richardson, 4 vol. port. 1 map. New York, F. P. Harper, 1905.

Smith, Miss Laura Alexandrine. The Music of the Waters. A collection of the sailors chanties . . . . 360 p. London, K. Paul Trench & Co., 1888.

Starbuck, Alexander. History of the American Whale Fishery from its earliest inception to the year 1876. 768 pp. Waltham, Mass., the author, 1878.

Stevenson, Robert Louis. Familiar Studies of Men and Books. (Any edition.) 342 pp. New York, C. Scribner's Sons 1905.

Stewart, Charles Samuel, 1795-1870. A Visit to the South seas, in
the United States ship Vincennes, during the years 1829
and 1830; including notices of Brazil, Peru, Manila, the
Cape of Good Hope, and St. Helena. By C. S. Stewart.
2 vol. 20 1-2 em. 365 p. New York, J. P. Haven, 1884.

Stoddard, C. W. South Sea Idyls. (Any edition.) 339 pp. New
York, C. Scribners, 1892.

————The Lepers of Molokai. (Any edition.) 80 pp. Notre
Dame, Ind., "Ave Maria" press (1885).

Swan, James G. The Northwest Coast or Three Year's Residence
in Washington Territory. 435 p. illus. 1 pl. 1 map. Harper & Bros. New York, 1857.

Thunberg, Charles Peter, M. D. Travels in Europe, Africa and
Asia. 1770-1779. English translation, 3rd ed. 4 vol.
Printed for F. and C. Rivington. London, 1796.

Towers, Walter S. A History of the American Whale Fishery.
145 pp. Philadelphia, (Pub. for University Penn., Series
in Political, Economy and Public Law, No. 20.) 1907.

Townsend, John K. Narrative of a journey accross the Rocky
Mountains to the Columbia River, and a visit to the Sandwich Islands, Chili, etc. 352 pp. Henry Perkins, Philadelphia, 1839.

Tucker, Sarah. The Rainbow in the North; a short account of the
First Establishment of Christianity in Rupert's Land by the
Church Missionary Society, New York, 1861.
Ditto . . . . London, 1851.

Tyrrell, J. B. A brief Narrative of the Journeys of David Thompson in Northwestern America. Proceedings of the Canadian Institute, Oct. 1888. Vol. vi, 1887-1888, pp. 135-160.

Washington Historical Quarterly, Edmond S. Many, ed. Wash.
University Press, Seattle, Wash., various volumes and dates.

Whall, Capt. W. B. Ships, Sea Songs and Shanties, Glasgow,
James Brown and Son, 1912.

Wilkes, Charles. Narrative of the United States exploring expedition, during the years 1838, 1839, 1840, 1841, 1842. 5
vols. atlas, maps and illus. Philadelphia, Lea, 1845.

Williams, Frederick Wells. Life and Letters of Samuel Wells.
Williams. 490 pp. port. New York, Puttman's Sons,
1889.

Wright, E. W. ed. Lewis and Dryden's Marine History of the
Pacific Northwest, Portland, Oregon. Lewis and Dryden,
1895.

A

ABBOTT, Mr., 33.
ADAM, Tillamook Chief, 122n.
ADAMS, John Quincy, 77n.
ADAMS, Will, 234n.
AFRICA, 42.
AINSLIE, Dr., 234n.
AINU, 163, 163n, 165, 261; Pronounced "eye-nose," "Inoes," 163; Islands, 170; Meaning of name, 164n; A Mongol people from Chinese Tartary, 163n, 164n, 169; Indigenous to Yezo, 163n; A subject people, 167, 168; Simple and kindly, 168; By occupation, fishermen, 163n, 166; Differ physically, mentally, morally from Japanese, 167, 168; No government of their own, 170; Physical characteristics, 164n, 168, 169; Resemble Hydras and Balla Coola indians, 168; Uncouth in person, wild in person, in dress, 169; Uncombed beards, unwashed faces, 169; Very hairy, 168; Fond of saki, 165; Abstain from meat, 163; Offer "grace" before meals, 165.
ALASKA, 104.
ALEXANDRIA, (B. C.), 102n.
ALEXANDRIA, Fort, 46.
ALLEN, Joseph of the ship, Moro, 150.
ALLEZ, Miss, 114n.
ALTAR, Japanese, 164.
ALMANAC, Japanese, 160.
AMBOW, Island of, 141n.
AMELIA, whaler, 134n.

AMERICAN crew, 195; Corvette, the Preble, 246; Indians, 227n, 169n, characterization of, 169n. Sailors, 195, 196; Sailors from whaler Lagoda, 195, 196, 246; Ships, see ships; Words used by Japanese, see English.
AMERICAN Fur Co., 32, 33.
AMERICAN Publishers, 19.
AMUR, 165n.
ANDREWS, Ruben of David Paddock, 139, 141, 145, 235.
APPLES, Japanese, 203.
APPLETON, 19.
ARROW Lake (B. C.), 107n.
ASA-HI-SHIMBUM (Rising Sun News-Morning Chronicle), 255.
ASSINIBOIA, appointment to governorship of, 107.
ASTOR, expedition, 75; First ship, the Tonquin, 80; Staff, Leading officer of, 77.
ASTOR, Mr., (John Jacob), 77n.
ASTORIA, 74, 77n, 78n, 80, 85, 92, 111; D. Thompson's arrival at, 111, 32.
ATHABASCA, 169n; Pass, 26, 96, 108, 112; Highest in Rocky Mountains, 108.
ATHABASCA River, 109n.
ATLAS, Japanese copy of English, 244.
AUSTRALIA, visited by Ranald MacDonald during "first gold diggins." 44, 45, 249; Champion of, 45; Gold rush, 44; Gold discoveries, 249n.

B

BAKER, Capt., 161, 235n.
BAKUFU, 173n.
BALL, John, 25, 39n.
BALL'S School, 25, 25n, 105n, 106n.
BALLARAT (Australia), 44.
BANCROFT, H. H., 86, 124, 124n.

BANCROFT, History of British Columbia, 100, 124.
BANK of Elgin, 116, 116n; Of Upper Canada, 116, 116n, 117; of Montreal, 116n.
BARKER, Capt. Seth of Boston, 85, 85n.

BARKER and Sturges, 85n.
BARNES, Miss Jane, 84n.
BARNSTON, George, 93n.
BARNSTON, Mrs. George, 93n;
BARNSTON, John G., 45, 102n.
BASSIE, Mr., 284.
BAS, (hashi) Japanese word for bridge, 169, 169n.
BAS de la Riviere, 30, 78n.
BASHEE (or Bashi) Islands, 145, 145n. 146.
BATAVIA, 161, 162n.
BATEAUX, 25
BATTAN Island, 145, 146, 224.
BAWL, John, 196n, 284, 285.
BEADS for prayer, 189.
BEAR, brother of Com-com-ly, 76n.
BEAVER river, 100n.
BEAVER skins, 56; Unit of exchange, 56.
BEAVER, steamer, 107n.
BEAVIT'S sledge, 28.
BED and covering, Japanese, 200, 222.
BEESWAX Junk, 121, 122n.
BELCHER, Point, disaster, 134, 135n.
BELLA Coola Coast Indians, 168, 168n.
BENGAL, 234n.
BENTNICK Arm, 46, 46n, 102n.
BIFFAR, Melcher, 196n, 285.
BIG Bend of the Upper Columbia River, 108, 112.
BIG Eddy of Upper Columbia, 108, 112.
BIG Head Edwards, Indian chief, 107n.
BIRTH of Ranald MacDonald, 92.
BLACK bear, 37.
BLUE Coat Boy, 108, 108n.
BOAT Encampment on Upper Columbia, 108, 108n, 110n.
BOATS, (see ships post.)
BOLON, Indian Agent A. J., 91n.
BOMBAY, 44.
BONAPARTE River, 45.
BONAPARTE mining district, B. C., 47.
BONIN Islands, 145.
BOOBY Island, 198n.
BOOKS, foreign possessed by Japanese, 226n; Japanese, 204;

Japanese footnotes in, 206; Japanese manner of noting respect for, 200; Wood cuts in, 205; Binding, 204.
BOSTON, vessels of in Northwest trade, 80, 81n.
BOULARD, Michel, 111n.
BOUNDRY Creek, B. C., 67.
BOURDEAUX, Michel, 111n.
BOURNE, Jonathan of New Bedford, 196n.
BOURNE, Jonathan Jr. of Oregon, 196n.
BOURNE, Jonathan Whaling Museum, 196n.
BOY, Chinook word for, 93.
BOYD, Dr. of Emburgh, 101n.
BOYD, Jacob, 196n, 284, 285.
BRADY, John, 195.
BRAZIER, 222.
BREAD, Japanese word for, pan, 242.
BRIDGEPORT, whaler, 139.
BRIGADES, 26, 55.
BRIGADES of H. B. Co., 55, 62, 63, 105.
BRITANNICUS, pen name of Malcolm McLeod, 255.
BRITANNICUS, letters, 101n, 255.
BRITISH Columbia, 98, 104; Bancroft's History of, 100, 124; Indians of, 186; Ranald MacDonald's return to, 249; Source of cattle in Central and Eastern part, 104.
BRITISH flag over Ft. George, 92.
BRITISH Man of War, 42.
BROTHERS, Canadian steamer, 33.
BROUGHTON, Captain, 234n.
BROWN, Capt. of the Peruvian, 142, 142n.
BUDD, Capt. John of Sag Harbor, 38.
BUFFALO grass, 103.
BULL, John, 196n.
BUNKER, Capt. Harry C., 156n.
BURIED treasure, 42, 43, 144, 145.
BURNETT, A. D., 20.
BUTLER, Capt. Thomas of Salem, Massachusetts, 85, 85n.
BUTTER not used by Japanese, 243, 243n; called boutre by Japanese after Dutch, 243, 243n.

C

E

GIFTS to MacDonald: Fruit, 188; Sweetmeats, 178, 180; Tea, sugar, pipe and tobacco, 181.
GLENCOE, 118, 118n.
GLOBE, whaler of New Bedford, 139n.
GLYNN, Commander of the Preble, 147n, 246, 274, 280, 284.
GODBEY, Capt., 38.
GODS, Japanese, of earth, of fire, of sea, of sun, 165.
GOLDTHWAIT, Ezra, 197n.
GOOD-SO, Japanese name for pork, 242, 242n.
GORDON, Capt., 234n.
GOVERNMENT of Inoes, 170; of Japan, 238, 239.
GOVERNOR of Nagasaki, 218, 219, 220, 261, 262; Description of, 219, 229.
GOVERNOR, (Oblique) or Vice-Roy (Tojo), 170.
GOVERNOR Marcy, steamer, 32.
GOVERNOR'S Palace, Battan Island, 145.
GOVOGRO Imai, Capt., 194, 194n.
GRACE said at meals by Japanese, 204; by Ainus, 165.

GRANDISON, Sir Charles, style of, 52.
GRAY'S harbor of 1792, 89.
GREAT Lakes, 40.
GREELEY, Horace, of the New York Tribune, 92.
GREELEY, Horace, 54, 92.
GREEN Lake Fort, 100n.
GREENPORT, whalers from, 139n.
GREGAN, (Guagan) Island, 139, 139n, 140, 143, 145.
GREGOIRE Francois, 111n.
GRENVILLE, Point, 121n.
"GREY Coat Boy," 108n.
GRIFFIS, Wm. Elliot, 22n.
GRIST mill, pioneer, 24n.
GROG (Saki), 161, 164, 165, 204.
"GROG-YES", Japanese name for Saki, 161, 162.
GUAGAN Island (see Gregan.)
GULF of Georgia, 99n.
GULF Stream, "Kuro Siwo." or Black River of the North Pacific, 121.
GURNEY, Mr. Ralph, 32.
GUTZLAFF, Rev. Dr., 123, 123n, 125.

H

HAGEWARA Matasak, (Hagaiwara Matasaku, 207n.
HAIRPINS, Japanese, 231.
HALF-breed, 24, 27.
HANNAN, Mrs., 49.
HAPPY Despatch, (Harra Karri) 237, 237n.
HARBRIDGE, 114n.
HARNEY, General, 91.
HARPERS, 19.
HARRA-Karri, custom of, 237, 237n.
HARRISON, Lake, B. C., 46.
HASKINS, Mrs. L. C. P., 19, 20.
HAWAIIAN Islands (see also Sandwich Islands) 137, 138, 137n, 138n, 146, 156, 196; Throne of, 41.
HAWES, Jasper, 95n.
HAWES' Pass, 110n.
HAYASHI, the elder, 218n.
HEIGHTS of Abraham, 104n.

HENRY, Alexander, 75n.
HENRY, William, 134n.
HERCULES, whaler, 134n.
HERMIT Kingdom, 38.
HERON, Francis, 121n.
HILDRETH'S History of Japan, 195, 240.
HOANGHO River, 147.
HOBARTTOWN, 235.
HOKADADI, 150.
HOLIDAYS, Japanese, 181.
HOLLEY, Mrs. Eleanor Haskins, 38.
HONG Kong, 138, 146, 148.
HORI, Ichiro, an interpreter, 226.
HORSEFLY Mining District, B. C., 47; Country, 47.
HOSAI Tani, a Japanese doctor, 206n.
HOUSES (see forts or trading posts)
HOWAY, Hon. F. W., 22n.

K

P

T

AFTERWORD

A CAUTIONARY note is in order for readers of this facsimile edition of Ranald MacDonald's memoir. In the years since its first publication in 1923, further research has revealed new information that clarifies and in some cases alters the interpretation of Professors Lewis and Murakami. Not all of the text's inconsistencies are addressed; for instance, there are a number of spelling errors throughout the book that have not been corrected. Those problems that are most troubling are discussed, however.*

MacDonald's relationships with his family, his claim that Colvile had been his boyhood home for several years, and his early lack of knowledge of his native ancestry are now called into question, along with a number of specific points in the manuscript. Some of this can be put down to the revisions and elaborations imposed on MacDonald's original text by his collaborator Malcolm McLeod, and some simply to faulty memory or lack of documentation.

Ranald MacDonald's remarkable story needs no hyperbole. Left to his own spare style of writing it would have had none. Unfortunately the original version of MacDonald's memoir has not survived and the manuscript followed in this edition is in the handwriting of McLeod, the McDonald family lawyer, who attempted to help Ranald MacDonald find a publisher and who

---

*EDITOR'S NOTE: Please refer to Jean Murray Cole's book on Ranald Mac-Donald's father, *Exile in the Wilderness*, for further elaboration on the myths and realities of the MacDonald family.

rewrote and "thoroughly revised" the tale according to his own lights.

(To avoid confusion with the spelling of the family name, please note that Archibald McDonald, Ranald MacDonald's father, always spelled his name "Mc," but I was told by Benjamin MacDonald's son, Arthur MacDonald, that the sons all agreed to change it to "Mac" in the 1850s—probably after Archibald's death in 1853.)

MacDonald himself welcomed McLeod's input. Sending some additional information to him in 1889, MacDonald suggested, "You will please hamer [sic] into shape so as to make it presentable in the book." He had left his "notes" on his adventures with McLeod while on a visit to his stepmother in St. Andrew's East, Lower Canada (Quebec), in 1853, before returning permanently to the West. In subsequent years, McLeod made several attempts to write something from them for publication and made reference to Ranald's adventures in letters to newspapers in the East. But it was not until the two men renewed contact with each other in 1889 that MacDonald actually participated in the rewriting of the manuscript. The correspondence they began then went on until the final months of MacDonald's life, and the original letters, in the archives of British Columbia in Victoria, reveal the process McLeod followed. In August 1889, MacDonald received a ten-page letter from his editorial mentor, outlining McLeod's plans for "the book" and asking for replies to twenty-five questions to "supplement" the journal. Many of Ranald's answers to these (primarily dealing with his experience in Japan) were incorporated, with few changes, in the present manuscript.

Lewis and Murakami, in editing the manuscript in 1923, were aware of McLeod's role in the evolution of the manuscript, though perhaps they did not realize how much he had imposed his own views and personality on it. Other material written by MacDonald has since become available, and in comparing those works with the present volume, it seems highly unlikely to me that some of the more exaggerated passages in this book could have come from the same hand. One very obvious example is the description of the wedding of Ranald's parents, the Hudson's Bay Company officer Archibald McDonald and Princess Raven, daughter of the legendary Chinook Chief Comcomly (pages 88 – 91). MacDonald gives his account in a letter to McLeod dated 10 August 1891: "Heard from an American Captain Buttler, who was present at the marriage ceremony of my Father to the Princess . . . that the King had 300 slaves with sea otter, land otter & Beaver skins to carpet from beach to the Great Lodge & as the party of white men passed the skins were taken up by the slaves and brought to the Lodge & made a present to the whites by the King. I told Captn Buttler that could not be my father for the H.B.C. had too great veneration of a Beaver skin to make a carpet of it. . . . No, he said, it was Macdonald." The details, essentially, are there, but the elaboration in the published version would seem to be McLeod's. One can also compare the straightforward description of the procession to Nagasaki (pages 212 – 14) with the account of the "Royal" wedding and conclude that the former had not been tampered with.

McLeod was the son of a fur-trade colleague of MacDonald's father. Archibald McDonald succeeded John McLeod in charge at the Hudson's Bay Company's Thompson River post (Kamloops) in 1826, when Governor George Simpson sent McLeod back east to Norway House. Malcolm McLeod was then four years old, and in 1830 he was sent to school in Scotland, to return after several years in Britain to complete legal studies in Quebec and be called to the bar of that province in 1845. There is no evidence that he was ever again west of the Rocky Mountains. McLeod's parents were living in Quebec when he returned to Canada, and he established his first law practice there, in St. Andrew's East, Argenteuil County, where the elder McDonalds had taken up residence in 1848 after retiring from the fur trade. It was there that he came to know the MacDonald family, and, when Archibald McDonald drew up his final will in 1852, McLeod was named one of the executors. McDonald died the following year and the executors renounced their power in favor of his widow, Jane Klyne McDonald.

McLeod, however, had access to Archibald McDonald's large collection of personal papers and journals (now in the British Columbia Provincial Archives). In 1872, McLeod edited and published *Peace River*—the elder McDonald's account of a journey from Hudson Bay to the mouth of the Fraser River with Governor Simpson in 1828—and according to McLeod's introductory remarks McDonald's widow had "allowed me the use of his 'notes.'" In his extensive footnotes and appendices, McLeod professes a familiarity with the route that could only have come from his voluminous reading on the subject and not from firsthand experience, as he sometimes liked to imply. He treasured a collection of papers his father preserved, notes of his experiences and letters from his Hudson's Bay Company colleagues, and used many quotes from them in his writing. In his attempts to promote the building of the Canadian Pacific Railway and to influence decisions about the route it should take through the mountains, Malcolm McLeod put much emphasis on his own experience, although it is hardly possible that any of his information came from the memories of a four-year-old. In a series of letters signed "Britannicus," which appeared in the *Ottawa Times* in the summer of 1869, he goes into minute detail about the geographical and climatic features of the land through which the railway would have to pass on its westward route to the Pacific coast, all of his information gleaned from secondary sources. In his mind he seemed to feel that he was an insider, that he had been there, and could speak with the authority of an old Northwester.

This eclipse of time was not restricted to McLeod's experience. It sometimes surfaces in relation to MacDonald himself, as when the botanist David Douglas appears in the manuscript (page 136). Ranald MacDonald's father shared Douglas's interest in natural history and spent many weeks travelling with the scientist during his sojourns in the Columbia district. The young MacDonald probably did meet the famous botanist, but he was barely a year old when Douglas first appeared on the coast in 1825 and only nine when the elder McDonald and Douglas met on Puget Sound in March 1833. It is highly improbable that Ranald MacDonald would have referred to Douglas as "my dearly loved friend and companion of the wild woods." Details in this passage were no doubt the result of McLeod's reading in the *Companion to the Botanical Magazine*, which published large segments of Douglas's North American journals from the 1830s.

There are many other passages in the book that can be attributed directly to McLeod—not only because of his tendency to overwrite but also because of his inclination to insert background and facts that would unlikely have been in Mac-Donald's purview. In November 1889, MacDonald wrote to McLeod: "Not having read the manuscript I don't know what you have inserted and what you have left out." When he finally received a copy of the first few chapters in October 1893, he assured McLeod that he was "pleased with it." The later chapters follow the straightforward style of Ranald's answers to McLeod's twenty-five questions, but the attentive reader will be able to pick out the frequent diversions and attribute them to McLeod.

Several important factual errors should be noted. Ranald MacDonald's father and Jane Klyne were married at Fort George (Astoria) "in the custom of the country" in 1825, and it was not until 9 June 1835, when they were together in the presence of a minister for the first time, that the formal church ceremony took place in Canada at Red River, now Winnipeg,

Manitoba (see footnote, page 94). The story of Jane Klyne's Swiss origins, which caused the editors some confusion (see footnote, page 83, and pages 94 – 97) is now known conclusively to be untrue. (The footnote places her at "Fort Rae," a misreading of the "pedigree" in McDonald's handwriting, which says "came to H.Bay in 1813," referring to McDonald himself.) Jane was the daughter of Michel Klyne, a French Canadian fur trader of United Empire Loyalist descent on his father's side, and Suzanne LaFrance, the Metis (French and Indian) daughter of another French Canadian voyageur. The Klynes were at Lesser Slave Lake in the early 1800s when Michel was an employee of the North West Company. He was in charge of the H.B.C. post Jasper House in the Rocky Mountains from 1825 to 1835, when he retired and moved his family to the Red River settlement (Fort Garry, Manitoba). He had no connection with the Swiss deMeurons (brought out to the settlement by Lord Selkirk), who left Red River and settled in the United States (footnote, page 97).

Another misconception on the part of the editors was to assume that "Master Ranald" wrote to his father from London, England, after leaving St. Thomas in the spring of 1842 (p. 37; not 1841 as on page 40). It is more likely that it was London, Ontario, Canada, a town not far from the Ermatingers' home, which would have allowed him time to reach Sag Harbor and sail from there on the whaling ship *Tuscany* that year (footnote, p. 38).

The assertion (on page 18) that Ranald "entirely lost touch with his family and friends at St. Andrew's" after he went back to the west in the 1850s is contradicted by the fact that he was in partnership with his brothers Allen and Ben in various mining and ranching ventures in the Cariboo country of northern British Columbia in the 1860s, was in touch with his stepmother up to the time of her death in 1879, and was remembered in her will. He was corresponding with Ben (then living in Idaho) in the 1890s. Another contact that precludes the suggestion that many of his family and friends in Quebec "believed he was dead" was his association with John and Alex Barnston, sons of George Barnston, a close friend and fur-trade colleague of Mac-Donald's father. Ranald MacDonald's half-sister Maryanne had married another of the brothers, Dr. James Barnston, of Montreal, in 1857; also their mothers were good friends, and the families visited back and forth frequently. MacDonald formed a partnership with John Barnston, who was practicing law in the Cariboo, to build a road from Bentinck Arm on the coast to the interior gold country in 1861, and in 1864 Alexander Barnston was one of MacDonald's fellow members of the Vancouver Island Exploring Expedition sponsored by the British Columbia Botanical Association of Edinburgh. MacDonald also mentioned in a letter to McLeod in 1890 that he kept in touch with events in eastern Canada as "a constant subscriber to the *Montreal Gazette*."

When living near the Colvile reservation during the last years of his life, MacDonald informally adopted the family of Angus McDonald, whom he and Ben both referred to as their cousin. Christina McDonald McKenzie Williams, a daughter of Angus, told William S. Lewis that MacDonald's father was her uncle, and this has been repeated by a number of historians. A check of their dates shows this to be untrue. Archibald McDonald was born in Glencoe, Scotland, in 1790, the thirteenth and last child of Mary Rankin (1741 – 1829) and Angus McDonald (1730 – 1814). Angus of Colvile was born in Ross-shire in 1816. It is possible that Angus was the son of one of Archibald's brothers or sisters, four of whom had married MacDonalds, but Archibald himself does not mention any relationship in his references to Angus in correspondence and journals written while Angus served under him at Fort Colvile in 1838 – 39; nor is any connection indicated in existing family records or in the archives of the Hudson's Bay Company. Cousins they perhaps were, but, if so, at some remove and of different generations.

It is something of a mystery why Ranald MacDonald claimed

not to have known of his Indian blood until later in his life. In a letter to McLeod dated 4 June 1891, he wondered "why my family kept it dark." It is unlikely that it was intentional. All children born to fur traders in the Columbia at that time were part Indian since there were as yet no white women there, and probably no one thought it necessary to mention. MacDonald himself acknowledges that he remembered the "old King" who called him "Qu'Ame" (Chinook for grandson), and that some of his father's friends called him "KumlyKumly."

MacDonald is mistaken in his claim that Colvile was his old home. The only time he was there was when he came from Fort Vancouver in April 1834 with Chief Factor Duncan Finlayson and spent a few days at the fort with his father before they all set out with the Hudson's Bay Company for Red River, where Ranald and his three half-brothers were to be enrolled in the school. It was, in fact, Fort Langley that MacDonald recalled when he says, "Here, during three or four years, with younger half brothers, under the tenderest, and best, in every way, of parental care, I spent what I consider to have been the very happiest days of my life . . ." (page 105). Archibald McDonald describes his family's life during those idyllic years 1829 – 33 at Langley in a series of letters to a friend in the east (now in the British Columbia Provincial Archives). This was the only time the family was all together, and Archibald McDonald tells of the "thriving school" he conducted there for his wife and young family.

The MacDonald family remained at Fort Langley until the spring of 1833, when Archibald McDonald was posted to Fort Colvile. Ranald MacDonald spent the following year at Fort Vancouver where he attended the school started by John Ball, while his younger brothers went with their mother, Jane Klyne, to stay with her parents at Jasper House. They were all reunited, briefly, in the spring of 1834, when Archibald McDonald left Colvile for a year's furlough abroad, taking Ranald with him as far as Red River, where he was to attend school with his brothers (pp. 106 – 07). It was not until the summer of 1834, several months after Ranald MacDonald left Fort Vancouver, that the Japanese shipwreck survivors were brought there by Captain McNeil (see footnote, p. 121), so it is clear that Mac-Donald had no direct contact with them (p. 127).

There are similar instances of misinterpretations and minor errors in historical fact in this version of the memoir, none of them intentional or serious. It is understandable when one considers the length of time between Ranald's adventure in Japan in 1848, and his attempts, in 1889, to recall for McLeod the details of his childhood and dates and events in the past. McLeod's flourishes do detract somewhat from the final manuscript, at least in modern eyes, but the reader can be grateful that he persevered in his attempts to preserve and publish Ranald MacDonald's story.

Jean Murray Cole   *Indian River, Ontario, Canada*

NORTH PACIFIC STUDIES SERIES

Explorations of Kamchatka: North Pacific Scimitar
[Opisanie zemli Kamchatki].
By Stepan P. Krasheninnikov. Translated and edited by
E.A.P. Crownhart-Vaughan.
1972

Colonial Russian America: Kyrill T. Khlebnikov's
Reports, 1817 – 1832.
Translated and edited by Basil Dmytryshyn and E.A.P.
Crownhart-Vaughan.
1976

Voyages of Enlightenment: Malaspina on
the Northwest Coast, 1791 / 1792.
By Thomas Vaughan, E.A.P. Crownhart-Vaughan, and
Mercedes Palau de Iglesias.
1977

The End of Russian America: Captain P.N. Golovin's
Last Report, 1862.
Translated with introduction and notes by Basil Dmytryshyn
and E.A.P. Crownhart-Vaughan.
1979

Civil and Savage Encounters: The Worldly Travel Letters
of an Imperial Russian Navy Officer, 1860 – 61.
By Pavel N. Golovin. Translated and annotated by Basil
Dmytryshyn and E.A.P. Crownhart-Vaughan, introduction
by Thomas Vaughan.
1983

Log of the Union: *John Boit's Remarkable Voyage to the Northwest Coast and Around the World, 1794 – 1796.*
Edited by Edmund Hayes, foreword by Thomas Vaughan.
1981

For Honor and Country: The Diary of Bruno de Hezeta.
Translated and edited by Herbert K. Beals, foreword by Thomas Vaughan.
1985

The Wreck of the Sv. Nikolai: *Two Narratives of the First Russian Expedition to the Oregon Country, 1808 – 1810.*
Edited with introduction and notes by Kenneth N. Owens.
Translated by Alton S. Donnelly.
1985

To Siberia and Russian America: Three Centuries of Russian Eastward Expansion, 1558 – 1867. A Documentary Record.
Edited and translated by Basil Dmytryshyn, E.A.P. Crownhart-Vaughan, and Thomas Vaughan.
Volume One: *Russia's Conquest of Siberia, 1558 – 1700.*
1985
Volume Two: *Russian Penetration of the North Pacific Ocean, 1700 – 1797.*
1988
Volume Three: *The Russian American Colonies, 1798 – 1867.*
1989

Juan Pérez on the Northwest Coast: Six Documents of His Expedition in 1774.
Translation and annotation by Herbert K. Beals, foreword by Donald Cutter.
1990

Voyages of the Columbia *to the Northwest Coast
1787 – 1790 and 1790 – 1793.*
Edited and annotated by Frederic W. Howay, foreword by
Bruce Taylor Hamilton.
Second edition, revised
1990

*Soft Gold: The Fur Trade and Cultural Exchange
on the Northwest Coast of America.*
Historical introduction and annotation by Thomas Vaughan,
ethnographic annotation by Bill Holm.
Second edition, revised
1990

*Bering's Search for the Strait: The First Kamchatka Expedition,
1725 – 1730 [V Poiskakh Proliva: Pervaia Kamchatskaia
Ekspeditsiia, 1725 – 1730].*
Evgenii Grigorevich Kushnarev. Edited and translated by
E.A.P. Crownhart-Vaughan.
1990

Ranald MacDonald: The Narrative of His Life, 1824 – 1894.
Edited and annotated by William S. Lewis and Naojiro
Murakami.
Second edition, revised
1990

COLOPHON

FIRST PUBLISHED by the Eastern Washington State Historical Society in 1923 in a limited edition of one thousand numbered copies, Ranald MacDonald's *Narrative* has long been out of print. As time passed, and interest grew about MacDonald's significance, it was evident that this book must be re-published. This Oregon Historical Society Press/North Pacific Studies Series 1990 photographic facsimile edition, with its added elements, is a tangible contribution to the growing scholarship on MacDonald and is another example of the Oregon Historical Society's commitment to publishing works about the North Pacific region, and to restoring to their proper place those persons who have had great influence on our region and on the Pacific Rim.

It is conjectured that the typeface used in the original edition was Métis Demi-Bold (not a bastarda), a face that could have been popular with itinerant Linotype operators who may have plied their skills throughout the Inland Empire during the 1920s. However, all efforts by persons expert in the history of typography have been unable to confirm any of this.

The typeface used for elements added to the 1990 edition (e.g., copyright page, the foreword, afterword, and colophon) is a photocomposition version of Plantin, an "Old Style" or "Garalde" face based indirectly on the generation of typography used by Christophe Plantin. Plantin was a renowned sixteenth-century Antwerp printer/publisher (the Plantin-Moretus Museum in Antwerp, Belgium, preserves his print shop as one of the finest "black art" exhibits in the world). The first modern adaptation of this generation of faces was designed for the Monotype Corporation by F.H. Pierpont in 1913. It was chosen for this edition by the Oregon Historical Society Press' book designer because of some similarities to the conjectural face outlined above.

Ranald MacDonald is printed on 55-lb. Glatfelter B-16, an archival paper. The endpapers are Mist Gray Rainbow Parchment. The binding cloth is Holliston Kingston 35799 (Slate); the foil stamping is Holliston M61 (Red Metallic); the headbands are Holliston red and black.

The production of this book was accomplished through the cooperation and professional skill of the following:

Typesetting—Irish Setter (English) and Asian Type-Printing Company (Japanese), Portland, Oregon

Printing and binding—Edwards Brothers, Incorporated, Ann Arbor, Michigan

This edition was produced (with additional necessary design elements) by the Oregon Historical Society Press.

ラナルド・マクドナルドの生涯